READER'S DIGEST FAMILY TREASURY OF

GREAT PAINTERS AND GREAT PAINTINGS

THE READER'S DIGEST ASSOCIATION, PLEASANTVILLE, NEW YORK
THE READER'S DIGEST ASSOCIATION LTD., MONTREAL, CANADA

LIBRARY OF CONGRESS CATALOG CARD NO.: 65-24672
PRINTED IN THE UNITED STATES OF AMERICA

"IF A PAINTER WISHES TO SEE beauty that enraptures him, he has the power to create it. If he wishes to see things that are grotesque . . . or are laughable, or are truly pathetic, he is the lord and master of them. . . . Whatever lies in the universe—in essence or imagination—he has first in his mind and then in his hand."

With these words Leonardo da Vinci hailed the infinite scope of his profession. Though four hundred years have passed, his view holds true wherever we look into the story of art. The creations of painters are as various as those of Rousseau, who made an Eden of fanciful jungles, and Bosch, whose medieval apparitions of doom and hellfire cast a spell of fascination over a Europe still bound by such beliefs.

Masters of art were as unalike as it would seem possible for men to be: Rubens, joyously content, directed a staff of assistants to produce "hybrid" Rubens canvases to fill the overflowing demand for his works; van Gogh, a tormented spirit, walked precariously along the razor's edge of self-destruction.

But, however different and fiercely individual, the great painters are intricately bound together in the tradition of art. They were taught by those who came before them; they taught and influenced generations that followed. They pictured for all men the worlds they lived in and the visions they saw.

Paintings themselves have often been more shocking than any actions of painters. Fouquet represented the king's mistress as the Madonna. In staid Spain, Velázquez was the first to paint a nude, though his magnificent Venus is discreetly turned away from the viewer. Matisse set off a storm of criticism with his first work that, forsaking realism, consisted of designs based on the human form. The controversial Picasso took apart our everyday vision of the world and turned it into disarrayed fragments.

Some painters—El Greco and Vermeer—were ignored for hundreds of years, and then rediscovered as geniuses. Others cherished their own masterpieces. Leonardo da Vinci kept the *Mona Lisa* for himself. Goya hid *The Nude Maja.* Corot's figure paintings—all three hundred of them—were found in his studio when he died. Turner haunted the auctions and bought back his own paintings at prices higher than those for which he sold them; "They are my children," he said.

The pursuit of self-glory led generations of the mighty Medicis to commission the works of master painters, and so it was with kings and popes, guilds, aristocrats, republics and millionaires, down to our own time. The withdrawal of patronage was a special purgatory for men of genius. Botticelli outlived the vogue for his style; Rembrandt lost his popularity; Courbet, leader of his era, died forgotten in exile.

Perhaps the bitterest of all tragedies in art has been the later worth of masterpieces by artists who struggled for recognition most of their lives. Today's price of a painting by Frans Hals (who couldn't pay the baker) would have made him a millionaire in his time. Within one month in 1965, a Monet was auctioned for half a million dollars, a Brueghel peasant scene sold for 230,000 dollars, and a Hogarth brought 150,000 dollars. Valued at nearly a billion dollars are the Italian masterpieces in a single gallery—the Uffizi in Florence.

Higher and higher the prices have climbed, as the world's museums, especially those in America, offer ever-increasing sums for great works in private collections. Now our museums are alive with exhibitions and lectures, as the tide of public interest in the "enrapturing beauty" of great art reaches its highest peak. In 1963 *Mona Lisa* drew more than 500,000 people in less than one month at the National Gallery of Art in Washington, D.C. Two years earlier, Rembrandt's *Aristotle Contemplating the Bust of Homer* was purchased for a record price of 2,300,000 dollars, and the number of visitors more than doubled (to 24,000 people daily) during the early weeks of its exhibition at the Metropolitan Museum of New York.

Beyond the elusive fame and the changing values and vogues, the drama remains—the story of seven centuries of art which is told in this book. In the opening pages the painters of our own time appear, beginning with Cézanne, who is considered the founder of modern art since he was the first to abandon realism that had reigned for centuries. In Part II, "The Age of Greatness," we return to the humble Giotto and the flowering of Western painting in the thirteenth century. After him, the great painters and paintings flow in succeeding ages, from nation to nation—the episodes and masterpieces that form the treasury of art.

Paintings which are today regarded as masterpieces—the sunflowers of van Gogh, the landscapes of Cézanne—were looked upon fifty years ago with shock and even derision. At the time, people were used to more conventional painters; Cézanne's deliberately distorted compositions, van Gogh's emotionally charged canvases were dismissed as the efforts of childish fools. The same sort of reaction greeted the work of Gauguin and Matisse and Modigliani, who were unafraid to paint decorative portraits or landscapes in a flat fashion—a style which had not been seen since the Middle Ages. As for the wonderfully revealing character portraits and café scenes of Toulouse-Lautrec, these were considered mere sketches. Today the works of all these men are loved and understood: the priceless originals of their paintings grace our museums; inexpensive reproductions grace our homes. In our own time the most famous and wealthy painter in the world—Picasso—has made new assaults on what is commonly accepted as reality, placing on his canvases parts of people and objects in strange and startling juxtaposition. Many profess not to be able to find anything of merit in his work, and yet all modern painting, indeed all commercial art, has been strongly influenced by it. Perhaps this is always the artist's greatest contribution—to reveal the world in unexpected ways, discovering new meaning in all the wonders that surround us

SELF-PORTRAIT

P. Cézanne

PAUL CEZANNE

1839–1906

Old Master of Modern Painting

CEZANNE BECAME the most famous painter of the nineteenth century. But he was a problem to his friends in Paris, to his family and to his townsmen of Aix, who, had he not been the only son of a rich banker, would have treated him as a fool. The painter—of whom Renoir said that he could not place two colors side by side without producing remarkable effects—was so terribly sensitive he was nicknamed "the man without a skin." No better proof of the total estrangement of the modern artist from the public is needed than the hostility which greeted Cézanne at every turn of his career. Men of today have adopted him as the one modern master, but year after year he was condemned to the critical lash. Of all his fellow painters, Cézanne was considered the arch offender.

Cézanne was born in Aix-en-Provence in 1839. His father was of Italian stock, the family coming originally from Cesena. His mother, of Creole ancestry, was a servant in the wealthy Cézanne household and, according to Tristan Klingsor, the French critic, "it was not until 1844 that she was married to the painter's father." The happiest period of Paul's life, in fact the only period of real happiness, was his early youth in Provence, where in company with Emile Zola, he wandered about the country filled with the hopes and dreams of a great career. The shrewd Zola was ambitious to write, and Cézanne, his future decided by a box of colors which his father had bought from a peddler, talked of Rubens and Veronese.

Though not a dull boy, he was surely not a prodigy. He took the second prize in drawing at the Aix Museum, overcame parental objections and, in his twenty-second year following Zola's example, went up to Paris. Here his troubles began. As is so often the case with the excessively

LANDSCAPE WITH VIADUCT

The mountain Ste. Victoire in southern France was the favorite landscape of Cézanne. Time and again he painted different views of it. This scene with a Roman aqueduct is the most celebrated.

CARD PLAYERS

Cézanne once remarked, "When a picture isn't realized, you toss it in the fire and start another." He made many paintings of card players—reducing the number of figures as he experimented—and destroyed all but five versions. The above, with two players, was the simplest and most "essential" of all.

STILL LIFE WITH APPLES

"You must sit like an apple! Does an apple move?" Cézanne snapped at a man who failed to keep still while posing for his portrait. The painter worked so slowly and had so much trouble finding models willing to endure lengthy sessions that he delighted in painting still lifes.

shy, he endeavored to disguise his fears by sudden eruptions of temper in which he cursed the official jury of the annual art exhibition, known as the Salon. To show his contempt for the conventional art of Paris, he affected a bohemian swagger.

Failing to pass the examinations for entrance to the Ecole des Beaux-Arts, Cézanne attended irregularly one of the more liberal academies and copied in the Louvre. For ten years he did not seem to get anywhere—he was attempting inventions for which he had no aptitude whatever. But there was merit in his abortive labors; he was never banal, and he had the instinct of the born colorist. His painful gropings did not commend themselves to the juries, however, and he went ahead at a snail's pace. Paris depressed him, and to recover his faith he returned each year to Provence to paint alone on his father's estate.

During the Franco-Prussian War (1870–1871) he devoted his working hours to open-air painting and his studio. About this time he married a plain and rather stupid woman from Aix, who seems nevertheless to have been an excellent wife to him. She had no notion of what he was driving at—but who did? She was perfectly satisfied to remain at home while he was away in Paris or on a sketching tour with other artists. It is a little surprising that he should have undergone the ordeal of matrimony, and more so that he should have begotten a son.

Encouraged by Renoir—one of the first to appreciate him—Cézanne exhibited with the rebellious Impressionists (see page 160) in 1874 and again in 1877. He was received with derision, and this reception hurt him. Having no need to sell his pictures and convinced by his own suspicions that he did not belong anywhere, not even among those befriending him, he began to spend more and more time in the South. On the death of his father in 1886 he became a rich man, but made no change in his abstemious mode of living. In 1895 Ambroise Vollard (then an art dealer, later Cézanne's biographer) took advantage of public curiosity over the government's refusal to accept Impressionist paintings in the gift of an art collection for the Luxembourg Palace. He hastily assembled about twenty-five Cézanne canvases in a small gallery and announced an exhibition. Vollard told of the public's reaction:

Another day I heard screams through the door. A young woman was struggling to break away from a man who held her with a grip of steel before a picture of The Bathers. *I caught this bit of dialogue: "How could you upset me like this? And I once took a prize in drawing, too!" Then the voice of the man: "That will teach you to be more respectful to me from now on!" Apparently the husband was compelling his wife to look at the Cézannes by way of punishment.*

Soon afterward Cézanne retired permanently to his estate in Provence. He was probably the loneliest of modern painters. His friendship with Zola had ended long ago; his townsmen shunned him. He was, as he said, only a painter: profound as regards art but in other departments of thought naïve and lacking in intellectual independence. At times a curious melancholy attacked him. In his last years he carried his canvas into the fields as religiously as his neighbors went about their business of sowing and reaping. But his harvest was far more uncertain. His difficulties in "realizing his sensations," as he put it, increased with time and his nervousness became almost pathological. He would get up at all hours of the night and poke his bald head—he was as homely as the bust of Socrates—out of the window to gauge the prospects for the gray weather which he deemed most friendly to his sensations. He grew more exacting, destroying canvases, throwing them out of his studio into the trees, abandoning them in the fields and giving them to his son to cut into puzzles, or to the people of Aix when they could not refuse the favors of a man of property. "I am one," he lamented, "who has a piece of gold, and can't make use of it."

At the beginning of the century a few connoisseurs discovered the gold. When Vollard arrived in Provence with intentions of buying on speculation all the Cézannes he could get hold of, the peasantry, hearing that a fool from Paris was actually handing out money for old pictures, produced from barns and outhouses a considerable number of still lifes and landscapes, demanding as much as 150 francs (30 dollars) for the windfalls! The old Master of Aix was overcome with joy. At last he was making a little stir in the world! But recognition came too late. In 1906 Cézanne died from a fever contracted while painting in a downpour of rain.

Cézanne's ambition, in his own words, was "to make something as solid and durable as the paintings of the museums"—meaning the masterpieces of Michelangelo and Raphael. To put it in another way, his aim was to achieve the monumental in a modern language of glowing, vibrating tones. It sounds very simple, but technically his method was minute, analytical and exceedingly complicated. He would reveal and compose forms in their material and rhythmical aspects through the juxtaposition of colors.

For example: Before Cézanne on a table lies a red apple.

From his experience of feeling and handling it he knows that the apple, in general shape, is a sphere, but as he studies it in the lighting of his studio his eye informs him that the contour is broken into planes of various intensities of color and tone. These divisions escape the casual glance of the layman; to the trained eye they are not only evident but confusingly numerous. The old painters, disregarding accidental reflections and shadows, would have taken a red pigment and modeled a spherical object by uniform gradations of one color—that is, by mixing neutral tones with the red to produce the shadows—a perfectly good method, but not Cézanne's.

His aim is to preserve the solidity of the apple, but at the same time to conciliate the rounded mass with the lights and shadows breaking up the form into planes. Thus he sees before him a sphere the *local* color of which is red, but he observes that the surface divisions, absorbing or reflecting light from different sources—blue from the table cover, green from the trees outside the window, yellow from the walls of the room—are not uniformly red but orange, blue-green or violet. He does not intend to copy the apple. He will keep the dominant color and the character of the fruit, but will heighten the emotional appeal of the form by a scheme of rich and concordant tones. He will harmonize the planes one with the other and establish their exact position in space; and he will preserve throughout a balance of red so as not to ruin the local color—he does all this so he may create a new and more exciting apple.

This tortuous process of *modulating* (as he named it) nearly killed the man. A single fruit, in which he needed to consider only the effect of one plane on another, was difficult enough. But how much more difficult was a collection of things in which he had also to consider the effect of one object on another—or the human figure and all its complexities—or a group of figures in landscape; no wonder he moaned that he was only a primitive blundering on an untraveled road.

No other painter of equal ability ever reserved for still life his strongest impulses to the creation of new and living things. In Cézanne's painting of still life, his "little sensation," as he put it, is realized. By sensation he meant his perception of forms: their effect upon him, the poetry they aroused within him, their size, structure and solidity, their relation to all his experiences. Cézanne restored to painting the preeminence of knowledge—the knowing of things. That is one of his chief claims to distinction. He is the original glory of Modernism. —THOMAS CRAVEN

SELF-PORTRAIT

PAUL GAUGUIN

1848–1903

Rebel in Tahiti

THE AUCTIONEER THOUGHT the paintings were really funny. Turning one upside down, he said with a loud laugh, "Look—Niagara Falls!" And he knocked it down for less than three dollars. Seven others sold for a dollar each. One went for thirty-five cents.

The painter Paul Gauguin had just died in the Marquesas Islands in the South Seas, and his effects were being sold in the nearby town to pay his debts. A fisherman, finding three trunks stuffed with canvases and drawings in the painter's shabby hut, did not bother to sell them. He dumped them into the sea. Today, in the islands, this is called the million-dollar mistake. It is not an exaggeration. In 1959 a dealer paid 369,000 dollars for a Gauguin painting. His finest canvases are almost beyond price. The master would have appreciated the irony; his lifetime earnings from painting came to about 15,000 dollars.

Security and comfort, however, meant little to Gauguin. What mattered always was an ideal. A wealthy stockbroker, he gave up luxury and ease—and, finally, civilized society—because he wanted to paint. Today he is recognized as one of the great modern painters. Van Gogh called him Master. Picasso acknowledges his debt. He gave painters everywhere a new interest in color and pattern for their own sake.

Paul Gauguin was born in Paris in 1848, son of an obscure journalist father and a mother descended from grandees of Spain. At seventeen he walked out of school, and for six years he followed the sea as a sailor. The rough life made the frail boy strong and, above all, gave him the dream that was to transform his life. Sitting on deck one night, he heard a shipmate describe life in the South Seas. Women were lovely and yielding there, fruit dropped from the

GAUGUIN'S PALETTE

THE BURAO TREE
The coconut-thatched hut beyond the tree in the painting above is believed to be where Gauguin lived shortly after he reached his Tahitian Eden.

TWO TAHITIAN WOMEN
The lack of modesty among people of the South Seas, so astounding to Victorians, fascinated Gauguin. He wrote back to France, "The Eve I paint . . . goes unclothed. Yours would be filled with shame."

trees, the sun shone every day and the nights were sheer magic. Gauguin made a mental note he was never to forget.

Back in Paris, aged twenty-three, Paul discovered he had a gift for making money on the stock exchange. Taking a job with a brokerage firm, he rose rapidly, invested wisely and was soon earning the equivalent, in values of today, of 40,000 dollars a year. He wore a high hat, went to work each morning in a carriage, was known at all the good restaurants.

To crown his career of middle-class conventionality, he married the daughter of a Danish civil servant. Mette Gad was a cool, practical blonde who wore the correct clothes, gave proper teas for the proper people and, in time, bore her husband five children. But by then Paul Gauguin had discovered painting. His wife was pleased at first that the good provider had found a congenial hobby. No harm in being a "Sunday painter." She had yet to realize that her husband was an all-or-nothing man. One of his paintings, called *Study of a Nude* (the model had been the family maid), was exhibited. A critic called it the finest painting of a nude since Rembrandt. Paul Gauguin's career in business slowed to an end after that remark. At the age of thirty-four he walked out of his brokerage office. Henceforth he would devote himself to painting.

Within a year he was penniless. The family home, with its fine furniture and rich rugs, was sold. Mette returned to Denmark, where the children would at least have enough to eat. Gauguin followed. The Danes mocked him as a man living off the bounty of his wife, sneered at his painting. He went back to Paris without Mette.

Gauguin has been vilified as a wastrel who abandoned his wife and children. Actually, he felt it was Mette who had abandoned him. Almost to the end he wrote her love letters, begging her to join him. "Love me well," he wrote from Tahiti fifteen years after their separation, "because when I return we shall be lovers again. It is a lover's kiss I send you, a betrothal embrace." She never rejoined him.

The Gauguin legend begins in 1885 with his return to Paris from Denmark. He lived in bare, icy attics, went about in tatters. Once he worked as a billposter for a few francs a day. Then, hearing that at Pont-Aven in Brittany there was an inn whose owner gave credit to painters, he borrowed enough money to get there. His stark landscapes and kneeling Breton women are products of this stay.

Still penniless, Gauguin went to Arles, in the south of France, to live with his friend Vincent van Gogh. The visit proved disastrous for van Gogh; the clash of their temperaments drove him into a fit of insanity (see page 18).

Gauguin returned to the inn in Brittany. A man of enormous vitality, he had enough strength left over after a normal day's work to do sculpture in wood and marble. Also he painted the walls and doors and ceiling of the inn's dining room, not to mention his wooden sabots, his walking stick and his fisherman's sweater.

Despite the approval of a few critics, the public considered Gauguin's paintings "grotesque." At forty-two he was still a pauper. Then Gauguin announced that he was going to the South Seas, to live and paint as a primitive. The favorite dream was at last to come true. His friends tried to dissuade him, but he was obstinate. An auction sale of his paintings provided passage money. In Tahiti—the year was 1891—he went into the back country and rented a hut overlooking a lagoon. His companion was a native girl whose face and body appear in many of his paintings.

Twenty-seven months later he returned to France, bringing many extraordinary canvases with him. Over forty-four pictures were exhibited. Only a few sold—to old friends, for a total of a hundred dollars. A critic wrote: "If you want to give your children a laugh, take them to the Gauguin exhibition." Gauguin cried when he read it.

Sadly, at forty-seven, he returned to the South Seas to live out the last miserable years of his life, first in Tahiti and then in remote Hiva Oa, in the Marquesas. He had contracted syphilis, for which in that day there was no cure; also, his leg was swollen and covered with eczema that refused to heal. He suffered dreadfully. "I wait here like a rat in a barrel in the middle of the ocean," he wrote.

Most of us imagine Gauguin lolling under the breadfruit trees while Polynesian belles sang and danced to amuse him. If he lolled, it was because his legs were eaten by disease, and he could not walk. If the girls sang to him, it was because he was going blind. "My lights are almost out," he told a doctor. He was the cleanest and neatest of men, but, alone and unable to care for himself, he died in 1903 in a filthy reed hut beside his last known canvas—a Brittany snow scene. Strange subject for a painting in the idyllic South Sea Islands!

Years after his death, when his name had become a legend, the scramble for his pictures began. Collectors found them in bars, brothels, boardinghouses. He had traded them for a bottle of wine, a day's lodging, or a moment of pleasure. They were usually put away in the attic or cellar, because the owners did not think them worth hanging. In Brittany, they had been used as floor mats or cut up and sewn together to make canvas shoes.

Not long before his death, Gauguin tried to explain, in a

written statement of faith, his strange and tragic life. "I believe," he wrote, "that art has a divine source and lives in the hearts of all men who have been touched by the heavenly light. Once having tasted the delights of great art, one is inescapably and forever dedicated to it."

Could he have explained more clearly? —GEORGE KENT

SELF-PORTRAIT

Vincent

VINCENT VAN GOGH

1853–1890

Soul in Torment

A YOUNG DUTCH FANATIC named Vincent van Gogh was serving as clerk in the London office of the Goupil art galleries. He had come to worship, silently, the daughter of his landlady. The girl rejected him and, sensitive and overwrought, he took the rebuff as seriously as he was later to take his troubles in religion and in art. The youth was transferred, lost interest in his work and left. A new devotion to religion made him heedless of all else, even the problem of making a living. During the next seven years he was to experience, through his religious fanaticism, the depth of misery and the heights of spiritual exaltation in a way destined to be significant to the development of modern painting.

In the Borinage, that black district of industrial Belgium, he practiced in 1879–1880 a form of early Christian communal life, giving to the miserable the clothes from his back, sharing his food until he had starved himself beyond possible return to full health and even giving up his bed. Shaken mentally, he nevertheless again in 1883 put to the test the doctrine of unselfish love. At thirty, when he had become an art student, he took into his rooms at The Hague a sickly prostitute, who brought with her one of her five children and was pregnant. He nursed her, paid her doctor bills, shared food or hunger with her; and he planned to marry her.

Frustrated in the end by the woman's restlessness, he had now set the pattern which his life in art was to follow. For no artist ever gave himself more self-destructively, more fanatically, more lovingly to painting than did the mad Dutchman. His was the story of the spiritual *exalté* who turned to art, pouring himself out in a fire of paint. No wonder that Freud's disciples found in van Gogh a perfect illustration of their darkest theories of art as a funnel for personal distress. Nor did the enemies of modern art fail to link the man's insanity with the distorted look of his painting.

Vincent van Gogh was the son of a small-town clergyman in southern Holland, near the Belgian border. He was born in March 1853, the eldest of six children. At twelve he was placed in a boarding school, but at sixteen he returned home as unformed and sensitive as ever. Egg-headed, small-eyed, red-haired, round-shouldered, excitable, given to moods of melancholy, he seemed like poor human material. His brother Theo, his junior by four years, had been the one member of the family who had understood and sympathized with him through his earlier difficult days. Theo was with the Goupil art firm, at the central galleries in Paris. To him Vincent appealed in his need, and there began one of the most touching records of fraternal trust known to the world of art.

Out of his own small earnings Theo began to send Vincent money so that he could study and paint. Vincent was even enabled, as he tramped the country fields and roads, to pay for his bread sometimes. When he could not pay, he begged. At Neunen, he suffered again the blighting effect of another tragic love affair and was driven in on himself in a way that may have contributed to the mental disorders which were to distort his life increasingly in the five years remaining to him. A woman older than he awakened his sympathy, then his consuming attention. To escape his passion she attempted suicide. It was his last effort to find happiness in a permanent love.

Theo met Vincent, on his request, in the Salon Carré in Paris and soon the brothers were together in a studio apartment in the heart of the artists' quarter, Montmartre. At first Vincent was delighted by the picturesque shabbiness of the streets, the cafés and the surrounding country. He threw himself excitedly into the business of painting what he saw around him. Now he was in the very heart of the Impressionists' territory. Van Gogh soon found that his real affinity was not for this school but for three men who had left their company to carry the torch of revolt a step further: for Cézanne (see page 8), usually considered the most monstrous painter among the outcasts; for Gauguin (see page 12), experimenting under the combined influence of Cézanne and of the Orient; and for Seurat (see page 18), obsessed with an experimental vision of color.

Vincent soon became depressed by the life of Paris. What had seemed gay at first was turning out to be superficial and tawdry. One day in February 1888, with characteristic kindliness, he cleaned his rooms in the studio apartment, decorated them with flowers and his own paintings and disappeared—to Arles, in the south of France. Nature newly glorious, humanity newly colorful—these gave wings to his brushes. As if by magic his art ripened. He gave himself passionately and heedlessly to painting.

Impressions crowded in on him—he must get them all down: the people, the cafés, the streets, the bridges, the farms, the orchards, the flowers. Animating all these subjects was the Provençal sun, giving them gorgeous color. The gay yellow of the sunflower was echoed in countless blossoms and was spilled in great patches over the fields of grain. Even that was not enough for Vincent: he often put the disk of the sun itself into his pictures. The reds were hardly less intoxicating to him. The tile roofs of the houses, the poppies studding the meadows, the painted boats, the fezzes and trousers of the Zouaves from Algeria.

Vincent (he now signed his pictures with his Christian name only) painted too the places that became familiar to him, his little house, night scenes in the café where he drank absinthe, the café terrace on the street at night. Or it might be small things that took hold of his imagination—a pair of old shoes on the floor, or a chair, a burning candle. Impossible as "artistic subjects" in 1888, these things were destined to take on immortality when he transferred them in thick paints, clumsily it seemed, to canvas. Fifty years later no discriminating seller of prints would dare be without colored reproductions of *The Yellow Chair* and the golden *Sunflowers* and the cramped *Bedroom at Arles. Les Déchargeurs,* a painting of workmen unloading a coal barge, was sold for 240,000 dollars in April 1965.

Vincent rented a house, for fifteen francs (three dollars) a month, in preparation for the arrival of Gauguin, from whom he had recently heard. He rashly spent everything Theo had sent him, making over the rooms and putting in beds and chairs and a gas stove. Gauguin, who had to fall back on Theo for fare, arrived in October 1888, and the two painters plunged into a life of incessant painting and talking. At first, it was good for both of them. But Gauguin, the more forceful character, was inclined to play the teacher. Increasingly they quarreled, taunted each other and drank absinthe to excess. After a few weeks of this ex-

SUNFLOWERS

Van Gogh often rose at dawn to paint his beloved sunflower all their freshness. He hung pictures of them everywhere in his house at Arles. To his eyes yellow was a symbol of life and he painted the whole house yellow to welcome Gaugui

THE HARVEST

The landscape above, considered to be one of van Gogh's greatest, was based on a detailed pen-and-ink drawing (top of opposite page). To his brother Theo, the artist wrote: "Drawing is the backbone of painting. I draw in color."

BEDROOM AT ARLES

While confined to the asylum at St.-Rémy, van Gogh nostalgically recalled on canvas his room at Arles, where he had spent the most productive months of his life.

istence, Vincent was on the verge of a mental breakdown.

One evening in a café he threw a wineglass at Gauguin's head. Gauguin carried him like a child to his room and put him to bed. The next morning he was worried and contrite, and asked forgiveness. But by evening madness was full upon him. Gauguin, walking in the dark street, heard footsteps behind him and turned to see Vincent running after him holding an open razor. A sharp word was enough to send van Gogh away. Failing in whatever violence he had designed against Gauguin, Vincent returned to the studio, decided to take his own life with the razor, then had the diabolical idea of fulfilling a jesting promise made to a prostitute—that he would give her "one of his funny ears." He sliced off part of his right ear, wrapped his head in towels, and delivered the severed member to the door of the brothel. Then he went again to the studio and fell into the stupor of exhaustion.

Gauguin telegraphed to Theo, and left for Paris. A doctor put Vincent on his feet in a few days, and helped him to get started again with his painting. But inevitably the impulse to push on "headlong" with his art brought his nerves again to the breaking point, and, after a violent fit, he was taken to the hospital. On his release he found the townspeople had turned against him. Finally, goaded by the taunts and jeers of small boys calling for his other ear, he made an unforgivable scene in the square. Soon he agreed to commitment to a private asylum at nearby St.-Rémy.

Between attacks he accomplished an enormous amount of painting for one so ill. Permitted outside the walls, he found the fields as colorful as those at Arles. But the cypresses came to obsess him; he painted them as no one else ever had—in a flaming torment of movement, of dark color, of twisting coils. Sometimes whole landscapes took on the look of tortured convolution.

In May he wrote to Theo: "I can't stand any more— I must move even for a last shift," and a few days later he was permitted to start for Auvers by way of Paris. Theo met him and he enjoyed a visit with Theo's little family and a gathering with old friends. Vincent was looking exceptionally well, they all remarked, and he behaved himself meticulously. He began to paint. But he could not resist the idea that he was finally foundering.

After a few weeks, anticipating the time when his next crisis was due, he borrowed a revolver and shot himself. He did not do a clean job. When Theo came, Vincent said: "I have failed again." He lingered on two days and died in the early morning in Theo's arms. —SHELDON CHENEY

PORTRAIT BY ERNEST LAURENT

GEORGES SEURAT

1859–1891

Wizard of Color

GEORGES SEURAT was twice as successful as Vincent van Gogh; that is, he sold two paintings in his lifetime. By nature he was a man serious, lonely and studious; and he asked nothing better than the opportunity to linger through a morning on the riverbank, studying effects, sketching. Visionary in the profoundest sense, he was nevertheless methodical and painstaking. Whatever he may have been lacking in emotional warmth, he was, fortunately, a "born painter." Here, as with Cézanne and Gauguin and van Gogh, there came into the company of Western artists a great simplifier, an antirealist, a creative designer.

Seurat was born in Paris of parents well situated. His father was a court attaché. Georges's schooling was orderly, and at eighteen he entered the Ecole des Beaux-Arts. He haunted the art-school library, indulging a passion for information about painting methods and especially about color theories. For a year he was away for army training. After his return, he sought light on his problem in the books of the French and American color-physicists. A drawing of his was shown at the Paris Salon in 1883—no small honor for a youth of twenty-three.

The largest of his works is the *Sunday Afternoon on the Island of La Grande Jatte.* This painting, 70 square feet, marked Seurat's arrival at maturity in the use of the method he had invented—one of precise painting in "pellets" of color. It established his right to claim advance beyond anything accomplished by the school of Monet and Pissarro. First shown, curiously enough, at the last Impressionist show, held in May 1886, the *Grande Jatte* turned out to be the sensation-piece of the event. When it reappeared at the radical *Indépendants* exhibition in the same year it stirred ridicule and controversy almost as had

LA GRANDE JATTE

For two years Seurat labored on his stylized painting of the popular island park in the Seine, only to have it jeered at when exhibited. A recent offer of a million dollars for this, his most famous, canvas was declined.

THE CIRCUS

The careful and fastidious artist spent many hours at the Fernando Circus, watching the acts and making sketches. Exhibited before completion, the painting was never finished because of the artist's sudden death—at thirty-one.

Manet's *Olympia* twenty-one years before (see page 145). Characters from it, especially the lady and the monkey, became the subjects of café and music-hall jesting. Critics put it down as a failure by reason of "too much science and not enough art."

Never did a painter rise above the limitations of his own theorizing more brilliantly than Seurat. His mind was seething with excitement over his researches. Apparently he believed that he had developed a watertight and foolproof formula.

Monet and Pissarro had made much, in the seventies, of the discovery that color gave a cleaner, brighter effect when the painter, instead of mixing his pigments upon the palette, set strokes of raw color of differing hues side by side on the canvas. The mixing was done in the eye of the beholder. But they had done this only fitfully, seldom producing a canvas without palette-mixed pigments.

Seurat's followers, the "neo-Impressionists," claimed to be scrupulously scientific. *All* color must be put on in touches—clean, round, without any mixing on the palette. *Pointillisme* (or "point-ism") was the name the French applied to this method. Only six "pure" hues were to be employed: the primaries—red, blue and yellow—and their complementaries—green, orange and violet. To the realists Seurat's paintings seemed frightfully unnatural. And the Impressionists, as well, disowned Seurat. Here was a caricature, they felt, of their methods of showing nature in an instantaneous mood, a fleeting aspect, harmonized atmospherically and mistily.

As long as he lived, Seurat was content to lean for his financial support upon his mother, who had been left well placed after her husband's death. He had a studio of his own; that was enough. Toward the end he had taken a mistress, unknown to his mother or to any friend, and a child was born in 1890. In the years from 1886 to his death in 1891 his known meetings were almost solely with fellow painters—van Gogh, Gauguin, Degas, Rousseau and others of the progressive-radical movements.

Seurat produced seven major or monumental works, and forty or fifty pictures of lesser size. *The Come-On,* depicting the free show put on for the public outside the doors of a French circus, is one of the most meticulous and decorative of Seurat's compositions. In the final years, he worked day and night. Whether through passionate devotion to painting or because of some trait of character, he drove himself without mercy. He was now an *Indépendant,* and marked as among the truly dangerous and subversive members of this rebellious group.

In 1891 he painted one of the most ambitious and successful of his works, *The Circus.* The horse is the quintessence of all spirited, prancing, decorative horses. The equestrienne is the very flower of gracefulness, femininity and artificial loveliness. The upside-down clown epitomizes acrobatics. Even each of the spectators is characterized lovingly, with a touch of tongue-in-the-cheek satire.

Almost the last recorded glimpse of Seurat finds him at a preview of the seventh *Indépendants* exhibition in 1891. *The Circus* hung on the wall. The veteran Puvis de Chavannes, one of the very few painters accepted by the radicals, arrived to view the works of the young insurgents. Seurat stood to one side to see what would be the effect of *The Circus* upon the master. Puvis glanced at the picture and then passed on without stopping. Seurat was chagrined and bitterly disappointed.

At this time he already was ill from overwork and from a cold contracted at the gallery. Hardly more than a week later he died—of an infection of the throat. Most of his paintings were still in his studio and they were divided among his mother, his suddenly discovered mistress (the child had caught his father's infection and died) and a few friends.

—SHELDON CHENEY

SELF-PORTRAIT

Henri Julien Rousseau

HENRI ROUSSEAU

1844–1910

Immortal Innocent

IN A ONE-ROOM LODGING with but one window, above a plasterer's shop in a cheap quarter of Paris, Henri Rousseau lived from hand to mouth in apparent serenity. To pay his rent and buy food, Rousseau did artistic odd jobs for his neighbors. He wrote letters for those who couldn't write. He taught diction to the corner grocer, violin to the milkman's daughters and cornet to would-be bandsmen.

Every hour that Rousseau could call his own he spent painting pictures. He couldn't sell them; they were self-

THE CART OF PERE JUNIET
The charm and naïve quality of Rousseau's genius extended even to such everyday scenes as this one. His gay outing in the Forest of Clamart with a grocer's family was painted from a photograph of the occasion. Rousseau is on the right.

THE EQUATORIAL JUNGLE
Jungle scenes are his most popular—perhaps because viewers feel his enchantment with nature and the primitive. The painter Max Weber said, "To enter his studio was like going into a fresh vineyard . . . he seemed full of love and joyous at the sight of the world."

trained, greenhorn art, and in those days—toward the close of the last century—they looked so childish that they aroused only amusement. Henri Rousseau was a gentle creature. Small in stature, round-shouldered, a friendly little man with a high-pitched voice, he caught you by the fervor in his eyes. He seemed to glow. Despite his humble clothes, his impoverished air, he vibrated happiness as if he kept inside him the secret of the joy of life.

Everything about him seemed simplehearted innocence: his naïve talk, the pictures he painted and his sincere reactions to people. When he first exhibited his painting *The Sleeping Gypsy,* those who gathered before it stood smiling and laughing. Rousseau mistook this for approval.

The artist himself thought so highly of *The Sleeping Gypsy* that he offered it to the town of his birth, Laval in Mayenne, believing, as he told them by letter, that people there might want to "possess a remembrance" of him. He was not offended when the town refused. As usual, he was touched with pity for those who did not appreciate his paintings. He had no doubts about his high place in the history of art and said that someday his work would be treasured. No one laughs at Rousseau's pictures now. Their rich, interlinking patterns of bright colors have been compared to Persian painting. His *Sleeping Gypsy* is considered a jewel of New York's Museum of Modern Art, for which it was purchased some years ago for 25,000 dollars.

Such a price would have astounded Rousseau. Throughout his life he rarely possessed as much as twenty-five dollars at one time. Born in 1844, the son of a poor tinsmith, Henri Rousseau often had to earn his bread after school hours. Always longing to paint, he could not afford art school. As a young man he served four years in the army. Returning to civilian life, he landed a tiny job as a toll-gate employe on the outskirts of Paris, and was always known thereafter as *Douanier*—tollkeeper.

During his struggles, he kept his goodwill—even in the face of personal tragedies. His first wife died in 1888, after bearing him seven children; only one survived beyond infancy. He married again, but soon was a widower once more. In 1893 he retired with a modest pension from the toll service and devoted himself full-time to his art. Rousseau painted with such hairsplitting care that a picture took him two to three months to complete. If luck was with him and he sold the painting, he would get seven or eight dollars for it. No matter! He'd give a party. Rousseau loved people. He invited as many as could crowd into his room over the plasterer's shop—neighbors, pupils, toll-gate workers and some old cronies. He would start the festivities by giving a violin solo, then perhaps play a trio with the milkman's daughters. The son of the grocer would recite a piece. The baker's wife would pick out something on the mandolin. The milliner's husband would blast away on the cornet. Eventually the whole company would fall to singing songs.

If there was a newcomer among the guests, Rousseau proudly pointed out his paintings round the walls, explaining details that might not be clear. When guests laughed at his paintings, Rousseau chimed in with a beatific smile. His neighbors continued to take his painting lightly even after art critics, connoisseurs and titled notables began to arrive at Rousseau's room with words of praise.

But some of his neighbors thought the sophisticates were making fun of Rousseau. Indeed, the intellectuals, his cronies, his pupils—all played jokes on him. One jokester sent him a letter as if written by a foreign millionaire, asking to buy all his pictures at princely prices. Another, dressed up to look like one of the most famous painters of the day, knocked on Rousseau's door and said he had come because one great artist should pay respects to another. The faithful Rousseau answered, "I've been waiting for you a long while."

The cruelest jest occurred when the artist, in the lonely ten years between his two marriages, fell in love with a woman who declined to marry him. A wag stepped in, pretended to intercede with the lady, and returned with a "yes" and a date for the wedding. Rousseau announced the happy news to one and all. When the bride failed to appear, Rousseau was crushed, and revealed painfully to his neighbors how he had been left in the lurch.

But he kept on painting. When he could work at his easel from dawn till dusk he was satisfied with life. In this almost saintly calm he created again and again outstanding pictures such as *The Toll House* and *Banks of the Oise.* In his later years he launched the culminating achievements of his career, a series of magnificent jungle pictures: lions stalking their prey in tropical thickets of jeweled colors, a tiger attacking a buffalo, a gorilla leaping upon a native spearman. *The Dream,* with a central figure of a nude woman on a red sofa in the midst of a jungle, caused a surprising stir at the *Indépendants'* exhibition in 1910. An artist counted over fifty tones of green in the riotous plant life.

Rousseau's wild animals he saw at the Paris zoo. His tropical foliage came from leaves and fronds and grasses he picked up at the botanical gardens. In back issues of the *Magasin pittoresque* he saw engravings of rare species of beasts. And a children's book heavily illustrated with animals was still another source of inspiration. The different motifs he wove together into a mood of his own—a fantasy, an art that was his unique creation.

Two years before Rousseau's death, Picasso arranged a big banquet for him in his own studio, inviting all the modern artists in Paris to meet their peer. Toast after toast was drunk in Rousseau's honor. To these friends—the authors Apollinaire and Jules Romains, the painters Weber, Braque, Vlaminck—he was no eccentric but one of the most original artists among them. In the midst of the speechmaking Rousseau fell joyfully asleep.

In 1909 his serenity was shattered by a criminal charge of fraud brought against him and a former pupil who had implicated him in a financial deal. Rousseau won his trial with dignity, even as his lawyer produced his canvases to show what a simple dupe he was. Those closest to him knew that his goodness was often taken for naïveté. To Apollinaire he wrote: "I hope you will avenge me for all the injuries and insults I have received."

Rousseau died in 1910 and was buried in a pauper's grave outside Paris, but soon his friends contributed money for a decent burial plot. Apollinaire wrote his epitaph, and Brancusi carved his tombstone. —MALCOLM VAUGHAN

THE LAUNDRESS
This illustration for the sheet music of a risqué cabaret song is one of Lautrec's most admired paintings. For his model he chose a Paris working girl, Carmen Gaudier.

PORTRAIT BY J. E. VUILLARD

HENRI DE TOULOUSE-LAUTREC
1864–1901
Strange Genius of the Moulin Rouge

HENRI DE TOULOUSE-LAUTREC was a man of noble lineage and ignoble appearance, descended in direct line from the Counts of Toulouse and the Emperor Charlemagne. But many whose paths he crossed called him a "dwarf of Velázquez," "little monster" and "hunchback."

A man who knew and understood him well was the poet and essayist Arthur Symons, who recalled meeting him for the first time in the café Moulin Rouge, where Lautrec

THE JOCKEY
As a youth, and before he became crippled, Lautrec was an accomplished rider. He loved races, and his posters and lithographs of horses as well as of café scenes greatly influenced modern advertising.

YVETTE GUILBERT
The popular singer did not resent Lautrec's good-humored caricature of her.

Lautrec met in the Moulin Rouge (the Red Mill in the photo) many of the figures of Paris night life whom he was to paint. Among the famous posters he designed for the cabarets is this interior scene.

' THE MOULIN ROUGE
eft) Entering the café, the artist himself aring a derby, and his cousin, in the top ', have just passed the entertainer La Goulue e Glutton), arranging her hair.

JANE AVRIL DANCING
One evening at the Moulin Rouge, Lautrec painted the delicate improvised dancing of Jane Avril. She later wrote: "It is to Lautrec that I owe my fame."

was a regular customer, and portrayed him in these words:

No one who was acquainted with Toulouse-Lautrec could ever forget him: nor have I ever seen a man so extraordinary and so sinister as he was. Every night one came on him somewhere in Paris, chiefly in Montmartre, in the streets, in the cafés, in the theaters, in the music halls, in the circuses. He walked, his huge head lowered, the upper part of his body, which was in perfect proportion, leaning heavily on his stick; he stopped—owing to the difficulty he had in walking—stared this way and that way; his black eyes shone furiously, eyes that amused themselves enormously; he began to speak in his deep biting voice and always in some unimaginable fashion—jests or jokes or bitter sarcasms, or single phrases, in which each word told; simple and brutal, mocking, serious and sardonic.

Until he was almost fourteen the young Henri was a normal child—normal in the sense that, although fragile, his physique was like other children's of his age. There is an early sketch where he represents himself with legs quite in proportion with the rest of his body. In 1878 he slipped on a hardwood floor and broke a thighbone. About a year later, while on a walk with his mother, he fell into a shallow gully and broke the other leg. The bones never mended as they should and his legs did not develop properly, whereas the torso did. He soon knew that he was destined to be crippled and deformed. In all future self-caricatures Lautrec exaggerated the disproportions of his pathetic physique.

Henri demonstrated an affection for drawing and picture-making at an extremely tender age. He was taken to witness the baptism of a baby brother, and when the registry was inscribed by those in attendance, the boy of four cried, "I want to sign, too!"

"But you don't know how to write yet," he was told.

The child retorted, "Then I will draw an ox!"

Oddly enough, in the light of his future style and subject matter, Lautrec's first teacher was one of the best animal painters of the day—René Princeteau. He quickly revealed his aptitude with pencil and brush and was enrolled in the studio of a successful and fashionable artist, Léon Bonnat, who approved of Lautrec's painting but said, "Your drawing is simply atrocious!"—this to one of the finest draftsmen of the time. Lautrec left Bonnat to take instruction from Fernand Cormon, in whose studio he met van Gogh and other young painters.

About 1884, now aged twenty, he went to live in Montmartre, which was rapidly becoming the haunt and home of artists who were leaving the Latin Quarter on the left bank of the Seine. To Henri's delight the great Degas worked in a studio situated across the court from his own.

In the matter of style, Degas (see page 146) was perhaps the greatest influence on the young artist. But Montmartre, with its cafés, its music halls, its circuses, bars and bordellos, really formed him. And nowhere in art does this aspect of Paris come so truly to life as in the lithographs, posters and paintings of Lautrec. He liked and understood the characters who inhabited it. He set them down in grease crayon and paint and rendered many of them immortal: the singers Yvette Guilbert and May Belfort; the dancers Jane Avril, Valentin and La Goulue; Footit, the clown; and a host of others.

Lautrec's greatest production came in the ten-year stretch 1887–1897. This is the period of his nocturnal journeys through Paris, of his gargantuan absorption of liquor —every conceivable ingredient going into the "cocktails" which he mixed for himself and his visitors. During these days and nights he visited the racetrack, the hospitals (to witness surgical operations), the law courts, the circus, the music halls and dubious "nightclubs." Of all this he has left us a graphic record. He made posters; he lithographed menus, song sheets and theater programs. He illustrated books and did series for portfolios. He made sketches for magazines. He painted portraits of writers and prostitutes, working always with a feverish intensity—like a man who knew he had little time.

Occasionally Toulouse-Lautrec made trips out of the country, visiting Spain, where he was impressed by El Greco and Velázquez. In Brussels he almost fought a duel when he rose to the support of a van Gogh painting, challenging a defamer who called van Gogh an ignoramus. He went often to England, finding himself at home with the people across the Channel—with men like Oscar Wilde, Arthur Symons and Whistler. In Holland he had an unfortunate experience. There the natives, especially the children, thought he was a freak from some sideshow and constantly gathered around him expecting him to entertain them, this being a common method for circus folk to obtain advance publicity.

The years of hard drinking and living and—let it be insisted—hard work began to take their toll. Friends and family knew that something had to be done. In February 1899, Madame de Toulouse-Lautrec consented to have her son placed in an asylum at Neuilly, near the Bois de Boulogne. The sanatorium was expensive and comfortable, and Lautrec, under good and intelligent care, made a rapid recovery. He was well aware of where he was being held and why. At this time, he addressed a poignant note to his father, the count: "Papa, here is an opportunity for you to act like a good man. I am imprisoned and everything that is imprisoned dies!"

During this period of incarceration, Lautrec drew his astonishing series of circus sketches, later published in two portfolios titled *Le Cirque*. Completely from memory, he represented the movement and color of the circus—the clowns, the dogs, the horses, the ringmasters, the acrobats. To this day it remains a most artistic, acutely observed record of circus life. The doctors at the asylum recognized this as no work of a madman and they consented to his release. Later he said: "I have purchased my liberty with my drawings!"

After coming out, he was accompanied everywhere by Paul Viaud, an old friend of the family, who was a devoted companion and watchdog. For a while Lautrec did well; he regained his strength, showed a renewed interest in his work and produced some splendid lithographs and paintings. But by the summer of 1901 Lautrec was in trouble again. He had taken once more to drink and to consorting with his old companions. His descent was a rapid one. His mother had him removed to the family estate at Malromé, and there he died.

—HERMAN J. WECHSLER

SELF-PORTRAIT

HENRI MATISSE

1869–1954

The Brilliant Designer

LATE IN HIS CAREER, when he had become one of the great artists of the twentieth century and his pictures of unshapely women were famous around the world, Frenchman Henri Matisse said, "If I met a woman in the street who looked like my paintings, I'd faint."

Modernist Matisse could paint natural-looking pictures when he wanted. Indeed, he put in fifteen years at it before he decided that art and nature are two different things. He was deep in a study of Oriental rugs and Byzantine mosaics

ODALISQUE IN RED PANTS
Odalisques *(harem women) painted around 1920 brought Matisse world fame. The one above was bought by the French government in 1921.*

WHITE PLUMES
With ostrich feathers, ribbon and straw, the artist fashioned the hat himself. He made dozens of sketches of the model Antoinette wearing it.

LADY IN BLUE
Bright hues flourished many years in the art of Matisse; but, for sheer daring, he probably never surpassed this color scheme.

THE DANCE
A folk dance Matisse saw at the Moulin de la Galette inspired this canvas, according to his son Pierre. Thus the oft-painted dance hall (see page 155) made one more contribution to art.

Paper cutouts like the Head of Hair *(below, right) were done in Matisse's last years, after illness forced him to give up easel painting. Strikingly similar was* The Dancer, *a 1909 drawing (below, left).*

THE ANEMONES AND THE MIRROR
Few painters have taken so much delight in simple household objects as Matisse. These flowers were in his hotel room in Nice, his first Riviera home after World War I.

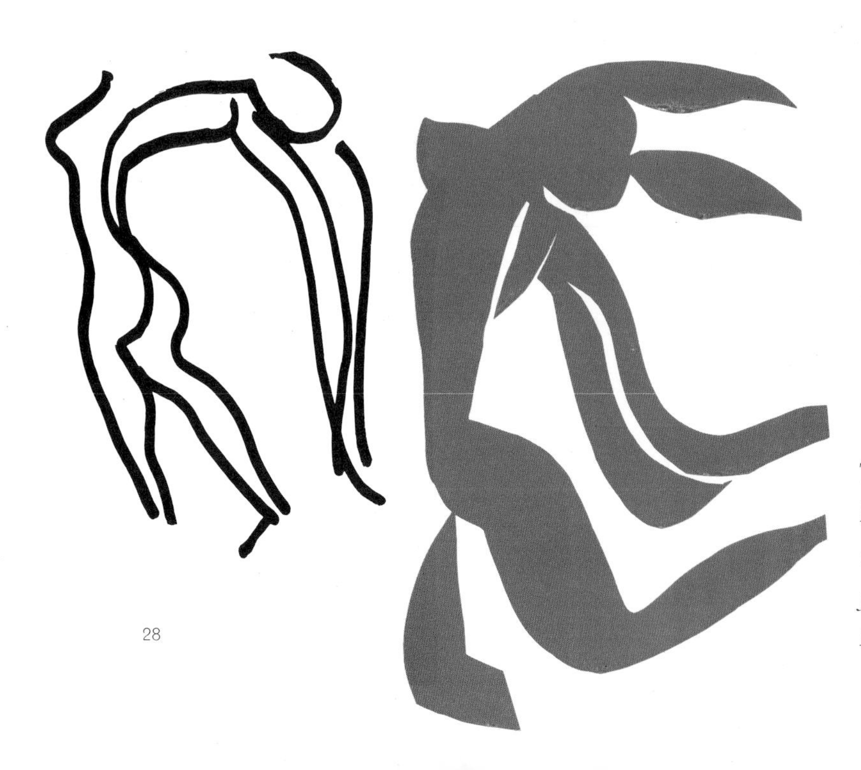

when it dawned on him that he could translate these patterns of color into pictures. From that moment on, Matisse's paintings became color designs rather than true-to-the-fact images. Sometimes the design is intricately intercurved, as in *Interior with Goldfish;* sometimes it is sharp-cut, as in *The Dance;* sometimes almost a checkerboard, as in *The Hindu Pose.* But always it is the color pattern, not the image, that most concerns him.

How he had to fight to win recognition! He was thirty-five years old, with a wife and three children, when, in 1905, he sent his first big nonfactual color design to the Paris Autumn Salon. *Woman with the Hat* burst upon the art world like an explosion. Almost overnight, Matisse was the center of a controversial group of artists who imitated his new style and who delighted in the derogatory name a critic gave them: Fauves (wild beasts). But fame eluded him. The public was outraged by the "spots and blotches" of his design. Crowds milled about in front of the picture, ridiculing the artist as a caricaturist, a madman.

But the picture sold. An American collector, Leo Stein, who had said at first that it was "the worst mess" he had ever seen, returned and bought the painting for around 100 dollars. The Matisses were glad to get the money. Often the artist had taken odd jobs to earn a living for his family. For years his parents had sent him 20 dollars and a sack of rice every month, but it was his devoted wife whose little millinery shop had supplied their main support.

The "mess" he sold for 100 dollars proved to be not only a trailblazer in modern art but also a stepping-stone for Henri Matisse. The buyer took him to call on his famous sister, Gertrude Stein, whose Paris living room was a meeting place for the vanguard in literature and art. Here Matisse's genius was recognized. Here he met another obscure artist—Picasso, great art critics like Bernard Berenson and Roger Fry, and wealthy collectors. His rise was painfully slow, but finally the artist was launched.

Encouraged by selling his first nonnaturalistic picture, he turned even further away from photographic painting and created *Joy of Life,* a large, almost abstract color design of nudes in a Garden of Eden. When Matisse exhibited it in 1906, the crowd again jeered, and even the artist's warmest advocate, Leo Stein, was appalled. But weeks later, after many trips to the show, Stein declared the big picture "the most important done in our time," and bought it.

That settled Matisse's future. Though he was increasingly denounced as an impostor, "art criminal" and "apostle of the ugly," he could make a living at his kind of painting, selling an occasional picture for 100, 200, perhaps 300 dollars. A couple of years later a wealthy Russian bought up a whole year's work, then commissioned *The Dance* and several other paintings. In a few more years, Matisse was one of the two most noted modern artists alive. The other: Picasso.

Yet Matisse remained the same simple, modest, hard-working fellow he had always been. Of medium height, robust, he was a redhead with regular features and, behind his spectacles, a warm twinkle in his eyes. He looked so much like a fatherly physician that friends called him "Doctor." As soon as it was financially possible, he took a little home in a suburb, from which he commuted to his Paris studio. In the suburb his children could get fresh air, and the artist could ride horseback and plant a garden, "just like any man."

Matisse now found himself hailed by many as the herald of a new art style, a distinctive way of seeing. Unimpressed, he made no effort to be startlingly new or to outmodern the latest moderns. Actually, his painting turned more conservative. It continued to be—like the art of the Persians and the Byzantines—an art of design, but it grew a little more natural-looking: the apples a bit more like apples, the women from time to time shapely, and even alluring.

One December, Matisse caught a fearful cold and went south to the Mediterranean coast. He fell so much in love with the sun-drenched Riviera that he stayed, moving into a high-ceilinged studio with hundreds of birds in cages and a huge window overlooking the sea. Here, year after year, he painted to his heart's content, the birds singing away above his head.

With the approach of old age, illness struck, and left him bedridden except for a couple of hours a day. Matisse ordered a tilt-top hospital table rolled over his bed, called for watercolors and oils and started painting again. Thus he worked for the last fourteen years of his life, until he died in 1954 at the age of eighty-five.

His last great work was a totally fresh departure, a venture into architecture—a modern chapel for a young girls' convalescent home in nearby Vence. Propped up in bed, he designed everything—the white-tiled building, stained-glass windows, candelabra, clerical vestments, altar crucifix and numerous wall paintings—including the *Madonna and Child,* and the Fourteen Stations of the Cross. The old artist said of his chapel: "It's my masterpiece."

But his "color patterns" are even more renowned. Museums and collectors the world over point to Matisse paintings as marvels of modern art. —MALCOLM VAUGHAN

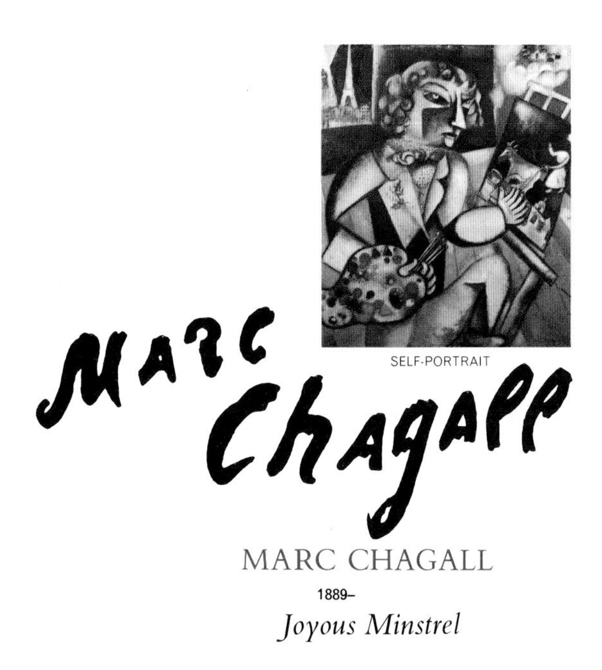

SELF-PORTRAIT

MARC CHAGALL

1889–

Joyous Minstrel

A CHANCE INCIDENT in his youth changed the life of the famous artist Marc Chagall, and altered the whole direction of his now unique art.

In the village of Vitebsk, Byelorussia, where he was born in 1889, he was visiting a friend. There was a knock at the door, then the voice of a girl that "sounded like a bird, like a voice from another world." He did not see the girl on that occasion. But later, when he met Bella, he was instantly attracted. "I feel she has known me always," he said. "My childhood, my present life, my future, too. There and then, I knew, this is she, my wife."

From that moment nearly every picture Chagall painted was a "love picture," a hymn in praise of womankind and motherhood. At first sight these might strike you as being bewilderingly fanciful. Blissful lovers stand on their heads, sail through the air, cuddle in trees. Other people walk around tooting horns, or sit on rooftops playing violins. Birds, beasts, even fish join the paean of joy. Such paintings had never before been seen. Bella recognized them as images of Chagall's rapture. This curly-black-haired fellow with electric-blue eyes was a poet.

Marc Chagall in the early 1900's was an uneducated nobody in a Jewish ghetto in Vitebsk. His father toiled in a herring warehouse. His mother eked out their living by running a little grocery store. Both his family and Bella's opposed their marriage. A penniless painter, an "outlandish modernist" to boot, he couldn't support her. Determined to develop his art and to earn enough money to make her his wife, he left Russia in 1910 for Paris.

Four years later Chagall returned to Russia to visit Bella. While he was there Germany declared war on Russia, and he remained in his homeland. A year later he married Bella, their parents finally having consented. The war was followed by the Russian Revolution, then the Communists, who tried to bend Chagall's talents to political purposes. Failing, they made him art director in one of their newly established children's colonies. Thereafter, Marc and Bella Chagall lived in poverty.

In 1923 they were able to return to Paris, and here found that Chagall had become famous. Paintings he had left with friends for exhibition in Holland and Germany were being praised by critics in many lands. Chagall began to paint anew—jubilant pictures which sold quickly. Every detail of these paintings reflects gaiety. They often center on a man holding a woman in his arms, or a woman snuggling a baby to her bosom. The colors take on vivid rainbow hues. Trees burst into exotic bloom; a horse plays a fiddle; a hen's egg lies in a golden nest; a cow leaps over a cottage roof.

Chagall bristles if you call these works fantasies or fairy tales. To him they are images of emotions, pictures of our subjective life. He says, "The inner world is perhaps more real than the visible world." The leaping cow, the fiddling horse, the fertile hen represent man's agelong dream of domestic bliss.

The Chagalls were still in Paris when France was invaded during World War II. They fled to a haven in the United States. His enchanting fantasies began to be interspersed with profound paintings of the Crucifixion and the sorrows of war. Suddenly in 1944 his wife fell ill and died, plunging him to the depths of grief. Eventually he returned to France, where, remarried, he once more began painting the scenes of his colorful, gravity-defying world.

There, too, he took up a monumental task he had begun some twenty-five years before: his etchings to illustrate the Bible. During the German occupation a faithful craftsman had hidden the plates Chagall had completed. The artist exhorted the engraver: "It must sing, it must cry; it is the Bible." When it was published in 1956, the great work not only placed Chagall in the front rank of etchers; it revealed his profound love for the divine.

Today he still paints the joys of every man and woman in love, "the eternal youth of humanity." But his art has become deeper, stronger. Among his most recent works is the group of twelve stained-glass windows for the synagogue of a hospital in Jerusalem. Another is the ceiling of the Paris Opera—a pastel blend of airy creatures who mirror the action on the stage below. They are evidence that his art today is a hymn to life itself.

—MALCOLM VAUGHAN

THE THREE CANDLES

Chagall celebrated each wedding anniversary with a painting of himself and his wife Bella. In 1938 the happy lovers embrace tensely, almost fearfully—the news of war had cast doubt upon their future.

modigliani

SELF-PORTRAIT

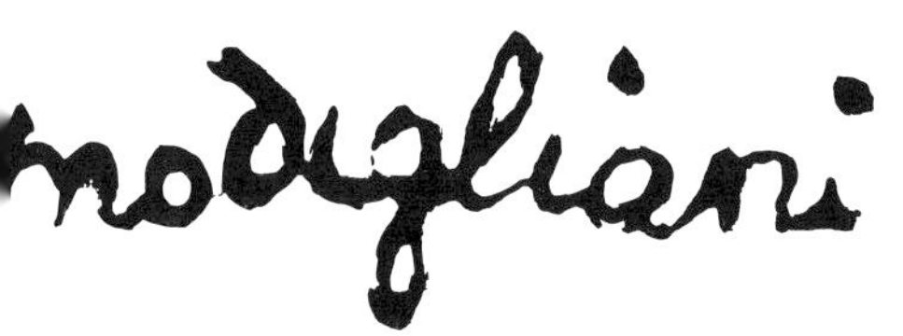

AMEDEO MODIGLIANI

1884–1920

The Ultimate Bohemian

HERE IS THE BOHEMIAN as legend generally paints him. Amedeo Modigliani was possessed of a mad frenzy to live out his brief span in excitement, adventure and impassioned work at his art. He had the temperament of a poet who expressed himself, not in rhyme, but with pencil line and brush strokes. He was decadent, as the world labels those poetic souls who concern themselves with wine, women and song.

People never forgot him—his aristocratic bearing, his handsome classical features, his diabolical pride. The artist Jacques Lipchitz recalls that when he first met him, Modigliani was chanting Italian stanzas from Dante's *Divine Comedy*. Other writers have also mentioned this habit of the painter who, to the end of his days, exhibited a passionate love for the poetry his immortal countryman wrote six centuries ago.

Modigliani was born in Leghorn, Italy, in 1884. His early influences, therefore, were Italian, and having developed an instinct for art, he had the works of the Renaissance masters available for inspiration and study. His first lessons in painting came at the age of fourteen, when he was instructed by one Micheli. At this time Modigliani was already suffering from a pulmonary disease which ultimately killed him. In the first years of the twentieth century he was sent to southern Italy to convalesce and, when somewhat strengthened by the salubrious climate, he traveled north to visit Rome, Florence and Venice. Here, of course, he saw some of the greatest Italian masterpieces of all time and perhaps developed that love of drawing which stayed with him to the end.

It was in 1906 that Modigliani came to Paris, where there were many influences at work to affect an enthusiastic youth

THE APPRENTICE

A social outcast, the artist often painted humble persons whose lives were as painful as his own. His compassion for a young boy worn out by hard labor was expressed at a time when Modigliani was kept from starving by a friend.

MME. HEBUTERNE

"Noix de Coco" (Coconut) was the nickname given Jeanne Hébuterne (opposite page) by her fellow art students. During the few years of their tragic romance, "Modi" painted many of the works that have made his name.

of twenty-two. He saw the art of Toulouse-Lautrec (see page 23), who favored sensitive line and the swift economy of great caricature. The tradition of Impressionism and, of course, the lasting influence of Cézanne were still in the air. For a time Modigliani was affected by this master. But the influences which really shaped him were the sculptured works of Constantin Brancusi and the carvings from Africa which were appearing in the Paris art world. Because of the former, he himself turned to sculpture for a while; the inspiration furnished by aboriginal masks is evident in many of his portraits. Other leading painters of the time whose work showed the impact of African art were Pablo Picasso, Georges Rouault and Maurice Vlaminck.

In 1909 Modigliani began to behave in that manner which contributed to his becoming a legend in the Montmartre and later the Montparnasse quarters of Paris. Tuberculosis was now well advanced and was ravishing his body. But he was not unaware of the fact—a knowing victim of his own disease. He drank unlimited quantities of alcohol and experimented with a variety of drugs, including hashish. Almost always penniless, he slept wherever he could find shelter—in a friend's bed or on the floor, sometimes in the streets. He lived and worked at the cafés. His destitution and need for food compelled him to sell his work for piddling sums or to exchange a painting for something to eat.

With the grand gesture of a millionaire he would hand out drawings as though they were bank notes in payment for a glass of whiskey which someone offered him. Always proud, he wanted no charity. One day, seated at a café, he made a rapid sketch of an American tourist. This he graciously offered to the young woman who had served as model. When she insisted that he add his signature to make it of greater value, Modigliani angrily took back the sketch and scrawled his name in huge letters across the drawing.

Vlaminck, in his book of memoirs, tells another tale to indicate how great was Modigliani's pride and how resentful he could become when he felt that advantage was being taken of his straitened circumstances. On one occasion he offered a group of his drawings to a dealer, who—not satisfied with the ridiculous price quoted by the artist—continued to plead for a further reduction. Whereupon Modigliani presented the entire lot to him at no charge. However, he first pierced a hole through the bundle of pictures, quickly ran a string through the opening, walked to the back of the shop and hung them on a nail in the toilet.

Modigliani began to gain general recognition as an artist when he exhibited at the *Salon des Indépendants* in 1910, and again in 1912. But long before this, the inhabitants of the bohemian haunts of Paris had taken him to their collective bosom, and he was widely known and loved as an artist and a man.

One of the most important events in his life was his meeting in 1916 with the Polish dealer and poet Leopold Zborowski, who became his constant companion in his adventurings around Paris. Modigliani has left us numerous portraits of the dealer and his family. Zborowski helped arrange for the sale of pictures at fairly respectable prices and in 1917 organized Modigliani's first one-man show, at the Berthe Weill Gallery.

In all that is written about Modi (as his friends called him) we find mention of his inordinate love for women. His affairs were many, and he has left portraits of most of his mistresses—Beatrice Hastings, diverse unnamed girls and finally Jeanne Hébuterne, who bore him a daughter. Many of these women posed for him in the nude, and he represented them with a candor and frankness so shocking to the authorities that the exhibit at the Weill Gallery was closed by the police. The cold nudity of Manet's *Olympia* was in many respects a less honest portrayal than his. No doubt Modigliani thought in terms of the painter's problems, designing and coloring the elongated bodies to produce linear rhythms and harmonies of subtle hue. Those who came to view his work had somewhat less pure sensations when they gazed at the undraped forms. This fact kept many of his pictures out of the museums for a time.

His portraits were generally received with no greater enthusiasm. When in 1922, after his death, an exhibition was arranged at the Twelfth Venice Biennial, an "eminent" critic described the canvases as "twelve ugly unformed heads that a child of five might have drawn." Here once again was that recurrent invention—the extraordinary, mythical "child of five" who always draws and paints better than the artist whose works are being exhibited!

It was the painter Moïse Kisling who brought word to Montparnasse that Modi had died suddenly. He had been in the hospital only two days. Jeanne Hébuterne threw herself on his dead body, covered him with kisses and returned to her father's house to leap to her death from a window, or a housetop—the report varies. Montparnasse was emptied of artists the day of Modigliani's funeral. They followed the hearse across Paris to see their friend laid to rest. This was in January 1920, and Modigliani had not lived out his thirty-sixth year.

His friend Jacques Lipchitz wrote: "Modigliani said to me more than once, 'I wish a short and intense life.' "

—HERMAN J. WECHSLER

SELF-PORTRAIT

Picasso

PABLO PICASSO

1881–

His Astonishing World

PEOPLE WHO DON'T LIKE unconventional art have said he is only spoofing the public. And the public itself has often scoffed at his works. When his masterpiece, *Guernica,* was first shown nearly thirty years ago, many thought it looked like a scattering of pieces of a jigsaw puzzle. Despite these reactions—or perhaps partly because of them—Pablo Picasso has become the most famous artist of the century. But a multitude of painters now following in his footsteps believe he has achieved something far greater than fame: he has liberated art from age-old academic tradition.

Picasso himself believes he is demonstrating that art and natural appearance are two different things. He can, however, paint conventionally when he wants to. For example, he can depict a ravishingly Eve-like woman—instead of a combination of lines, forms and colors which may, according to his mood, have elephant ears, two noses, three eyes, and resemble a potbellied stove.

It was in his teens, after painting numerous realistic pictures, that Picasso began to feel he was merely imitating nature. Within a short time he evolved what few artists are ever able to: a style of his own. The pictures he painted in this period—blue-tone-dominated portrayals of blind beggars, sad, solitary drinkers, poverty-stricken mothers—were seminaturalistic. The "Blue Period" proved but the first in a lifelong procession of original styles. He also became a remarkable sculptor, etcher, ceramist and graphic craftsman. For sixty years he has been one of the most varied artists who ever lived.

This son of an impecunious art teacher was born in Málaga, Spain, in 1881. From the age of seven the child was always drawing. His marvelous technique soon began to attract attention. At sixteen his painting won honorable

LOLA

By 1899 the eighteen-year-old Picasso had won high art honors in his Spanish homeland. A realistic work of that year was a portrait of his sister (above).

WOMAN IN BLUE

What painter most influenced the amazingly original Picasso? Some say Toulouse-Lautrec. The lady in this 1902 work could indeed be about to visit the Moulin Rouge *(see page 24).*

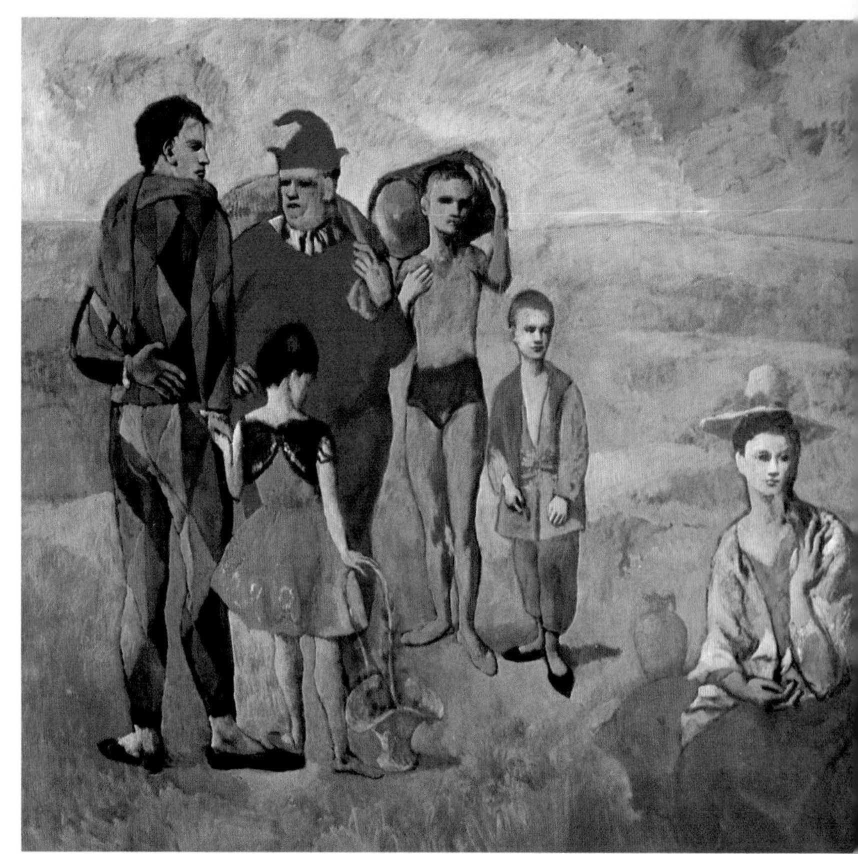

(2) FAMILY OF SALTIMBANC

(1) POOR PEOPLE ON THE SEASHORE

(3) GERTRUDE STEIN

(5) WOMAN IN W

(1) The Blue Period painting reflects the pover Picasso experienced during his early days in Pa (2) In the warm tones of the happier Pink Per the artist pictured his Montmartre circus friends (3) Picasso said, "Everybody thinks the portra not like her, but in the end, she will look like the portrait." (4) The clown, the harlequin an

(4) THE THREE MUSICIANS

(6) GIRL BEFORE MIRROR

(9) WOMAN AND TWO GIRLS

(7) GUERNICA

monk blend into the camouflage of Cubism.
One of the artist's most famous paintings,
portrait belongs to his Greek-Roman or Classical
iod. (6) His Gothic Stained Glass style was
inguished by brilliant colors and heavy outlining
ilar to that of Georges Rouault (see page 181).
The black-and-white wartime masterpiece
(see page 38) was created in two months from
a hundred studies. (8) This lithograph
series is a favorite of the artist, who once said,
"For me the bull is the proudest symbol of all."
(9) Painted in his eightieth year, when
he was experimenting in subject matter, the
portrait does not fall into any new trend.

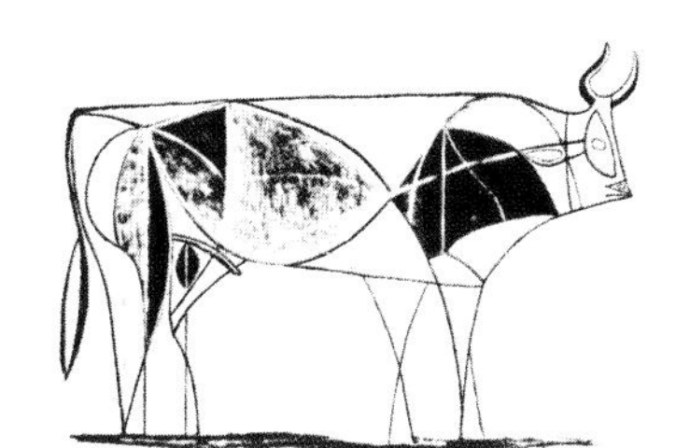

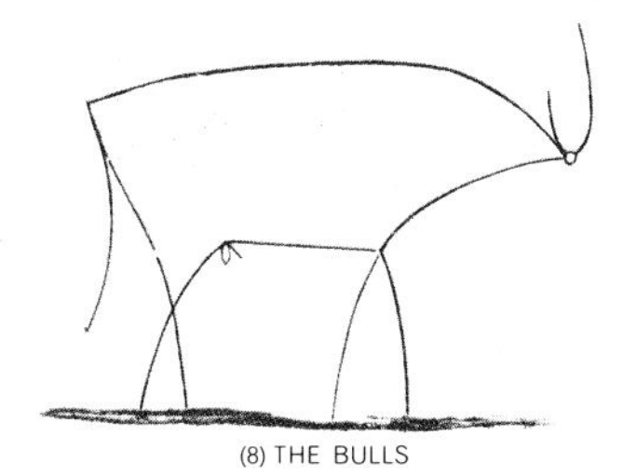
(8) THE BULLS

mention at the National Exhibition of Fine Arts in Madrid. The next year, 1898, he took the gold medal in a show in his home town of Málaga. So great was his father's faith in the boy's genius that he handed over his savings to enable his son to go to Paris at nineteen.

Picasso lived in want for the next ten years. At one time he shared a single bed with a writer, working at night while the writer slept and sleeping all day while the writer worked. To keep from freezing one night, he had to burn all the drawings he'd made that year—drawings which today would sell for thousands of dollars.

Short and thickset, with glossy black hair and jet-black eyes—"the bold eyes of a bull"—young Picasso looked more like a day laborer than an artist. His blue overalls and pullover completed the impression. During his first five years in Paris he turned out two hundred paintings—as many as some artists produce in a lifetime. Though a number of them were exhibited, they rarely sold.

In 1906 Gertrude Stein gave a boost to Picasso's career. He painted her portrait, and she and her brother, the art collector, persuaded their acquaintances to buy his works. Many years later she said of the portrait: "For me, it is I, and it is the only reproduction of me which is always I, for me." This fitting comment is a choice sample of the style of the writer who coined the famous "A rose is a rose is a rose"!

After several years in which his work was influenced by primitive objects, Picasso made the most powerful innovation in twentieth-century art. By taking literally Cézanne's search for "the cylinder, the sphere, the cone" in nature, he interpreted what that Master had pointed toward. Among the myriad artists Picasso attracted were prominent Fauves, who now dropped their bold expressive combinations of color for the almost drab "Cubism." These were Rouault, Vlaminck, Raoul Dufy and Georges Braque (see page 183). Matisse, known as "King of the Fauves," gave Cubism its name—disparagingly, but it stuck—and went on his own colorful way. Among the many styles created by Picasso, none has had as much impact as the Cubist.

In April 1937, news of the destruction of the Spanish town of Guernica by planes of the German Luftwaffe led the expatriate Spanish artist to create, in less than two months, his famous *Guernica*. It became the most talked-about painting of the time. What did the huge jigsaw puzzle mean? What to make of the speared horse, the bull, the light bulb, the burning house, the dead soldier grasping the sword? Why the newsprint-like design in the horse's hide? What was Picasso for, what was he against? And on and on. The topical questions are no longer of pressing interest. But for many people, *Guernica* is among the greatest paintings of the century because it has expressed with overwhelming eloquence the tragic, troubled soul of our disordered age.

Just over two years after *Guernica*, world war came again to Europe. In Paris, the Germans forbade Picasso to exhibit his pictures but otherwise did nothing to keep the artist's hands from continual work—this despite Picasso's unconcealed hatred of all they stood for. When a German officer, visiting his studio during the war, asked him if he had painted *Guernica*, he replied: "No, you did!"

After the liberation of Paris in 1944 Picasso gave out the news that he had joined the Communist Party, an affiliation from which he may have wavered. Moscow, despite his efforts on behalf of the party (his lithograph of a white pigeon became the symbol of their 1949 Peace Congress), denounced Picasso's art.

From his first marriage in 1918—to Olga Koklova, a Russian ballerina—Picasso's son Paul was born. He is the father of three other children: Maïa, Claude and Paloma. Today he lives in "destitute grandeur" with his young wife, Jacqueline Roque.

Years ago Picasso said he'd like to be rich and live like a poor man. The wish has come true. A self-made millionaire, he eats simple food, dresses like a peasant.

Picasso's affluence shows itself uniquely in the accumulated property of an artistic lifetime: his homes in Paris and the south of France are topsy-turvy jumbles, piled with pictures, pottery, books, press clippings, interesting stones he has picked up, shells, gnarled roots. When he moves, the hodgepodge is carefully crated and carried to the new house, where the crates stand unopened in the midst of fresh accumulations.

Now in his eighties, Picasso still does a prodigious amount of work—most of it by night, following lifelong habit. Painting swiftly and spontaneously, he has been known to finish three pictures in a day and a half. His Spanish secretary, a close friend for over sixty years, described Picasso as a "molten mind comparable to a volcano in constant eruption." It might be said that this volcano has broken apart the life it touches, and created a strange volcanic world of its own.

Picasso's unconventional pictures of a transfigured world have influenced thousands of other artists. Whether they will appeal to future generations only time, the great art critic, will tell. —MALCOLM VAUGHAN

THE AGE OF GREATNESS

Why did so many of the world's great painters appear within fifty years, in Italy, around 1500 A.D.? Leonardo da Vinci, Michelangelo, Raphael, Titian and others were all fiercely sought after by popes and rulers. Artists were the most honored of men. Three centuries earlier, Europe had begun to change astonishingly, as cities grew and merchant classes rose. The great cathedrals were built in the thirteenth century. Painting was then almost entirely religious, confined to the adornment of churches, with a flat two-dimensional style—known as Byzantine in the Eastern Church and Gothic in the Western. Beginning with Giotto, the first great artist to win fame in his lifetime, men learned to create three-dimensional effects, as well as the wonders of perspective and light. And they began to paint the worlds about them—women and knights, forests, palaces, battles. All this the geniuses of the High Renaissance—that period of the rebirth of learning after the Middle Ages—fell heir to. And they produced marvels such as the world has never again achieved—the discerning portraits of da Vinci, Michelangelo's magnificent human figures in motion, the divine beauty of Raphael and Titian's miracles of color and light

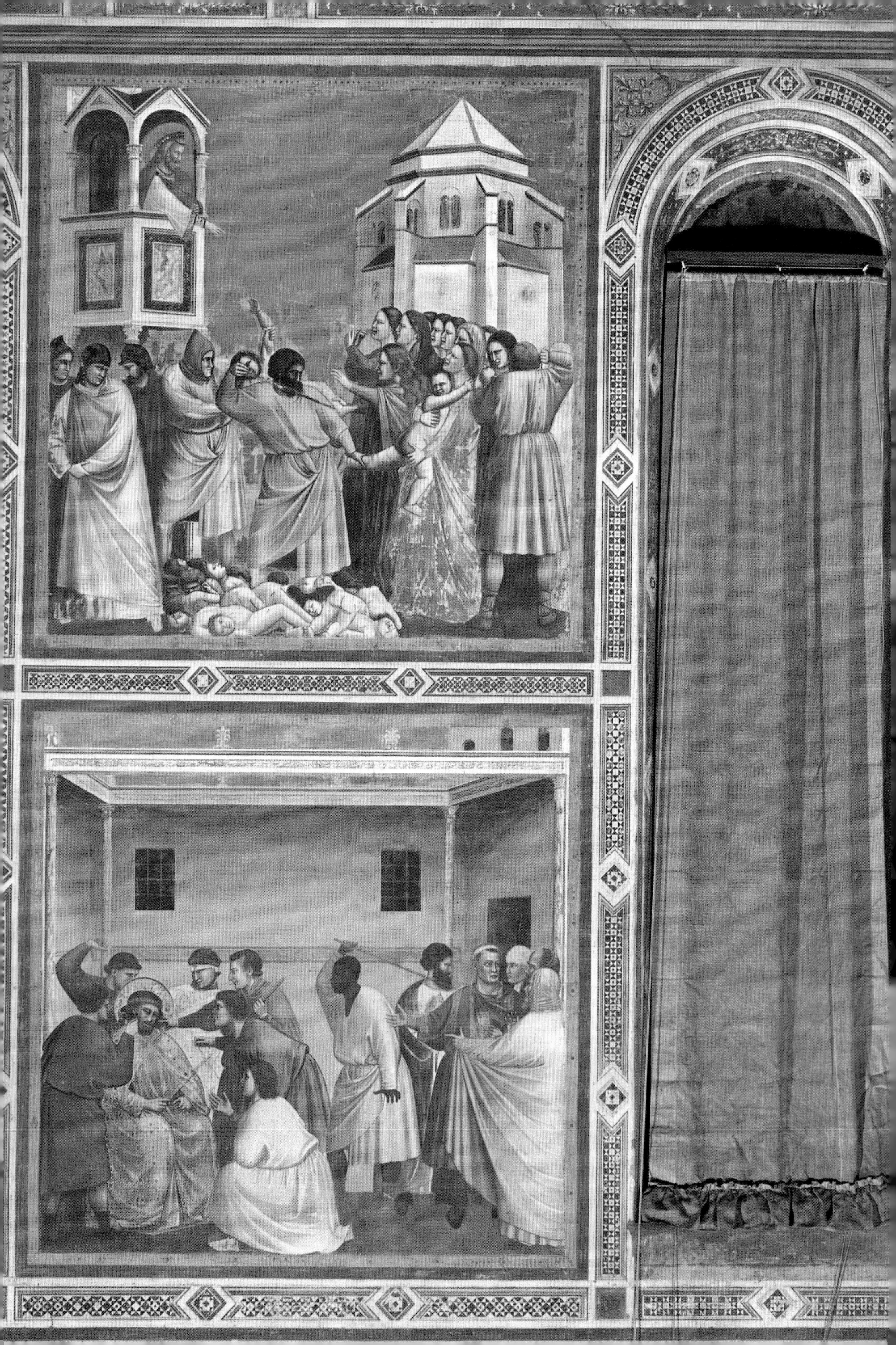

GIOTTO

1276?–1337

A Boy Who Changed Art

Giotto's best-preserved works are in the Scrovegni Chapel at Padua (above). Enrico Scrovegni, a well-to-do citizen, invited him there about 1305 to paint a series of frescoes upon the life of Christ and the Virgin Mary. The large panels (opposite, above) show The Massacre of the Innocents*—soldiers of Herod killing babes lest the newborn King live to gain the throne—and (bottom)* The Flagellation of Christ *before He was led away to be crucified. The small portraits of holy men may have been done by Giotto's assistants. In the center is a confessional.*

ACCORDING TO A TALE told for centuries, an artist, trudging along a mountain road in Italy, passed a shepherd boy sprawled upon a large flat rock. The boy was drawing on the rock with a burnt stick—charcoal. The artist, glancing down, couldn't believe his eyes. He was looking at the most lifelike image of a sheep he had ever seen.

"Who are you?" he asked the boy.

"My name is Giotto. My father's a farmer, and I'm his sheepherder. We live up there."

The boy and the artist climbed to the farm cottage, and the artist talked at length to the father, telling him that Giotto possessed extraordinary talent and ought to be trained. In the end the father agreed that the artist, Cimabue, Italy's greatest painter of that time, might take Giotto as an apprentice. The boy would grind colors, mix paints, wash brushes, while being taught how to paint.

That boy's talent for making an image lifelike was to change the history of art. For it was Giotto, in the late thirteenth and early fourteenth centuries, who started a new tradition of painting by turning away from the austerity and flatness of Byzantine art toward the mastery of perspective and of nature.

He based his painting on what he saw. When he painted a tree it looked like a tree. The people he painted looked like human beings. You could read in their faces the types of persons they were. You could even feel their emotions: fear, grief, happiness, love. From the day Giotto's pictures began to be seen, other artists imitated him. The greatest painters of later times—Raphael, Leonardo da Vinci, Michelangelo—all acknowledged their debt to his novel way of painting the world as it appeared.

Giotto was keenly religious, as were the majority of his contemporaries. A spiritual tide was then sweeping over Europe. Thousands of men and women were fascinated by the beautiful mysteries of faith. This was due to a great extent to the influence of Francis of Assisi, who had died about half a century before Giotto was born. Francis was a rich merchant's son who gave away everything he owned, even his shoes, and went about ever afterward in a simple and austere robe, barefoot.

MEETING AT THE GOLDEN GATE
Legendary tales of Christ's family were loved in Giotto's time. From one of these, he showed Joachim and Anna meeting at the "gold-gilded" gate of Jerusalem, after the Angel has told them they will become parents of the Virgin Mary.

THE BETRAYAL BY JUDAS
The face of every disciple or soldier reveals his allegiance in the drama created by Giotto, the first great storyteller in Western painting. He depicted not only the kiss but the cutting off of a soldier's ear by the disciple Peter.

ST. FRANCIS PREACHING TO THE BIRDS
This picture marvelously tells of the universal love in St. Francis' heart. Birds listened "as if they had the use of reason," when he told them to praise their Creator, who gave them feathers to fly through life without care.

Francis was dedicated to helping others, especially those in direst distress—paupers, outcasts, lepers. He wanted to prove by his own example that God is love. In so doing he himself became the most beloved man of his era; two years after he died he was canonized.

A church was built in Assisi and named for the saint. When it was finished, young Giotto was called to help paint on its inside walls the story of St. Francis' life—a vast picturebook of twenty-eight scenes in a rich variety of colors. When those walls were unveiled, people gaped, spellbound, at the lifelike pictures. Nothing of this kind had ever been seen before. Today, six centuries later, tourists from around the world still flock into the church and stand before those paintings in awe and admiration.

Another beacon of Giotto's art that still draws art lovers in wonder is the Scrovegni Chapel in Padua. Here he painted a series of scenes that in their power to evoke emotion rival those of any other master. It is said that the poet Dante, on first visiting the chapel, was struck dumb by these frescoes, "so truly did they represent nature."

Giotto's wonderful combination of heart and skill made him the foremost artist of his time. Praise, homage, fame were lavished upon him; kings and dukes invited him to their palaces and sought to commission him. Giotto remained unimpressed. He painted for them and accepted their money (enough to support his wife and five children in every comfort) but he never lost his modesty. When other artists tried to address him as "Master" he would not allow it.

Even though Giotto achieved unsurpassed greatness in painting, he excelled in more than one art. He was also a sculptor, a poet, a composer and an architect. Of the honors heaped upon him, perhaps the highest was the resolution passed by the public officers of Florence, who asked him to come to live there so that "by his presence many can have the advantage of his learning." When he accepted, Florence gave him the title of city architect and contracted with him to design their cathedral bell tower, or campanile. The humble Giotto's creation is still one of the most famous towers in the world.

At his death, in his sixties, he was revered by the plain people as well as by art connoisseurs. Later the greatest of the Medicis, Lorenzo the Magnificent—patron of the arts in fifteenth-century Florence—had this epitaph carved on the painter's tomb: "Lo, I am he . . . to whose right hand all was possible, by whom dead painting was brought to life, by whom art became one with nature. For I am Giotto."

—MALCOLM VAUGHAN

SELF-PORTRAIT(?), JAN VAN EYCK

THE VAN EYCKS

Hubert: 1366?–1426; Jan: 1370?–1440

The Discoverers

ABOUT 1420 the van Eyck brothers appeared: two painters in oil, marvelous technicians and the greatest artists of the North in their time.

Hubert and Jan van Eyck were not the first to use the oil medium, as was once believed; nor were they oil painters in the modern understanding of the term. "Oil and varnish," according to Sir Charles Holmes, the modern English critic, "had long been employed as surface protectives for work in tempera (paintings in which the colors are tempered with yolk of egg), but the van Eycks were the first to make them clear and tractable, so that they could be mixed with the colors and used for the painting itself."

In the northern countries, the damp climate was destructive to frescoes; the great cathedrals, built to admit every possible ray of light, had no room for wall decorations, and oil painting came to the fore. The great art of Flanders (now part of France, Belgium and the Netherlands) began with the van Eycks and ended two hundred years later with Rubens (see page 87). The wealth of Flanders was the talk of Europe; the cities—in spite of feudal kingdoms elsewhere—were democratic communities. Illiteracy was unknown and the spirit of the people was strong and hearty. Along with this material prosperity, the art of painting developed to a degree of excellence that is an endless source of despair to modern artists. It is now nearly six hundred years since the van Eycks and their followers painted their portraits and altarpieces, and yet these look as though they were done yesterday!

Before a century had elapsed, the van Eycks' new method was adopted by the other European schools; Leonardo da Vinci used it, and so did all the Venetians. Their discovery was prized as a miracle by their countrymen, and in St. Bavon Cathedral of Ghent, the bones of the right arm of Hubert, the elder brother, were enshrined in a casket and placed above the door as a sacred relic.

Jan van Eyck outlived his brother many years and was sent by the Duke of Burgundy on confidential missions into Spain and Portugal. He was a portrait painter, and he ranks with the greatest. Acrid, unflattering and cold-blooded, he examined the human face with an infallible eye and compelled it to yield the psychological secrets of the sitter.

Hubert excelled in the organization of many figures and objects into a single unit, but Jan organized the smallest components of the face into a striking countenance. The man had a biological passion for probing into homeliness. Instead of leaving out wrinkles, wens and blemishes, he seemed actually to add to them, blending innumerable details into a speaking reality. Sometimes he signed his pictures with a great flourish, but the signatures are superfluous: the heads reveal not only the subject but the maker—as precise a personality as ever got itself into paint.

His *Marriage of Giovanni Arnolfini and Giovanna Cenami* is one of the prizes of the National Gallery, London, and one of the most desired paintings in the world. According to a former director, this picture of an acrid little shrimp of a man and his timid bride is the one painting above all others which the majority of visitors would love to carry away. Part of the picture's charm lies in the discovery of the exquisitely painted details: the string of amber beads against the back wall, the oranges, the mirror with its frame decorated in perfectly distinct miniatures of the Passion of the Lord, the one burning candle and the extravagant signature in Latin—*Jan van Eyck was there, 1434*. The picture is an example of a great artist's simple humanity and his honest love for domestic things.

Although their processes are no mystery, the formula for the van Eycks' oil glazes and the manipulation of their pigments remain a secret. All painting in oil will deteriorate in the course of time, and nothing can stop it. But no artist has ever matched the clean and brilliant color, the perfection of the finished surfaces, and the durability of these Flemish masters.

Besides perfecting a new means of painting, the van Eyck brothers explored and conquered the mechanics of picture-making. They mastered and taught linear and atmospheric perspective and revolutionized the medieval notions of landscape.

The apocalyptic vision unfolded on the twelve panels of their joint masterpiece, *The Adoration of the Lamb* in the St. Bavon Cathedral, holds the splendor of a new dawn. In

MARRIAGE OF GIOVANNI ARNOLFINI
The first great Western artist to portray personal events of life, Jan van Eyck attended this Flemish wedding where the couple performed their own ceremony. The reflection in the mirror includes the artist.

ST. GEORGE AND THE DRAGON

True to the Renaissance, Uccello appears to take chivalry lightly, with his imaginative dragon and demure maid. St. George saves Princess Cleoddinda, a final sacrifice for the city of Selene to the threatening dragon.

A section of the painting as i (above) gleams with new life the restored work (right). Uc painted The Rout of San Romano, *a series of panels long, in 1452 for Cosimo de'*

UCCELLO'S SIGNATURE, FROM A PANEL OF THE ROUT OF SAN ROMANO

the central panel of the upper tier of this altarpiece stands Christ the King of Heaven, grave and ruddy; a hairy John the Baptist in a green gown; a piquant Virgin Mary; choirs of full-lipped Flemish angels earnestly singing; and Adam and Eve in their scrawny nakedness.

Nowhere else in Flemish painting, or for that matter in all painting, is there a picture of so many small, precise forms—pebbles, precious stones, leaves and flowers, banners, brocades, tiled patterns and carved woods—drawn with the minute observation of the miniaturists.

The van Eycks had that rare faculty of imagination, the power to take the familiar and charge it with their own intense feelings and experiences so that the ordinary man is carried into a world that is fresh and enchanting.

—THOMAS CRAVEN

PAOLO UCCELLO

1397–1475

The Experimenter

DURING HIS LIFETIME Paolo Uccello was set down by his more practical neighbors as a harmless crank; inasmuch as his idiosyncrasies ran to graphs and abstractions they were humorously condoned. It was said that he would stay up all night with his studies—drawing eighty-sided polygons and other such oddities. When his wife begged him to go to bed, he exclaimed: "Oh, what a delightful thing is this perspective!"

He was one of those early Florentine painters who had no time for minor graces of painting—melting color, tender sentiment and smooth textures. They conquered the stubborn questions of technique and the basic principles of art by willpower and unremitting toil.

THE ROUT OF SAN ROMANO

Reproduced here for the first time anywhere—following nearly six years of restoration by the National Gallery of London—is a panel of the earliest known masterpiece employing visual depth *(for definition see left column below). To see how the painting formerly appeared, compare its vivid colors with those of the unrestored section on the opposite page.*

Uccello's geometric chalice and circular ornament show the science behind his new perspective.

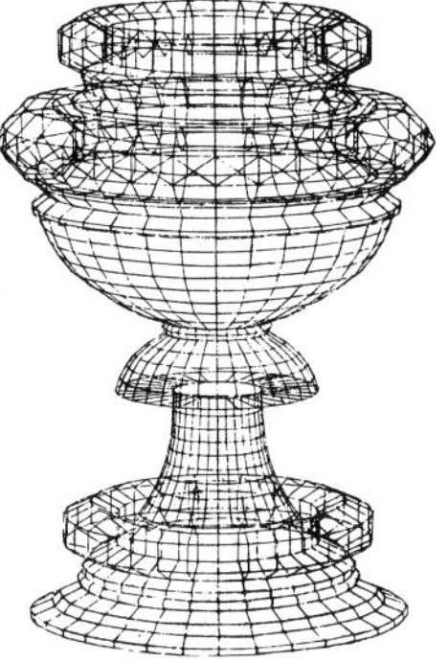

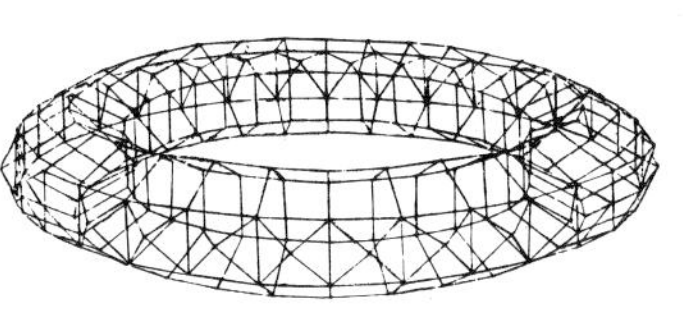

Uccello's mastery of perspective was among their greatest achievements. This barber-surgeon's son was absorbed with devices used by artists to give depth to a scene—converging lines, foreshortenings and receding planes. In the words of a sixteenth-century biographer of Italian painters, "He sought a method of placing his figures standing on planes, and revealed how they should diminish in proportion as they recede, which before had been done haphazardly by others." To make his strange discoveries, "Uccello began to stay alone, almost wild, without household routine for weeks and months, and without letting anyone see him."

Not too surprisingly, the reclusive painter was also a timid man. Once he was engaged to do a series of paintings on the lives of the Holy Fathers at San Miniato: It seems that little was served to Uccello at the abbey but cheese. Meek though he was, he decided not to work there any longer. When the abbot sent for him, he was never at home. One day two of the younger friars caught up with him, even though he tried to take to his heels. "Why don't you come finish your work?" they asked. "It's your abbot's fault," Uccello replied. "He has everything made with cheese—even cakes and soups. If this goes on, I shall not be Paolo, but cheese." Laughing, the friars went off and told the story to the abbot, who called Uccello back to work—with the promise of more appetizing fare.

In battle scenes and historical settings Uccello found his most noted means of presenting his solutions for the problems of linear perspective; he was probably the first to treat these subjects in art on a major scale.

Uccello's *Rout of San Romano*—three large panels painted for the bedchamber of one of the Medicis, the most prominent and powerful family of Florence—celebrates the defeat of the Sienese by the Florentines in 1432. *San Romano* has long been admired—and justly so—for its quaintness, its childlike gaiety and its naïve playfulness. But it would be a mistake to suppose that Uccello, intent on painting a realistic battle picture, had blundered onto a nursery masterpiece. He was a scholar, a precisionist, a mathematician of distinction. The wonder and youth of the Renaissance fascinated him, and his *San Romano,* alive with clashing planes, radiating lines (projecting lances among them), is strangely modern. In its geometrical horses there is a foretelling of the Cubism of modern art. In its clear-cut, detailed design, its pattern of linear science and color—constructed by the most advanced technician of his time—there is movement, rhythm. There is a fantastic vision of figures that are more tin soldiers than knights, more hobbyhorses than steeds.

Another famous painting by Uccello is *Sir John Hawkwood,* a memorial to the English mercenary who led troops for Florence. It is a larger-than-life pictorial substitute for a statue, the customary equestrian monument.

In his last year, the retiring, single-minded artist withdrew altogether from the outside world after a slight from his fellow artist and longtime friend, the renowned Donatello. The story was told by his early biographer that Uccello, painting a picture of St. Thomas placing his fingers in the wound in Christ's side, "had made a planked enclosure so that no one could see his work until it was finished." Visiting Uccello, Donatello saw the covered picture and asked:

> *"What work is this that you keep it closed off?" And Paolo answered him: "You will see, that's all." Donatello did not want to press him further, thinking as usual that in time he would see a miracle.* [Later Paolo uncovered his painting for Donatello, curious to hear his opinion as to how the picture looked to him.] *Donatello, after looking the picture over very carefully, said: "Ah! Paolo, now that it is time to cover up, you uncover!" Then, Paolo, seriously saddened, realized he had received severe censure for that labor when he had expected praise; and, humbled, having no more courage to go out again, he shut himself up at home, studying perspective, which kept him impoverished and in obscurity until his death. . . . But there can be no doubt that his work, so "delightful" to him, has been invaluable to those painters who came after him.*
>
> —THOMAS CRAVEN

FRA FILIPPO LIPPI

1406?–1469

Amorous Monk

DESPITE HIS ADVENTUROUS LOVE LIFE, and perhaps because of his sensitivity to the beauty of women, Fra Filippo Lippi's finest pictures are of the Virgin. They fall short of ethereal spirituality, but they convey a deep sense of soft delicacy and infinite tenderness. With Fra Lippo, as he was known, the Holy Family became an Italian family, surrounded with homely incidents, and the Virgin took on a greater liveliness than any painter had shown before. To the feminine charms of his Madonnas, Filippo added an airy grace that passed down to his apprentice Botticelli (see page 52).

Filippo, son of the butcher Tommaso Lippi, was born in Florence in a poor street behind the monastery of the Carmelites. According to Giorgio Vasari, the biographer, he was orphaned at two and reluctantly reared by an aunt, who rid herself of him when he was only eight by entering him in the Carmelite order. Instead of studying the books assigned to him he covered their margins with caricatures. The prior, noting their excellence, set him to copying the frescoes that the famous artist Masaccio (see page 163) had just painted in the Carmelite church. Soon the lad was painting frescoes of his own in that same church; they have disappeared, but Vasari thought them as good as Masaccio's. "Of his time there were few better than [Filippo]," wrote this biographer in 1550. "Michelangelo has always praised him."

At the age of twenty-six (in 1432) Filippo left the monk's community; he continued to call himself Fra (Brother or Friar), but he lived in the outside world and supported himself by his art. Vasari tells a story that tradition has accepted, though we cannot be sure of its truth.

> *Filippo is said to have been so amorous that when he saw a woman who pleased him he would have given all his possessions to have her; and if he could not succeed in this he quieted the flame of his love by painting her portrait. This appetite so took possession of him that while the humor lasted he paid little or no attention to his work. Thus, on one occasion when Cosimo de' Medici* [the ruler of Florence] *was employing him, he shut him up in the house so that he might not go out and waste time. Filippo remained so for two*

ADORATION OF THE MAGI

One of the earliest paintings of the great Medici collection of Florence, this ranks with the finest of the fifteenth century. The worldly monk Fra Lippo sets Mary before a stable, amid Oriental pageantry, peacocks and awestruck bystanders. The many gorgeous details may have been inspired by the visit in 1439 of the Patriarch of Constantinople and the Emperor of the East.

days; but, overcome by his amorous and bestial desires, he cut up his sheet with a pair of scissors and letting himself out of the window, devoted many days to his pleasures. When Cosimo could not find him he caused a search to be made for him, until at length Filippo returned to his labors. From that time forward Cosimo gave him liberty to go and come as he chose, repenting that he had shut him up . . . for, he said, geniuses are celestial forms and not pack asses. . . . Ever afterward he sought to hold Filippo by the bonds of affection, and was thus served by him with greater readiness.

In 1439 "Fra Lippo" described himself—in a letter to Piero de' Medici, the son of Cosimo—as the poorest friar in Florence, living with and supporting with difficulty six nieces anxious to be married. His work was in demand, but apparently not as well paid as the nieces wished. His morals could not have been notoriously bad, for we find him engaged to paint pictures for various nunneries. At the convent of Santa Margherita in Prato (unless Vasari and tradition err), he fell in love with Lucrezia Buti, a nun or a ward of the nuns. He persuaded the prioress to let Lucrezia pose for him; soon they eloped. Despite her father's reproaches and appeals she remained with the artist and sat as the model for many Virgins. Their son was the Filippino Lippi of later fame as a painter.

The wardens of the cathedral at Prato did not hold his adventures against Filippo; they engaged him to paint the choir with frescoes illustrating the lives of St. John the Baptist and St. Stephen. These paintings, now much damaged by time, were acclaimed as masterpieces—perfect in composition, rich in color. Alive with drama, they depict the climactic scenes of the dance of Salome on one side of the choir and the stoning of Stephen on the other. Filippo found the task too wearisome for his mobility; twice he ran away from it.

In 1461 Cosimo persuaded Pope Pius II to release the artist from his monastic vows; Filippo seems to have thought himself also freed from fidelity to Lucrezia, for he was no longer in Prato. The wardens of the cathedral exhausted all schemes for luring him back to his frescoes. At last, ten years after their inception, he was induced to finish them by Carlo de' Medici, Cosimo's illegitimate son, an apostolic notary. On the scene of St. Stephen's burial Filippo exercised all his marvelous powers—in the deceptive perspective of the architectural background, the sharply individualized figures surrounding the corpse, and the stout proportions and calm, rotund face of Carlo reading the services for the dead.

A few years later the city of Spoleto invited Filippo to tell the story of the Virgin again in the apse of its cathedral. He labored conscientiously, passion having cooled; but his ability failed with his passion, and he could not repeat the excellence of his Prato murals. Amid this effort he died in 1469, poisoned, it was said, by the relatives of a girl he had seduced. The story is improbable, for Filippo was buried in the Spoleto cathedral. There, a few years later, his son, on commission from Lorenzo de' Medici, built for his father a splendid marble tomb. —WILL DURANT

GENTILE AND GIOVANNI BELLINI

Gentile: 1429?–1507?; Giovanni: 1430?–1516

A Dynasty of Venice

THE ACHIEVEMENT of Giovanni Bellini was probably one of the rarest in art: the variety of his Madonnas. The wonder is that he could have maintained such inspiration in painting so many of them—more than seventy. They are all sisters, neither mystical nor deeply affecting, but self-possessed and splendidly Venetian. Much of their distinction must be attributed to their color—a fusion of reds, greens and blues with subtle distribution of light. *The Madonna of the Trees* is perhaps the finest.

Giovanni, the first of the Venetian masters, was the great glory of the Bellini family, who were the earliest leaders of art in Venice. Jacopo, the father, was an eccentric and inquisitive old gentleman and a great traveler. He wandered through Italy, notebook in hand, visiting Florence and Rome and making sketches of all sorts of things—elaborate architectural settings, animals, antiquities, mountains, cities and Madonnas. Jacopo is remembered in art for his endless curiosity and for sharp, carefully outlined sketches, which won the admiration of Leonardo da Vinci. His notebooks were carefully preserved by his sons.

In Padua, Jacopo Bellini acquired a scientific knowledge of painting from the famous artist Andrea Mantegna (see page 165). Later he gave his daughter in marriage to Mantegna, and trained his sons Gentile and Giovanni in Mantegna's technique. Gentile, less imaginative than his brother, gained renown for his church decorations and his portraits, but his position as one of the founders of Venetian art rests mainly upon his processional pictures. His masterpiece, *Procession of the True Cross,* a view of St. Mark's Square during a religious festival, is a reflection of the Venetian love of display. It shows a crowd of choristers and

PROCESSION OF THE TRUE CROSS, *by Gentile Bellini*

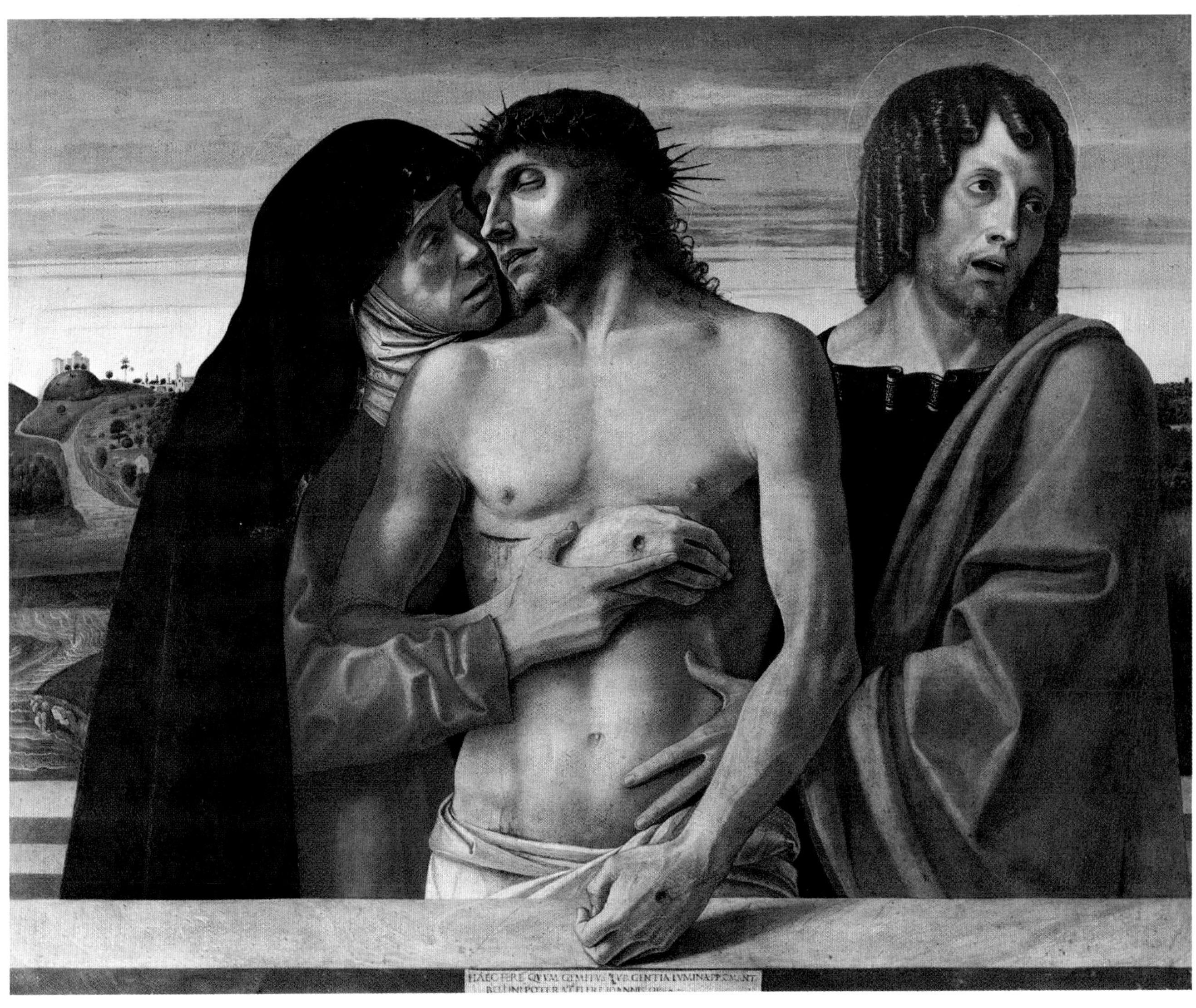

PIETA, *by Giovanni Bellini*

The main square of Venice, painted by Gentile, looks much as it does today. A fire in the Doge's palace (right of the cathedral) destroyed many works by Giovanni, whose first masterpiece was this fresco of the dead Christ. Giovanni probably introduced oils to Italy.

candle-bearers; dignitaries fetching up reliquaries (sacred objects); groups of sightseers; and, in the ringside seats on the balconies, the overlords sipping wine and looking very high-class indeed. Turning from the religious tradition, which had never been very marked in Venice, Gentile entered into the pageantry of the city, portraying the stately crowds, the marching priests, the background of light and air and color.

The most illustrious member of the family was Giovanni, who lived to the ripe age of eighty-six and passed through many stages of development, painting portraits, allegories, altarpieces, landscapes and pastorals. If his fame has been overshadowed by his pupils Giorgione and Titian, it is because his followers profited by his discoveries and carried them forward to a higher degree of perfection.

The rulers of Venice were patriotic souls, jealous of their city and not a little conscious of their own superiority. To preserve their likenesses in a style befitting their official station, they wanted an artist whose works were pleasing to the eye and not contradictory to their own ideas of distinction. They found their man in Giovanni Bellini, a mild-mannered artist who could be depended on to paint truthfully but without harshness, for his inclination was to discover in his subjects the pacific integrity of his own nature.

Today, Bellini's portraits are exceedingly rare. For his *Portrait of a Youth,* now in the National Gallery in Washington, D.C., Andrew W. Mellon, financier and philanthropist, paid 280,000 dollars. In this picture Bellini produced a work which shows the grave quality and line of his training in Padua, but which has a richness of color that makes it a glory of Venetian painting. Another example of Bellini's genius is *Doge Leonardo Loredano,* a late work and as impressive a portrait as the hand of man has produced—noble in characterization, beautiful in color and faultless in execution.

Giovanni was a man of uncommonly good sense and reasonableness. He was incapable of the tragic passions, but he was above banality. And, in his use of light and color to bind his forms together into a harmony of tones, he anticipated Rembrandt.

As artist and practitioner he was serenely prosperous from youth to extreme old age. When Titian attempted to obtain his official post, he was annoyed but not vindictive. Albrecht Dürer, the great German painter and engraver, in 1506 pronounced Bellini "the grand old man of art, and the best and most courteous painter in Venice."

—THOMAS CRAVEN

SELF-PORTRAIT

SB.

SANDRO BOTTICELLI

1444?–1510

Poet of Spring

IN ART MUSEUMS EVERYWHERE, the paintings of Botticelli are besieged by artists struggling to capture in copies his magician's touch. In his own Florence, postcards and color prints of Botticelli outsell those of all other masters. And millions of reproductions of his works grace living rooms throughout the world.

What is it about Botticelli that places him among our most beloved of artists? For one thing, the beauty of his elongated bodies; also, his soft, unblemished faces and the delicacy of those "Botticelli hands" that we can recognize a mile away. But there is more: something strange, elusive, wistful gives all his works an otherworldly look and strikes chords that lie deep in our soul.

Born in 1444 or 1445, Botticelli was a child of Florence's golden age. The artistic springtide known as the Renaissance was in its early phases. Sandro—short for Alessandro —was one of the youngest children in a large family. His father, Mariano Filipepi, was a tanner. His brother Giovanni's nickname, *Botticello*—"little barrel"— was handed down, like an ill-fitting coat, to the thin Sandro. Soon common usage had replaced his family name with "Botticelli," and he was stuck for life with that well-rounded alias.

Though Sandro's first biographer, Giorgio Vasari, himself a painter, tells us that the boy "quickly mastered anything he liked," he was loath to settle down to reading, writing and arithmetic. So Sandro worked in a goldsmith's shop. But he was restless; painting was on his mind. His father apprenticed him to Fra Filippo Lippi (see page 48), whose free-and-easy ways may have soured the young man on the idea of marriage, for Botticelli remained single all his life. When a friend asked him the reason why, Sandro told him he once dreamed he was married and woke up so scared that he ran from his room and walked the empty streets till dawn.

Still, it is largely as a painter of women that Sandro was to make his reputation. His *Fortitude*—in which a young mother appears to watch a child at play—along with several luminous *Madonnas* and the graceful *Judith,* drew the twenty-five-year-old Sandro to the attention of the city's ruling family. A mighty dynasty, whose fortunes rested on finance, the Medicis governed Florence with a velvet glove, careful not to disturb the outward trappings of a sovereign republic. Lorenzo the Magnificent, the reigning Medici, was a titanic figure destined to give his stamp to an age. Vivacious, pleasure-loving, a poet in his own right, he gathered around him the philosophers, the painters, poets and musicians who made fifteenth-century Florence the glittering center of European culture.

When a local merchant, Giovanni Lami, commissioned Sandro to paint an *Adoration of the Magi* for an important altarpiece, the artist painted all the leading members of the Medici family into the picture. The three Oriental kings are senior Medicis. Lorenzo is the youthful knight on the far left, holding a sword. His opposite, on the far right, is Master Botticelli, the poor tanner's son himself: a blond, lean, well-built fellow with heavy-lidded eyes, high cheekbones, a strong nose, a willful mouth and a long chin.

Three of Sandro's most celebrated paintings are intimately linked with his attachment to the Medicis—three paintings which, should all the rest of Botticelli's work go up in smoke, would still proclaim him one of the great original artists of the Western world. One of these pictures —*Pallas Subduing a Centaur*—shows the goddess Athena taming a shaggy Centaur, and symbolically compliments Lorenzo on his triumph over chaos and disorder. Like its two more famous companions, *Springtime (La Primavera)* and *The Birth of Venus,* the *Pallas Subduing a Centaur* delights in Greek mythology.

The Birth of Venus—one of the best-known paintings ever done by an Italian hand—is self-explanatory: the beautiful Goddess of Love, having just risen from the sea, beholds, with dreamy eyes, the world. The winds waft her toward the shore, while an attending maiden stands ready for the landing with a resplendent cloak.

Springtime is more complex. In front of a thick orange grove, we see eight nearly life-size personages—nine, if we count the airborne Cupid—acting out a charade. The picture's central theme, richly embroidered with Greek myths, is Love. Sandro assigned the center of the stage to a demure, ethereal Venus. On her right, the Graces—

YOUNG MAN WITH A MEDAL
Soon after he set up his studio, Botticelli gained the patronage of Lorenzo de' Medici. Lorenzo's eldest son, the weak Piero, holds the medallic image of Cosimo, the first great Medici, as a symbol of protection. Piero's reign over Florence lasted only two years; he was driven out by the reformer Savonarola.

filmily dressed deities of love and beauty—perform a rhythmic dance, while the god Mercury, reaching into the sky, dispels a cloud. On Venus' left, a clever byplay illustrates the great awakening of nature: Zephyr, a puffy-cheeked wind sprite, chases a sultry nymph, Chloris, whose breath turns into flowers as she runs and who, before our eyes, changes into a smiling, flower-strewing Flora. Love wins, and spring is here.

Some see in the blue-eyed Flora, shortlived Goddess of Spring, none other than the lovely Simonetta Vespucci, while the distracted, handsome Mercury could be her old admirer, Giuliano de' Medici. Whoever the models were, *Springtime* is the great Botticelli's crowning masterpiece.

His fame brought the painter an invitation to Rome from Pope Sixtus IV in 1481. There he painted some papal portraits, and three murals representing Biblical subjects for the recently built Sistine Chapel in the Vatican.

Returning home after eighteen months, Sandro was the painter of the hour. But Florence's golden era was losing its first bloom. A fanatical Dominican friar, Girolamo Savonarola, bent on reforming the corruption-ridden Church and society as well, was preaching fire-and-brimstone sermons. When Savonarola directed his thunder against the Medici regime, the people rose against their

THE BIRTH OF VENUS
From Port Venere, the traditional site of Venus' birth in the sea, came the perfect Renaissance beauty, Simonetta Vespucci. In her memory Botticelli painted Venus. Her husband's cousin Amerigo Vespucci gave the New World its name.

SPRINGTIME (LA PRIMAVERA)
Springtime*'s female figures, with the exception of the one on the right, are said to be modeled after Simonetta. Botticelli had painted her from life years earlier for a tournament banner of her chivalrous champion Giuliano, brother of Lorenzo.*

ruling family. For more than three years Florentines enjoyed a tense, precarious peace under the friar's virtual dictatorship. But when the Pope himself ordered Savonarola silenced, they turned at last against their idol. One day in 1498 they crowded into the town-hall square to see the brilliant and courageous rebel—condemned for heresy—hanged by the neck and burned.

No Florentine as sensitive as Botticelli could have lived through those soul-searing days without being severely shaken. He plunged into the gigantic job of illustrating Dante's *Divine Comedy,* covering sheepskin sheets with pen-and-ink designs that are among his finest works. Botticelli's *Mystic Adoration*—his last great painting—is full of dark allusions to the Apocalypse; it was painted in 1501.

The rest is silence. For even while the master, now in his late fifties, was working steadily away, a race of giants was growing to maturity. Leonardo da Vinci, Michelangelo and Raphael, all younger than himself, were evolving a new, colossal style. Gradually dropping out of circulation, Botticelli spent most of his time in his snug country house, or tending his vines and fruit trees. He died in 1510, amid the bursting of a Florence springtime and was laid to rest in the small graveyard of All Saints Church, in the parish of the tanners.

—ERNEST O. HAUSER

SELF-PORTRAIT

LEONARDO DA VINCI

1452–1519

Genius of All Arts

"*The life that is well spent is a long life.*" The man who wrote those words lived, by that standard, for centuries, and he lived not only one life but ten. Leonardo da Vinci, in addition to being one of the great painters in the golden age of painting, was a multiple genius of science. He was a modern man, born in that morning of today which we call the Renaissance; he foresaw or invented much that science has spent 450 years in finding out.

Da Vinci even suggested the atomic theory of matter. He envisioned where this might lead when he wrote:

There shall come forth from beneath the ground that which by its terrific report shall stun all who are near it and cause men to drop dead at its breath, and it shall devastate cities and castles. It shall seem to men that they see new destruction in the sky, and flames descending.

Leonardo was born on April 15, 1452, the son of Caterina, a sixteen-year-old peasant girl, and Piero da Vinci, a lawyer. To prevent Piero from marrying the lowborn Caterina, his parents hastened to wed him to a girl of good family. Following a custom of the times, Piero da Vinci bought his love child from the mother and took him as an acknowledged son. Leonardo was never allowed to know his mother, though he knew she existed. His startling beauty and quick wit made it easy to forgive his faults, which he never shook off—elfish practical joking, unlimited self-confidence, and daydreaming.

The boy, growing up on the family estate near Florence, idled over that lovely countryside until parasol pines and winding streams, dreamy crags and delicate wild flowers sank into his soul, to emerge later in those jewels of landscape with which he adorned his paintings. Music he loved and could play enchantingly; verses came lightly to his lips. All life was to him his teacher, as he ransacked the world for its treasures.

When Piero da Vinci discovered his son's first drawings, he placed him as an apprentice in the studio of Andrea del Verrocchio (see page 166). Verrocchio was jack of all the trades at which Leonardo was to become master—painting, sculpture, architecture, music, geometry and natural history—so that teacher and pupil were delighted with each other. In and out of Verrocchio's studio were other young artists—among them one named Botticelli—who became Leonardo's best friends. Together they argued the world to rights, or played outrageous pranks, or wrestled, or tamed horses—one of Leonardo's favorite sports.

Or you might have found da Vinci wandering the courts and churches of Florence to study their art treasures, or strolling with the leading mathematicians, astronomers, geographers of the day, devouring all they knew. Leonardo studied the sciences, not in addition to his art but as part of it. To him there was no essential difference between art and science. Both were to him ways of describing God's one universe.

When he came to paint, Leonardo flung over chill, naked fact the glowing cloak of beauty. His knowledge, his peerless draftsmanship were concealed with a conjuror's sleight. How he loved life can be seen by turning over the hundreds of pages in his sketchbooks. Here on one sheet may be seen the contorted features of soldiers killing and dying, there a young woman kneeling in prayer. It is said he would follow beautiful or grotesque people around all day to study them. He visited the hospitals to watch old men die, and hastened to see a criminal hanged. He loitered to watch the innocent greed of a baby at its mother's breast. Secretly, for it was frowned on, he dissected a human body that his brush might accurately paint "the divine proportion."

Indeed on no science did Leonardo spend so much time as on anatomy. Our muscles he demonstrated to be the levers they are, and he revealed the eye to be a lens. The heart he proved to be a hydraulic pump, and showed that the pulse is synchronized with the heartbeat.

Yet it was as a lyre player that Leonardo, when about thirty, was recommended by Lorenzo the Magnificent to Ludovico Sforza, called "the Moor." Sforza, treacherous, practical and brutal, was the tyrant behind the throne of Milan. Reading Leonardo's letter he was persuaded he could use him. For this man da Vinci says that he is the inventor of a portable bridge useful in pursuit of an enemy; that he has devised suction pumps for emptying the moat

THE VIRGIN OF THE ROCKS
In Milan, Leonardo painted this Madonna, with babes John and Jesus, and an Angel (pointing to indicate the presence of God). The artist kept it, making a copy with his pupils for the duke, his patron.

PORTRAIT OF CECILIA GALLERANI

When Leonardo arrived in Milan, the great beauty and queenly style of this lady had captivated not only Ludovico Sforza, the power of the city, but its people as well. She was probably also the model for The Virgin of the Rocks.

of a besieged castle; that he has schemes for a self-propelling armored car to open paths for infantry!

When Leonardo went from sunny Florence to frowning Milan, he found that his duties included the installation of plumbing for the duchess' bath as well as painting the Moor's proud, cold mistress. He also built an elaborate system of canals for the city. As an expert on fortifications he was sent to the Alps to secure the valleys against invasion from the north. And there, in the lovely Engadine, he saw the smoky twirl of the waterfalls spilling from hanging valleys, traced the tilted strata of the rocks, and from their niches lifted flower and fern in reverent fingers that were to place them on canvas where they live forever.

From this experience, and from the memories of his boyhood, was born *The Virgin of the Rocks,* where landscape and flora enhance with their wild sweetness the holiness of the adorable Mother, the Angel as beautiful as we dream an angel to be, and the Child curling baby fingers in blessing over his playmate, St. John.

What once was one of the world's greatest paintings, *The Last Supper,* Leonardo painted on the wall of a convent hall, on plaster unsuited to pigments. Within twenty years a creeping damp caused mildew and flaking to disfigure the painting. Later a door was callously cut through the wall; and when Napoleon's soldiers came they amused themselves by shooting at the figures of Christ and the Apostles. Then generations of "restorers" distorted the picture. The last, best and tenderest of the resto-

rations may have brought it back to something like the original, but if it were not for Leonardo's many preliminary sketches, and copies by other artists made when the picture was fresh, we would scarcely know how passionately *The Last Supper* was conceived and executed.

Another of Leonardo's paintings, one that ranks with *The Last Supper* as the most famous in the world and one that is even more talked about, is his portrait of Lisa Gherardini, wife of Messer Giocondo of Florence. Painted about 1503, this, his last great picture, is known to us as the *Mona Lisa,* or *La Giaconda.* Though a lady of wealth and fashion, the Mona Lisa wears a dark dress and no rings—perhaps signs of mourning for her child recently dead. Less the likeness of an actual woman than the embodiment of one of da Vinci's daydreams, the Mona Lisa smiles enigmatically at some vision just behind your right shoulder, as you view her.

Leonardo actually finished very few paintings, though his sketches and studies run into the thousands. When at last he began to paint, he might work for days, scarcely taking food. Again he would sit all day in front of his work and add but three strokes. The next morning he might wash out everything and begin again. It is doubtful if he ever considered any work finished to perfection; perhaps that is why he signed almost nothing.

And all this time that da Vinci was painting like a god he dared to dream, as have few mortals, of the conquest of the world by science. The sky was no limit to his soaring speculations, nor was the sea too deep, and into both he plunged, in imagination. He learned why birds take off into the wind, understood how the slotted wing helps them mount more steeply.

His earliest plans for a flying machine suggest a dragonfly, or again a bat. He expected the wings to flap and imagined his aviator lying face down in the frame and rowing the air with the wings. Then, first of men, Leonardo hit on the idea of a propeller for locomotion. In his model the "prop" beats horizontally, with the fuselage hanging below it, like a helicopter. As da Vinci foresaw it, the machine would rise straight into the air, but lacking a light engine he could never test his theories.

Yet one flight he did, it seems, attempt, in what was probably a glider. With infinite precautions and secretiveness, this was constructed on a high building and, according to a single reference that has come down through the ages, it was finally launched, possibly with da Vinci at the controls! But the flight was a failure, and apparently Leonardo never made another attempt.

Leonardo designed prefabricated portable houses, rolling mills, a screw-cutting machine, a bulldozer, a spinning machine and a harbor dredge. He was the first man to mount a magnetic needle on a horizontal axis, thereby giving us the compass as we know it today. He devised a diving bell and a life preserver. He planned large cruising submarines but destroyed his plans. For, said he, men are so wicked they cannot be trusted with such a secret, lest

THE LAST SUPPER

Christ has just said, "One of you shall betray me," and each disciple, stunned, replies "Is it I?" The author Bandello wrote that Leonardo painted the great mural for whole days, then stopped to study it for days. He searched for, but never found, a suitable model for Christ's head.

MONA LISA

Leonardo wrote: "Paint the face in such a way that it will be easy to understand what is going on in the mind." Yet the most famous portrait in the world possesses a smile that has become the symbol of mystery.

they "practice assassination in the bottom of the seas."

Leonardo was the first scientist to understand fossils as being the impress of extinct animals that lived when the rocks in which they are found were but sediment on the ocean floor. For the earth, he told men, was not just 5000 years old. His pioneering studies in geology persuaded him that it must have taken the River Arno 200,000 years to build its flood plains.

A century before telescopes and Galileo's time, da Vinci hit upon the idea that the earth is not the center of the universe but moves around the sun in an elliptical orbit; that the earth is but a planet, looming no larger in the solar system than the moon in comparison with the earth; that the stars are distant "worlds," vastly larger than they seem, and the sun is but one of their number.

No wonder that eyes which could see so much look tired! To judge from his self-portrait, done about 1510, Leonardo was an old man at fifty-eight, venerable and profound, but somewhat disappointed. It was as if the many lives he had tried to live in one had consumed his frame. He had had to flee Milan when it was invaded by the French and the Sforzas were driven out. He sojourned in several cities and, when it was safe, drifted back to Milan, where he had to accept odd jobs as an engineer and chance commissions as a free-lance artist.

In his day Leonardo enjoyed a reputation at once more popular than and yet not so high as he does today. Our deep respect for his science was not matched in his age. As an artist, of course, he had a superb reputation. It was not without rivals; after all, he lived in the times of Botticelli, Raphael, Michelangelo and Titian. But the art-loving population of fifteenth-century Florence crowded about him, and when one of his sketches was exhibited they packed and pushed like movie fans at a "personal appearance." City-states and men of great wealth bid for him; kings asked him only to grace their courts; for Leonardo was, in himself, a cult. And yet he was a lonely man at heart. He probably never knew another human being capable of meeting him on his plane.

The last years of da Vinci were passed in ease near Amboise, in central France, where he had gone to live at the invitation of King Francis I. His visitors avoided noticing his paralyzed hands. Never had his conversation been more versatile, never his presence more courtly, nor his smile more understanding. Perhaps Death herself wore that smile—that light on the lips of mystery and wisdom which da Vinci alone ever captured—when she came for Leonardo on May 2, 1519. —DONALD CULROSS PEATTIE

LIKENESS OF THE ARTIST FROM HIS SCULPTURE

MICHELANGELO BUONARROTI

1475–1564

Monarch of His Time

"PAINTING ISN'T MY ART," protested the sculptor Michelangelo. "Let Raphael do it." But Pope Julius II insisted that he paint the ceiling of His Holiness' private chapel, called the Sistine. For the next four years Michelangelo was practically a prisoner—first of the Pope, then of his own fever of inspiration.

Never was a more forbidding task set for any artist. The Sistine Chapel is a dark, narrow box of a place, higher than it is wide. The ceiling space is interrupted by dormer-like windows, which results in eccentric curves and angles. All this—10,000 square feet of it—was to be filled with frescoes: paintings in fresh, damp plaster.

Up the ladders, into the scaffolding, went Michelangelo, to lie on his back and paint overhead. Working in a slavery of creation, he often forgot to eat or sleep; he drove away one assistant after another, and locked the door to all but an old servant. Only to the thunder of Julius' cane would the artist open. Julius didn't understand art, but he knew grandeur when he saw it. He knew also that life is short. "When, when, will it be done?" he would storm.

Finally Julius said, "It's done, I tell you. Get down off that scaffolding or I'll have you thrown off." Quailing, for he *had* fallen off once, Michelangelo agreed to let in the world of art, fashion and priesthood.

There above them, as if Genesis were blazoned on the sky, was the story of Creation, of the Fall of Man, and the Deluge! God, with a commanding gesture, is seen dividing the Firmament. He breathes upon the dust, and lo, there is Adam, in His image, God's finger just quitting Adam's, while Man gazes with adoring eyes into his Maker's face. And Eve, under the shelter of the Almighty's arm, turns her gaze, in eagerness and fear, upon her lord and master.

Prophets and sibyls fill the difficult spaces. There are 343 major figures in the ceiling, every one sublime; each has the power of sculpture.

Michelangelo's deepest love was not painting. Throughout his long career, the artist's brush had to be practically forced on him. The hammer and chisel were his most meaningful companions; they enabled him to find in stone an emotional fulfillment he never found among his fellow men. He liked to jest that he sucked in his profession with his foster-mother's milk. As an infant, he had been put out to nurse with a stonecutter's wife.

Michelagniolo di Ludovico Buonarroti Simoni was born in 1475 at Caprese, where the Tiber rises in central Italy. His mother died when he was six, and not till he was past sixty would he again know a woman's tenderness. He grew up in a harsh male world, with selfish, mediocre brothers who sponged on him all his life, and a grasping, complaining father. At school the boy did poorly. He was always drawing pictures and he drew them on the walls at home, too. So he was beaten. As this did no good, he was beaten again, and harder. In the end the physical courage was thrashed out of the frail body. But the artist remained unbroken.

Eager to get financial profit out of the refractory boy, Buonarroti senior sent him at thirteen to the studio of the famous Domenico Ghirlandaio in Florence. Here he had his only lessons in painting. One day, when several apprentices were studying a drawing of a female figure by their eminent teacher, Michelangelo picked up a broader pencil and corrected it. Worse still, Domenico saw that the forward boy was right. So Michelangelo soon found himself ushered out of the shop (with the highest recommendations). He landed in the art factory of Bertoldo, the sculptor who was turning out pseudoclassical statuary for Lorenzo de' Medici.

Michelangelo was employed in roughing out blocks of marble in the Medici gardens. Every day the young shoulders grew stronger, the eye surer—so sure that when Lorenzo happened on a carving made by the boy from a piece of waste marble he took him into his palace, cloaked him in velvet, had him served with his sons. At that princely table, where poets and scholars clustered, readings took the place of chatter. Here the youth heard the great thoughts of Plato, the mighty lines of Dante. A second talent—poetry—was born in him; he was to become the author of seventy-seven sonnets that in their sincerity seem to be hewn out of his very soul.

It was a soul great as some ancient prophet's, full of

THE LIBYAN SIBYL and Sketch
Contrasting with the male prophets of the Sistine ceiling are five female sibyls, or pagan oracles. In her book, a divine daughter of Zeus foretells the Creation, Adam's fall and the Flood. The drawing is the most valuable one in America.

THE CREATION OF MAN

THE PROPHET JEREMIAH

THE PROPHET JONAH

THE SISTINE CEILING

In "lunette" spaces above the twelve windows, the master was to paint the Twelve Apostles. But an overwhelming purpose seized him. Seven great prophets and five sibyls took their places, and over their heads in the central portion of the ceiling rose nine of their visions, which were the episodes of God and Man. From the creation of the sun and earth to the advent of Noah, the epic unfolded over Michelangelo's scaffold. In eight small spandrels just over the windows were the ancestors of Christ. The great corner spandrels became heroic scenes of the saviors of Israel, Moses and Judith, Samson and David. Atop the twenty pedestals between the windows sat giant nude youths, representing humanity as yet not saved.

sublime visions and moral passion. Yet his human personality was pitifully faulty. Arrogant, touchy, harsh of tongue, the youth got his nose broken in a quarrel with an older apprentice. The disfigurement lasted for life and went deeper than his face. For he who worshiped beauty now thought himself repulsive. Of medium height, with overdeveloped shoulders, he may not have been a handsome young man, but the years were to make unforgettable the wrinkled face; the bitter, generous mouth; the hazel eyes filled with an almost Biblical sorrow and love.

In 1492 Lorenzo died, and his son Piero could think of no better employment for Michelangelo than to summon him one winter morning to make an enormous snowman in the palace courtyard. Soon the young artist fled the city and drifted ultimately to Rome. There Michelangelo produced his first masterpiece, the *Pietà*—a Madonna holding the dead Christ on her lap. He overheard visitors ascribing the work to another artist, so he stole at night into the church where it then stood and chiseled his name on it, leaving it the only signed Michelangelo in existence. It stands now in St. Peter's.

Shortly after his return to Florence the next year, Michelangelo began to wrest another great work from an adversary that may well have been unique in an artistic life that never lacked for enemies—the stone itself. City officials owned a piece of ruined Carrara marble nearly fourteen feet high. Decades earlier, a sculptor had blocked it out impracticably narrow and thin and had carved a deep gash near the base. Though many artists eyed it, none could solve the problems of its odd shape.

For nearly three years, Michelangelo toiled, hidden behind a high board fence, to meet the challenge of the ruined stone. Passersby heard only the clank of steel on stone, the thwack of mallet on chisel. When the judges viewed what he had done, they awarded him 400 gold florins (2000 dollars) and his choice of a site for his work. Unblushingly, Michelangelo selected the most conspicuous place in Florence—before the great, grim palace in the Square of the Nobles. Forty men labored four days with windlass and rollers to move the statue of the Biblical hero to the spot.

This is David, the killer of Goliath, the giant. Every flaw of the original block has been turned into perfection. The excessive height and thinness became the compact body of a towering athlete; the gash at the base is the space between the stalwart legs. Every cord and sinew, every vein in the readied limbs is shaped with exquisite precision. *David,* like all Michelangelo's great works, is more than a statue; it is a living truth—as alive today as 450 years ago.

But while Michelangelo was uttering through his art such timeless truths, the times he lived in were rent with corruption and religious dissension. Worldly extravagance had bankrupted not only the fiscal but the moral treasury of the Vatican. As a result, half of Europe rose in the Protestant revolution. Italy was invaded by French, German and Spanish armies and torn with civil war. Pope Clement VII, now in the Vatican, marched on Florence. In her peril, the city of artists called on her greatest son. For months Michelangelo was in charge of fortifying hills and placing cannon.

Out of the bloodshed and fear of these times emerged Michelangelo's work of profoundest calm—the Medici tombs. To visit them—and the stream of visitors never ceases—you go to the chapel adjoining the church of San Lorenzo in Florence and enter a room, of Michelangelo's designing, that lays a finger on the pulses and stills the restless spirit. There, on opposite walls, are the two tombs, one for Lorenzo de' Medici, one for his brother Giuliano. Clad in light armor, his hand on the sword across his knees, young Giuliano gazes with unsatisfied desire at the years he did not live to enjoy. This figure is popularly called *The Active Life;* its opposite, *The Contemplative Life,* shows a brooding Lorenzo, secretive hand at his mouth, a helmet shading eyes that are looking down lonely perspectives to death.

In 1533 Pope Clement summoned the aging artist to one more exhausting task. The wall of the Sistine Chapel, behind the altar, remained to be decorated. So, for five years, the sculptor painted again—*The Last Judgment,* that moment when the angels sound the trump of doom, when graves give up their dead, when kings stand naked as their slaves before the awful Judge, when the righteous are chosen, and the damned fall down to everlasting torment.

Michelangelo was old now—older than his years, worn with struggle over colossal tasks. For a brief time he enjoyed a deep friendship with a noble lady, Vittoria Colonna. To her, as to no one else, he poured out his dark and lofty thoughts. When death claimed her, he became almost a hermit in an obscure little house in Rome. He behaved like a penniless man, when in fact he supported his brothers and had a fortune in cash hidden in his studio. Secretly he gave dowries to poor girls of virtuous character that they might make good marriages.

Yet, in his late seventies and eighties Michelangelo won new fame as an architect. He was still a novice when he was appointed to complete St. Peter's, a roofless shell nearly fifty years after its cornerstone was laid. Many builders had worked on it; the only thing all plans had in common was size, for this was to become the world's biggest church. The task took so long that Michelangelo had time in between to design other buildings all over Rome—churches, palaces, bridges, museums. His style came to dominate the Eternal City like a mighty anthem, its chords frozen into stone.

Some of Michelangelo's plans for St. Peter's were never carried out, but the great, double-shelled dome is all his, and it caps the mighty basilica with glory, as it capped his life. Engineers said it was impossible. But slowly, tier on tier, the great stone bubble rose, magnificent in proportion, each tier creeping out in seeming defiance of gravity as it approached the center. It was a race with death. "I am so old," he said, "that death drags at my mantle." Before he died at eighty-nine, Michelangelo Buonarroti saw his work completed—the biggest and most beautiful dome in the world. Filled with light, with organ thunder and the choir's rejoicing, a vast and airy climax of power, it holds—if anything on earth can hold—a last echo of this titan soul. —DONALD CULROSS PEATTIE

PLATO AND ARISTOTLE
The figures of the two famous Greeks (above) form a detail from The School of Athens. *Finest of four frescoes Raphael painted in the Vatican, it portrays the greatest of the ancient philosophers and scientists. Raphael chose the head of Leonardo da Vinci for Plato.*

SELF-PORTRAIT

RAPHAEL VRBINAS F

RAPHAEL SANZIO

1483–1520

The Divine Painter

RAPHAEL SANZIO died on his thirty-seventh birthday; his body lay in state in his studio by the side of his unfinished *Transfiguration,* and the whole of Rome flocked in for a last glimpse of the "divine painter." During his short working life, he lived and painted in an atmosphere of princeliness and popular idolization such as no other artist has enjoyed. His high position in the affection of the world has continued for more than four centuries.

The preeminence of Raphael in the popular imagination is based largely on his Madonnas and his *Transfiguration,*

HOME OF RAPHAEL
Raphael was born in this fourteenth-century house at Urbino, Italy, and lived there until he was fourteen years old. Raphael's painter father gave his son his first art lesson in this house. Today part of it is used as a gallery to display the work of local artists.

RAPHAEL VRBINAS
M
DIIII

but it would be wrong to suppose that his fame has been kept alive solely by the mass appeal of sweetness and light. Artists of almost every period have looked long and intently at Raphael's paintings. Two approaches, the emotional and the critical, arrive in the end on common ground—for Raphael's intention was to make living people of the utmost gracefulness and serenity of mood. He succeeded, for his figures are but reflections of himself.

Raphael's Madonnas differ greatly in pose and treatment, but not radically in sentiment. *The Madonna of the Goldfinch,* one of the best, was painted during his early twenties in Florence. Its emotional appeal is half classical and half Christian—a composite of the sensuous and the saintly. This Italian woman is not of the modern world: she expresses a type of perfection arrived at by one of history's most sensitive artists, whose ideal was expressed in faultless proportions and a refinement of sentiment which will probably never be surpassed in its popular appeal. His heart and talent were dedicated to beauty.

As if by exact calculation, Raphael's career falls into three periods: his early training under Perugino, the master painter of Perugia, whose mannerisms he absorbed; his Florentine years, from 1504 to 1508, when he molded himself in the new style by yielding to the influences of Michelangelo, Leonardo da Vinci and Masaccio; and his Roman triumph, from about 1508 to his death. In this period he developed his capacities as a mural decorator and gave new life to classical figures.

He has been described as the great harvester, the man who moved from influence to influence—absorbing and assembling, and transforming all that he had extracted from others into his own style by the ineffable grace and loftiness of his personality. He was one of the most gifted painters the world has seen, and it is no wonder he was called divine. He was never disturbing; he seemed to rise with godlike ease above all others, to achieve a symmetrical completion in his life that made Michelangelo appear boorish and uncivilized. He could do no wrong; he was gentle to the point of effeminacy, and yet he could exercise undisputed authority over fifty assistants.

A new challenge brought Raphael inevitably to Rome. In Florence he had received word from the famous architect Donato Bramante, his distant kinsman serving Pope Julius II, that His Holiness was considering him as the artist to decorate some rooms in the Vatican. The artist, then twenty-four years old, charmed the churlish old pontiff—and everybody else except Michelangelo, who was at that particular time at work in the Sistine Chapel.

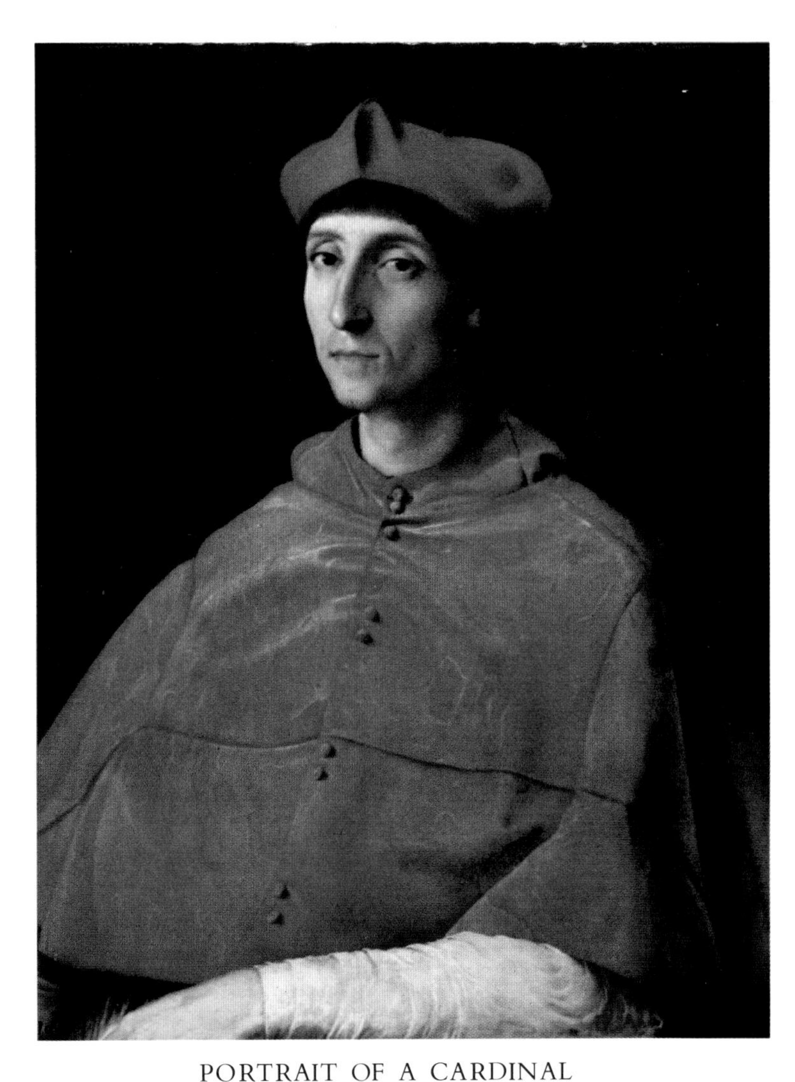

PORTRAIT OF A CARDINAL
Believed to have been painted about 1510, when Raphael was twenty-seven, this portrait shows a Prince of the Church whose identity has been lost over the years. The Renaissance biographer Vasari makes the interesting comment that Raphael himself hoped to be made a cardinal by the Pope as a reward for his work—an honor that never materialized.

MARRIAGE OF THE VIRGIN
(Opposite page) In the altarpiece painted for the Church of San Francesco, Raphael tells the legend of how Joseph was selected to be Mary's husband. The suitors were brought together, each bearing a branch from a dead tree. When the lifeless branch carried by Joseph suddenly burst into bloom, he was regarded as the chosen one.

No empty walls being available, the impulsive Pope commanded the frescoes in some of the rooms to be erased; and Raphael, a tender soul, wept to see the murals of his old teacher Perugino and other painters washed down the Vatican drains. Though sensitive, he was very determined and went to work energetically. With his corps of assistants he covered room after room with meetings of pagan and Christian folk—the ancient groups representing Philosophy, Law, Poetry and History in a stage setting called *The School of Athens;* the contrasting groups forming a religious drama, the *Dispute of the Sacrament,* which had to do with the ceremonies of the Christian faith. Some of the frescoes clearly showed the influence of Michelangelo, but the Pope did not mind. Nor did anyone, save the great man who lay on his back on the scaffold beneath the Sistine ceiling. "The young man from Urbino," said Michelangelo sarcastically, "has been lurking in my chapel."

In one room Raphael designed and executed, also with the help of assistants, *The Fire in the Borgo.* It commemorates a miraculous event in the career of Pope Leo IV, who appeared at a window in the Vatican, made the sign of the cross and so put out the fire. Raphael was not by nature a dramatic artist, but so great was his versatility that he produced splendid muscular figures in action, utilizing the powerful forms of Michelangelo with a grace of gesture and a flow of drapery that were unmistakably his own. In addition to all these labors and despite his delicate health, he was the inspector of monuments and antiquities in Rome, Bramante's successor as architect of St. Peter's and, in his spare time, the painter of many easel pictures.

Raphael's art was constantly fertilized by the styles of other painters. He was extremely impressionable, but his receptivity was guarded by a fine intelligence and he never abandoned himself unreservedly to a single influence. He painted as he lived, sensitive to all forms of life but surrendering to none, and retaining in his fame a golden equanimity and a charm of manner so captivating that the world did not stop to consider that he was more pagan than Christian and not exactly a saint in his private behavior. The Madonnas he painted as a young man in Florence, with coolness and deliberation, reveal purity of form and refinement of spirit rather than vitality and firmness of structure. In his later years in Rome he painted portraits—not virginal sublimations—in which classical poise is united to warm humanity. These portraits represent the highest attainments of his genius.

The development of Raphael was the old story of the enrichment of a man's art by direct experiences. Not that his painting is a diary of his physical or emotional adventures—but his best and most original conceptions of the human form came from his observations of men and women and not from the study of other paintings. The facts of his life are not altogether clear, but the legend that he was perpetually addicted to sensual pleasures is flatly denied by his immense productivity. In a diplomatic moment he was betrothed to the niece of a cardinal—but the engagement lingered on until his death. There is ample evidence, too, that he was passionately attached to La Fornarina, the baker's daughter, who some believe to have been the original of *La Donna Velata* and the model for the Virgin in *The Sistine Madonna.*

Whatever the identity of the model, the veiled lady remains his most majestic conception of womanhood. In contrast to the lymphatic and drooping Madonnas of his early youth, the woman in *La Donna Velata* is superbly erect and alluring, direct of glance, richly attired, but chastened by the veil. The composition, with its intricate weaving of lines—its beautiful pattern of folded satin grays and whites against a dark ground—is Raphael's masterpiece in portraiture.

In describing Raphael's last illness the historian Vasari, often unrestrained and inaccurate, for once mentions no names. He merely relates that Raphael "dismissed the object of his attachment from his house, but left a provision for her in his will." Raphael, worn out by hard work at the height of his genius, had caught a fever; he died ten days later on Good Friday, 1520. —THOMAS CRAVEN

GIORGIONE

1477–1510

Beholder of Dreams

HIRE ARTISTS to paint warehouse walls? It seemed the thing to do in Venice early in the sixteenth century. For Venetians in those days felt that life without color was dead. And German traders in the bustling commercial city had their own lusty sense of art—weren't some of them from Nuremburg, city of the celebrated German etcher, Albrecht Dürer? So they put part of their profits into two warehouse murals and had the luck to choose two immortals for the task.

The paintings soon succumbed to salt moisture and the sun. Only vague blotches remain. But even these tell of

CONCERT CHAMPETRE

The artist may have had no intention of creating a realistic scene. Many believe this to be a fantasy of two Venetian men who, lulled by the beauty of the scene and the music of the lute, are dreaming of Greek nymphs in the midst of a blissful episode. No known legend or myth inspired this painting.

ADORATION OF THE SHEPHERDS

Giorgione painted his religious pictures, of which this is the best preserved, while still under the influence of his teacher, Bellini. As none of Giorgione's paintings was signed, they have been frequently attributed to Bellini or Titian, the two geniuses closest to his career.

the talents of both Giorgione da Castelfranco, then about thirty years old, and his friend Titian (see page 74). Giorgione's real name is not known; an old story made him the love child of an aristocrat and a woman of the people. In 1490, at about thirteen years of age, he was sent from Castelfranco to Venice to serve as apprentice to Giovanni Bellini. He developed rapidly, won substantial commissions, bought a house, painted a fresco on its front and filled his home with music and revelry; for he played the lute well, and preferred gay women in the flesh to the loveliest of them on canvas.

What influences formed his wistful style it is hard to say, for he was quite unlike the other painters of his day. Probably the decisive influence came from letters rather than from art. Italian literature was taking a rural turn; Sannazaro published his *Arcadia* in 1504; perhaps Giorgione read these poems and found in their pleasant fancies some suggestions of idealized landscapes and amours. From Leonardo—passing through Venice in 1500—Giorgione may have acquired a taste for a mystic, dreamy softness of expression, a delicacy of nuance, a refinement of manner that made him, for a tragically brief moment, the summit of Venetian art.

Among the earliest works attributed to him—for in hardly any case can his authorship be assured—are two wood panels describing the exposure and rescue of the infant Paris; the story is an excuse for painting shepherds and country landscapes breathing peace. The first picture that may be regarded as his—*The Gypsy and the Soldier*—is a typically Giorgionesque fancy: a casual woman, nude except for a shawl around her shoulders, sits on her discarded dress on the mossy bank of a rushing stream, nurses a child and looks anxiously about her; behind her stretches a landscape of Roman arches, a river and a bridge, towers and a temple, curious trees, white lightning and green storm-laden clouds; near her is a comely youth holding a shepherd's staff—but richly garbed for a shepherd!—and so pleased with the scene that he ignores the gathering storm. The story is uncertain; what the picture means is that Giorgione liked handsome youths, soft-contoured women, and nature even in its moods of wrath.

About 1504 he painted, for a bereaved family in the town of his birth, the *Madonna of Castelfranco*. It is absurd and beautiful. In the forefront St. Liberale, in the shining armor of a medieval knight, holds a lance for the Virgin, and St. Francis preaches to the air; high aloft on a double pedestal Mary sits with her babe, who leans out from His high perch. But the green-and-violet brocade at Mary's feet is a wonder of color and design. Mary's robes fall about her in wrinkles as lovely as wrinkles can ever be. Her face has the gentle tenderness that poets picture in the ladies of their dreams; and the landscape recedes with Leonardesque mystery till the sky melts into the sea.

Giorgione's genius lay in conception rather than coloring. When he painted the *Sleeping Venus,* he might have thought of her in purely sensual terms as an inviting formation of molecules. Doubtless she is that, too, and marks the passage of Venetian art from Christian to pagan themes and sentiment. But there is nothing immodest or suggestive about this Venus. She lies asleep, precariously nude in the open air, on a red cushion and a white silken robe, her right arm under her head, her left hand serving as a fig leaf, one perfect limb outstretched over another raised beneath it. On her face is a look of innocence and peace. Seldom has art so simulated the velvet texture of feminine surfaces, or so conveyed the grace of a natural pose.

In another work—the *Concert champêtre* or *Pastoral Symphony* of the Louvre—the pleasure is frankly sensual and yet once more has all the innocence of nature. Two nude women and two clothed men are enjoying a holiday in the countryside. A patrician youth, in a doublet of gleaming red silk, is strumming a lute. Beside him is a disheveled shepherd painfully trying to bridge the gap between a simple and a cultivated mind. The aristocrat's lady, in a graceful motion, empties a crystal pitcher into a well. The shepherd's lass waits patiently for him to attend to her charms or her flute. No notion of sin has entered their heads; the lute and the flute have sublimated sex into harmony. Behind the figures rises one of the richest landscapes in Italian art.

Finally, in a similarly titled picture in the Pitti gallery of Florence, *The Concert,* desire seems primitive and irrelevant, and music has become a bond of friendship. At the left a plumed youth stands, a bit lifeless and negative. A monk sits at a clavichord, his beautifully rendered hands on the keys, his face turned round to a bald cleric. The cleric lays one hand on the monk's shoulder, and holds in the other a cello resting on the floor. Has the music ended, or not yet begun? It does not matter. The silent depth of feeling in the countenance of the monk is what moves us. His every fiber has been refined, and his every sentiment ennobled, by music; he hears it long after all the instruments have been mute. His face, not idealized but profoundly realized, is one of the miracles of Renaissance painting.

Giorgione lived a short life, and apparently a merry

one. He seems to have had many women, and to have healed each broken romance with a new one soon begun. Vasari, biographer of early Italian artists, reported that Giorgione caught the plague from his last love; all that is known is that he died in the epidemic of 1510 at the age of thirty-three.

His influence was already extensive. A dozen "Giorgionesque" minor artists painted rural idylls, conversation pieces, musical interludes, masque costumes, in vain efforts to capture the refinement and finish of his style, the airy overtones of his landscapes, the guileless eroticism of his themes. He left a follower who was to stir the world: Tiziano Vecellio—Titian, who became the greatest Venetian of all.

—WILL DURANT

SELF-PORTRAIT

TITIAN

1477–1576

Glorious Venetian

AT HIS EASEL ONE DAY in the palace of Charles V, emperor of the Holy Roman Empire, the painter Titian dropped his brush. The emperor, ruler of half the world, hurried forward and picked it up. Charles' admiration for Titian was unbounded. He honored him as a count and a Knight of the Golden Spur, and made his children nobles of the empire. For a painter, these honors were without precedent, and the ambitious courtiers did not fail to point this out to the emperor. He silenced them by remarking: "We can create counts without number, but we cannot create another Titian."

During his life he became indeed the one and only. His three mighty rivals—Michelangelo, Leonardo and Raphael—all died before he did, leaving him the undisputed master of his time. Kings sent their envoys to his home to implore him for pictures.

The widely heralded artist was unique in his versatility. He painted vast altarpieces alive with ecstasy and Christian

NYMPH AND SHEPHERD

Nude scenes of literature and legend were the fashion for half a century during Titian's life, and he made great use of them. In this work, which he painted when he was in his nineties, he depicted Angelica and Medoro, lovers in an Italian classic.

MALTESE DOG

Little is known about the subject of this oil sketch done on brown paper. Yet dogs appear so frequently in Titian's paintings that it is not too farfetched to imagine the shaggy pet delightedly greeting his master on his return to the studio.

PORTRAIT OF A YOUNG MAN
The painting to the right has been referred to by some as The Englishman. *Others state it is the portrait of a young Florentine man of law named Ippolito Riminaldi. Still others believe that Titian's model was Ottavio Farnese, grandson of Pope Paul III.*

tenderness; he also did lusty alcove pictures—bacchanalias, pastorals and an endless parade of Venuses. He created battle scenes swarming with incident, including as many as one hundred figures; and he did hundreds of portraits which were not only good likenesses but psychological studies—all in a style that became the model for those who followed him. Van Dyck, Rubens, Rembrandt, Velázquez drew their inspiration from this artist who won the awe of kings.

Titian the human being was also unique, for he lived, according to some scholars, to the age of ninety-nine, always in robust health. He survived all his contemporaries and to the end produced masterly works. His *Shepherd and Nymph,* one of his most sensuous paintings, was done during his last years. Titian died in a plague which carried off fifty thousand people, one quarter of the population of Venice. Even in death he was honored. The ordinary dead were loaded into carts at night and ferried off to a remote island for burial; Titian was given a ceremonial burial in a church adorned with his pictures.

It was a wonderful age—a gold-and-scarlet age. When Titian was a boy, the big news was the discovery of America. As he grew older, Henry VIII sat on the throne of England, Lucrezia Borgia pursued her toxic career, Martin Luther started the Reformation. Soon Calvin was preaching in Geneva; Erasmus was lecturing in Paris and Basel; Rabelais was writing. Venice, which had been queen of the seas and mistress of the Orient, began descending slowly in a blaze of vice and glory. From far and wide men came to visit the city—to enjoy its beauties, to learn from its savants and men of art.

Many artists of the free-and-easy Renaissance were rascals and worse—thieves and wastrels—but Titian was a good husband and father, a sure friend, a man of dignity. Up to the end he could be seen, a lordly figure in skullcap and gown, strolling the streets of Venice followed by disciples and admirers. People hurried to make way for this painter friend of royalty and of papal dignitaries. When Henry III of France came to the city, he had only one desire—to see Titian at work in his studio.

Born at Pieve di Cadore in the Italian Alps about 1477, Tiziano Vecellio—to give him his full name—was descended from peasants and soldiers. A legendary story says that at seven the boy pressed the juice from flowers and painted a *Madonna and Child* on the wall of his home. He was poor, and he never went to school, but he had the good fortune to have a father who recognized his talent and sent him, at nine, to an uncle in Venice to learn the craft. It was

LA BELLA

The subject of one of the finest of all portraits may be the same young woman who posed for Titian's masterpiece on the opposite page, and some say she is the Duchess of Urbino. Obviously highborn, the lady is dressed in a manner suitable to her station in life.

VENUS OF URBINO

Titian painted the picture to the left for the Duke of Urbino about 1538. This Venus is almost identical in pose to a Venus painted by Giorgione many years earlier, which Titian completed when his friend and associate died.

the beginning of a career that rose to wealth and fame. No painter was more venerated, none more honored, than this man who had begun life as a crude mountain boy.

After studying design and color with a maker of mosaics, he went to the studio of the great Giovanni Bellini, who was an excellent teacher. Noting his pupil's passion for color—and his weakness with form—Bellini kept him at his drawing. But it wasn't Bellini who turned the key that was to set free Titian's genius. It was instead a student of Bellini, known as Giorgione, who was himself to become an immortal painter. A charming individual, irresistible to women, Giorgione revolted against the rigid style of Bellini and began painting people as he saw them—freshly, lyrically. Titian was entranced, and soon he too was laying on his colors with abandon. Their pictures were very much alike; experts still debate which of the two painted certain canvases.

Giorgione left Bellini, and one day Titian gathered up his brushes and followed him. When a newly erected building, the Fondaco dei Tedeschi (German Warehouse), needed frescoes on its outside walls, Giorgione got the contract (see page 68). He did the front, facing the lagoon; Titian the rear, which looked out on a narrow street. As they worked, people watched and talked; when they were done, there was still greater comment and Titian's work won the higher praise. Giorgione could not forgive him. It was the end of an idyllic friendship. An unhappy Titian could not understand such envy. When Giorgione died two years later, Titian completed some of the paintings his friend had left behind.

With Giorgione dead and Bellini a very old man, Titian was officially named "First Painter of Venice" and soon obtained an important commission—to do an *Assumption* for the Church of the Frari (Friars). It was a huge work, nearly 23 feet by 12, with giant figures and flaming color. All Venice came to the unveiling; only a few persons applauded. The church fathers postponed payment. But soon the church swarmed with artists, studying and copying the picture. More convincing than the painters was an agent from the Spanish Court. He hefted a bag full of gold pieces and offered to buy the painting on the spot. Titian got his money . . . from the friars.

Despite his success, Titian remained faithful to his mountain home, visiting it whenever he had a few free days. In his painting you will rarely find canals or gondolas. The rugged steeps and gnarled trees of his native Alps intrigued him more. To keep house for him he brought down the daughter of the local barber, a girl named Cecilia. She bore him two sons, both out of wedlock. But when she fell ill, not long after the birth of a daughter, Titian, who could have won a wealthy and titled bride, called for a priest and a goldsmith. The former read the marriage lines; the latter supplied the rings. After his wife's death the painter was desolate.

Titian, the good father, arranged the marriage of his daughter, Lavinia, giving her a huge dowry. She died before him. His firstborn, Pomponio, caused Titian disappointment, for, though he had guided him toward the priesthood, the boy proved unsuited for the Church. Orazio, his other son, was taken by the same plague which killed his father.

In his early days Titian was still under the influence of Giorgione. His paintings scintillated with all possible hues, a harmony from the distance but dissolving close at hand into a pattern which seemed to have a being quite apart from the forms composing it. In the painting of flesh his method produced the most splendid results. He would paint carnation on white and white on white, adding a bit of blue and a bit of green, until at last he had flesh so real you felt it would bleed if touched with a knife; here were veins and arteries and the grain of the skin. The golden red-yellow hair of Titian's women has made his name a word in many languages. And no man painted the nude with such fidelity. No smooth, marble beauties for him, but the living creature.

In the last half of his long life Titian spent much of his time in a round of travels from palace to palace—painting murals on walls, doing portraits of emperors and kings, archdukes and cardinals. The Pope himself sat for his portrait. The painter was now strictly the professional, never touching brush to canvas or plaster unless he had an order from one capable of paying. If the buyer was slow, Titian would nudge him in a letter, and another—and another. It didn't matter if the man owing money was a king; the letters kept coming.

A scholar of the time marveled at Titian's ability when, past seventy years of age, he worked, drank wine and entertained to the late hours—arising the next morning refreshed and ready for a new day. His home in Venice had a lovely garden and in it he was host to many great artists and patrons of the day.

Velázquez said of him: "We must look to Venice for the good and the beautiful. I would give first place to Titian; it is he who carries the flag." In a thousand studios the lessons taught by the son of mountain people descended to new generations of painters. —GEORGE KENT

MASTERS OF OLD EUROPE

Outside Italy, while Michelangelo was still painting in Rome, artists of the North were following the early lead of the van Eycks, evolving a genius of their own. The clear, cold climate inspired fineness of detail and harsh realism. In Germany, first Dürer and then Holbein, with incredible precision, made the most exact portraits that painting has known. Monsters of medieval belief were set down with eerie reality by Jerome Bosch, and scenes of swarming peasant life were first portrayed by Pieter Brueghel. It remained for El Greco, a Greek, to capture the grand manner and carry it from Italy to Spain, where he formed a style so new that today it still stands alone. Another, the Flemish Rubens, after eight years in Rome, brought home to Antwerp a challenge of color and drama and glory that was the equal of Titian. Under Rubens' magnanimous influence, the abundantly gifted Van Dyck and the great Spaniard Velázquez fashioned marvelous royal portraits that linked the rich Italian past and the northern present. At the same time, there appeared the more warmly human portraits of Rubens' countryman, Frans Hals. Then the unbelievable occurred. In Amsterdam, a painter rose to the summit of northern artistry—a philosopher in painting. His name was Rembrandt. After him, as after the great Italian age, such giants were not to appear again for a long time, with one exception—Vermeer, called the "perfect painter."

PORTRAIT BY JACQUES LEBOUCQ

Jeronimus bosch.

JEROME BOSCH

1450?–1516

Explorer of the Afterworld

"ALL FLESH IS GRASS." Sometime or other, Jerome Bosch read these solemn words of Isaiah and a vision shaped itself within him, one unlike any that an artist had imagined before. He saw perished grass, in the form of a great hay cart. Atop the load was a curious party. A seated youth strummed the viol for a girl who sang from a sheet of music. Behind them two lovers, standing, shared a kiss. At one side an angel knelt disregarded on the hay. At the other an elfin winged creature, wearing a Pope's tiara, danced and played upon his nose, which was extended in the form of a flageolet—a kind of flute.

Behind the hay wagon rode a Pope with other dignitaries. Between the wheels and in front of the wagon, nuns, priests and laymen struggled to get aboard. Nearer, a man held down his foe while inserting a dagger just above the collarbone. In the foreground a procuress whispered to a girl, a quack advertised his wares. Beneath the wheels several revelers had fallen, but the wagon continued its journey toward the mouth of hell, half concealed by a trapdoor. Leading the way was a throng partly human and partly grotesque combinations of fish and animals. Above the hay wagon, Christ stood below a rainbow of promise, his hands outstretched, beseeching.

When he painted *The Hay Wain,* Bosch gave to this complicated yet lucid vision two companion panels—a prologue and an epilogue to mankind's urgent march toward the eternal burning. The prologue shows the Garden of Eden. The creation of Adam and Eve, the temptation, and the expulsion are below. High in the heavens is the Creator, and beneath Him, an obscene flight of tiny fiends and poisonous insects, probably symbolizing Satan and his fallen angels. The epilogue reveals the torments of hell,

THE HAY WAIN

The fantastic creatures populating many of Bosch's paintings appear here in his first major work. The wagon represents the world, dragged by demons. Mankind follows—lovers, princes, gypsies—all on the road to Purgatory.

THE CONJUROR

(Right) Few Renaissance paintings show humor. depicted the conjuror (a "demon" with an owl in basket) deluding onlookers while a thief pilfers a

CHRIST BEARING THE CROSS

One of his last works, this is recognized as Bosch's finest. The cruel faces are strikingly similar to caricatures by his contemporary Leonardo da Vinci. Christ bears the gigantic tree of the Cross; a breast-plated soldier bears down to increase Christ's torment. Lower right, the Bad Thief grimaces; above right, the Good Thief reveals his terror of death. At lower left, St. Veronica, after offering her kerchief to Christ to wipe His brow, discovers on it His miraculous image.

where demons travestied as animals go about their dreadful business, served by apes—in a land of fantastic towers, reeking chimneys, ladders and gallows.

Little is known of Bosch, the unique visionary, in whose art certain underground shudders of the late Middle Ages reached the surface and produced results that influenced later artists from Brueghel to Dali. In the records of the religious order of Our Illustrious Lady's Brotherhood of Heertogenbosch, Jerome Bosch appears as a member, and his death is noted in 1516. This tells us that the strange, sardonic, life-denying spirit which was Jerome Bosch was nevertheless a Catholic in good standing. We also know that he was married and well-to-do. Between 1493 and 1512 we have some half-dozen notices of payments or contracts for pictures, designs for stained glass, and sculptures in the Flemish town of Heertogenbosch; the works themselves have perished. A portrait in pen and ink at Arras shows a very haggard and unkempt old man, surely beyond sixty. So, counting back from his death in 1516, he was born somewhere about 1450.

During his early activity, Jerome Bosch painted the traditional religious subjects, but even at this stage his originality shows itself. The older Flemish painters had adopted a conventional "distance"—that is, the main group and action were forward, almost filling the frame, but never crowding it. Bosch often set his figures well back and provided them with a spacious and somewhat competitive setting. Thus he was among the first, if not the first, to minimize the dramatic importance of his subject, making it merely an interesting happening in a world where other things are taking place.

In his tragic subjects, however, he pushed his group well forward, often showing only a cluster of heads, anticipating the "close-up" of the motion picture. These are the greatest Bosches, and the art of painting offers few parallels for them. This device of close-up presentation finds its most memorable expression in Bosch's *Christ Before Pilate* and *Christ Bearing the Cross*. In the latter picture the Christ is noble and pathetic; other faces are more distorted and frightful. Unlike the noble and dignified Italian Christs who always dominate the situation, Bosch's Jesus is just a dogged little preacher, hopelessly trapped and resigned to His fate.

The originality of Bosch extended even beyond his rendering of sinister visions or of the persecution of Christ. He was also the first to treat the peasant as a central subject, thus initiating a type of painting that the Netherlands was to excel in for several hundred years.

A generation or more after Jerome Bosch's death, the Florentine historian Guicciardini noted in Flanders that Bosch "was a noble and amazing inventor of fantastic and bizarre things." This referred not to his religious or rustic pictures, but to what men of his time called his "dreams" and what a modern man might call his nightmares. Of these *The Garden of Delights* is the most famous.

For Bosch was the spokesman of the terrifying belief in sorcery, witchcraft and all manner of diabolism, which in a century of frequent pestilence and constant wars had become the obsession of Western Europe. As the old, protecting faith waned, these superstitions became tortures. It was the century of Dances of Death, in words or in paint. Jerome Bosch made this netherworld of the troubled soul peculiarly his own and, save for the work of a few inferior imitators, completely exhausted it.

The painting of the dying Middle Ages ended, in Bosch, if not happily, at least with a promise and a prophecy. Something more racy, less limited by religious and courtly convention, was on the way. The people were to become subjects for the painter. Bosch had brought their follies and inner fears into visibility. Other painters were to make charmingly visible their ordinary walk and conversation.

—FRANK JEWETT MATHER, JR.

SELF-PORTRAIT

HANS HOLBEIN

1497?–1543

He Portrayed an Era

THE HOLBEINS, like the numerous musical Bachs of northern Germany, were more than individual artists. They were members of a clan of painters who for the greater part of an entire century were recognized as the undisputed leaders of their own particular trade. Hans' grandfather was a master tanner at Augsburg, in southern Germany, but, as the civilization of the Middle Ages depended as much on leather as we do on cotton and synthetics, a master

HENRY VIII

ANNE OF CLEVES

SIR THOMAS MORE

EDWARD VI

ERASMUS OF ROTTERDAM

PORTRAIT OF A MAN

JANE SEYMOUR

While court artist to Henry VIII, Holbein painted many portraits of the famous, such as Sir Thomas More and Erasmus. He portrayed two of Henry's queens—Jane Seymour and Catherine Howard—and traveled abroad to picture prospective brides. Princess Christina of Denmark, approved of in this manner, refused to go to England without two heads—"one to come home with," she said. Holbein so enhanced plain-looking Anne of Cleves that Henry proposed. Upon seeing her, the king called her a "Flanders mare." He divorced her after six months.

tanner in those days was a personage of great importance. As such he was held in great respect by his fellow men, and when the emperor paid the town an official visit, Holbein was there to greet him as a member of the official reception committee.

The old leather man had two sons, Hans and Sigismund. Both of them became well-known painters, and the elder of the two, Hans, in turn became the father of two first-rate artists, Ambrosius Holbein and Hans Holbein the Younger. In time the fame of the young Hans greatly overshadowed that of the father. Similarly the fame of half a dozen Bachs has made us forget that at one time or another there have been literally dozens of Bachs, each one of whom in his own humble way has contributed somewhat to the development of music.

When Hans Holbein the Elder got into financial difficulties, his sons left their native Augsburg and moved to Basel. That happened in 1515. Hans was about seventeen years old.

Four years before, *In Praise of Folly,* the dangerous social satire by the great Dutch writer Erasmus, had been a tremendous success. So much so that his Basel publisher, Joannes Froben, decided to print a private illustrated edition. Young Hans Holbein seemed the ideal artist for the job. Later, in 1523, Holbein's three portraits of Erasmus established his international reputation. Through the years, the illustrations by Holbein have become almost an essential part of the works of Erasmus.

Hans also did a number of chores in Basel and nearby cities, specializing in decorating the walls of private houses and public buildings, and making quite a name for himself in those plague-ridden days by the gruesomeness with which he painted *Dances of Death.* These popular works by Holbein showed Death dancing merrily with every sort of citizen from the Pope and emperor all the way down to the village idiot. Eventually Hans came to the conclusion that the local market was nearly exhausted and that he had better look elsewhere for more remunerative orders. Holbein was no dreamer who believed in art for art's sake! He had acquired a wife and she had presented him with several children, who needed a home and an education. He meant to provide for his family as best an enterprising artist could.

In this decision he may also have been influenced by the terrible depression that hit Europe around the year 1520. The sudden influx of the many millions which Spain had taken out of the gold mines of the New World completely upset the simple economy of the Middle Ages. Everywhere prices rose skyward. Agriculture was hit worst of all, and the discontent of the starving peasants greatly aided the labors of Martin Luther. For the Reformation, confiscating the wealth of all churches and monasteries, was a godsend to those unfortunate paupers, and they were among the most ardent followers of the famous rebel from Wittenberg.

Basel, a distributing point for merchandise from the Mediterranean, was one of the first cities to feel the depression. Artists must have patrons if they are to live, and Holbein, shrewdly anticipating the breadlines that would soon be forming, packed up his brushes and his colors and made for England, where there was law and order. While anarchy reigned supreme in every other part of Europe, the British monarchy, by placing itself at the head of the movement that demanded far-reaching ecclesiastical reforms, had been able to avert the threat of civil war that haunted other nations.

The first trip of young Holbein to England was an unqualified success. He carried a letter of introduction from Erasmus to Sir Thomas More, the favorite politician of Henry VIII. In Windsor Castle there are not less than eighty-seven drawings that Holbein made during his first visit—a veritable portrait gallery (and sometimes rogues' gallery) of all the men and women who played a part during the reign of King Henry VIII. Holbein was a most faithful portraitist. Nothing escaped his eye. The slightest details of the client's face and garments were put down.

In the year 1528 Holbein returned to his home town. His baggage this time contained a sketch of Sir Thomas More, which the latter had asked him to give to his old friend Erasmus in Basel, the only city on the mainland where a man of his tolerant tastes could still hope to live in peace. It was the last likeness of Sir Thomas that Erasmus was to behold. A few years later that noble head lay in the dust, cut off by order of the same sovereign whom the wise and broad-minded Thomas had served with such singular loyalty.

Our sturdy Swiss painter, however, was not interested in politics. He carefully avoided doing anything that might arouse the king's ire. So in 1532 we find him once again in England, as busy as a beaver and gloriously basking in the favor of "good King Hal," who was a scoundrel and a rogue but who had certain essentially human qualities which greatly endeared him to his loving subjects.

During this second visit Holbein finished a great many more pictures than during the first one. He had perfected his technique to a point beyond which no man could hope to go. While contemplating these pictures, one feels that if the people there represented had not actually looked the way he depicted them, they should have done so. His contemporaries appreciated his work at its true value, and Holbein was able to provide home and shoes for his wife and children as he had hoped to do when he set forth upon his perilous voyages. His own town honored him with an offer of lucrative commissions and a pension if he would return permanently. The doors of England's mightiest mansions were wide open to him. But not a vestige of carelessness or indifference ever entered his work. Until the end he remained the faithful workman who intended to give his clients the best there was in him, just as his grandfather, the old tanner, had given his customers the best hides that money could buy.

In the fall of the year 1543 one of Hans Holbein's most popular series of woodcuts was suddenly enacted in life. The plague broke out in London. And when the "Dances of Death" were in full swing, young Hans (he was just past forty-five) was stricken and called to join in the grim festivities. Death danced one of his most renowned portraitists off to the cemetery. —HENDRIK WILLEM VAN LOON

SELF-PORTRAIT

P. Brveghel. Fe.

PIETER BRUEGHEL

1520?–1569

Spectator in a Peasant Land

PEASANT CROWDS, landscapes swarming with the activities of men: these were Brueghel's major interests. He did not individualize the faces or model the flesh. He refused to picture a person for art or history, but preferred to show men, women and children walking, running, jumping, dancing, playing games—in all the varied animation of life.

He harked back to the scenes of his childhood and delighted to contemplate the fun and feasting, music and mating, of the peasantry. He and a friend on several occasions disguised themselves as farmers, attended village fairs and weddings and—pretending to be relatives—brought presents to the bridegroom and bride. On these outings Pieter Brueghel took his sketchbook, for among his extant drawings are many of rustic figures and events.

Though Brueghel's paintings of peasant life led to his being dubbed "Peasant Brueghel," he was a man of culture who read Homer, Virgil, Horace, Ovid, Rabelais, probably Erasmus. The Dutch historian Karel van Mander described him as "tranquil and orderly, speaking little, yet amusing in company, delighting to horrify people . . . with tales of ghosts and banshees"; hence, perhaps, his other sobriquet, "Droll Brueghel." His sense of humor leaned to satire, but he tempered this with sympathy. A contemporary engraving shows him heavily bearded, with a face bearing lines of serious thought.

Brueghel may have derived his name from either of two little villages named Brueghel; one of them was near the birthplace of Jerome Bosch (see page 76). There he might have seen several church paintings by Bosch, the man who influenced his work only less than nature itself. At about twenty years of age, Brueghel went to Brussels, and was apprenticed to Pieter Coecke. This painter had begotten a daughter, Maria, whom Brueghel dandled in his arms as a child—and whom he later made his wife.

He moved to Antwerp and found work with a publisher. But in 1552 he followed the custom of his craft and went to study painting in Italy. He returned with a sketchbook thick with Italian landscapes, but showing no visible Italian influence in his technique. Back in Antwerp, he lived with a housekeeper, whom he promised to marry when she stopped lying. He recorded her lies with notches cut into a stick; and having no stick for his own sins, he renounced her when the notches overflowed.

During this period he followed Bosch in seeing life as a needless hurrying of souls to hell, and became known as Bosch the Second. In the *Triumph of Death* he visioned a ghastly cutting off of limbs—skeletons attacking kings, cardinals and peasants with hatchets, stones and scythes, corpses riding in a cart—one more variant of that "Dance of Death" which flits through the art of this somber age. He seems to have searched for ugly peasants; he never lets them smile or laugh; if he gives their crude faces any expression it is one of dull indifference, of sensitivity beaten out by the blows of life. He was impressed and hurt by the apathy with which the fortunate bear the misery of the unfortunate, the haste with which the living blithely forget the dead.

Brueghel's religious pictures reflect the same somber

mood. They have neither the grandeur nor the light grace of Italian pictures; they merely reinterpret the Biblical story in terms of Flemish faces, dress and climate. They rarely reveal religious feeling; most of them are opportunities for painting crowds. The people who jostle one another to see Christ carry His cross seem heedless of His suffering and are anxious only to get a good view.

Around the age of thirty Brueghel married Maria Coecke, who had reached eighteen, and granted her wish to live in Brussels. In this Brueghel family, there were now not only Pieter, his painter wife and in-laws, but there would follow four more generations of artists. At his new locale, Pieter developed no taste for, nor commissions from, the aristocrats that Titian found it so profitable to portray. Brueghel painted only simple people. Even his dogs were mongrel curs that could be found in any city alley or rural hut. He knew the bitter side of peasant life and sometimes depicted it as a multitudinous confusion of fools, but he loved to paint the games of country children, the dances of their elders, the riot of their weddings. In *The Land of Cockayne,* the peasants, exhausted with toil or love or drink, sprawl out on the grass dreaming of Utopia. It is the peasant, Brueghel seems to say in these happy pictures, who knows how to play and sleep as well as how to work and mate and die.

Before Brueghel landscapes had been painted as backgrounds and appendages to human figures and events; he made the landscape itself the picture, the men in it mere incidents. He was oppressed by the vast perspective of nature—that immensity of sky under which all human events seem drowned in insignificance. In *The Fall of Icarus,* the sky, the ocean, the mountains and the sun have absorbed the attention of the painter, and of the participants; Icarus is two unnoticed legs ridiculously sinking into the sea.

The art and philosophy of Brueghel culminate in the

HUNTERS IN THE SNOW
Most remarkable of all Brueghel's landscapes, here is one of many that show a bird's-eye view; even the Alps appear in his Flemish scenes.

ILDREN AT PLAY
ɔposite) Some two hundred children are engaged ighty-four sports. Of the artist's incomplete ɛs on "The Ages of Man," this was the first.

five paintings that remain of a series planned to illustrate the moods of the year. *The Wheat Harvest* pictures the cutting and stacking of the sheaves, the workers lunching or napping beneath the visible heat and stillness of the summer air. In *The Hay Harvest* a farmer sharpens his scythe, sturdy women rake the hay, men pitch it to the top of the wagonload. *The Return of the Herd* heralds winter—the skies darkening, the cattle guided back to their stalls. Finest of the series is the *Hunters in the Snow:* roofs and ground are white; dwellings range in an amazing perspective along the plains and hills; men skate, play hockey, fall on the ice; hunters and their dogs start out to capture food; the trees are bare, but birds in the branches promise spring. *The Gloomy Day* is winter scowling its farewell. In these paintings Brueghel reached his peak. He caught the unconscious unity of a village, a crowd, a wave of life.

What does Brueghel mean to say? Is he merely jesting, laughing at man as a grotesque "forked radish" and at life as a silly strutting to decay? He enjoyed the lusty swing of the peasants' dance, sympathized with their toil and looked with indulgent humor on their drunken sleep. Some of Brueghel's pictures, as we have seen, are Biblical parables, like *The Sower;* others, following Bosch, take proverbs for their themes. *The Blind Leading the Blind* shows a succession of dull-eyed peasants, cruelly ugly, following one another into a ditch; and *Netherlandish Proverbs* illustrates, in one teeming painting, nearly a hundred old maxims, including some of Rabelaisian fragrance.

We do not know which of these was Brueghel's real philosophy, nor why he gave up the battle so soon, dying in his forties. He bequeathed to his wife an ambiguous picture, *The Merry Way to the Gallows,* a masterly composition in fresh greens and distant blues with peasants dancing near the village gibbet—and perched on this a magpie, emblem of a chattering tongue. —WILL DURANT

SELF-PORTRAIT(?)

δομήνικος θεοτοκόπουλος ἐποίει

EL GRECO

1541–1614

Modern Master of Old Spain

THE SUN WAS SHINING in Toledo. It was spring—the river Tagus sparkled and sang, wild flowers bloomed on the red-brown hills. But in the home of the painter El Greco it was dark, almost black. The shades were drawn; no lights burned. When a friend dropped in to invite him for a walk, the artist replied, "No, the sun will interfere with the light inside of me."

It is a revealing anecdote, for El Greco was a man of intense religious feeling, living much by himself and within himself. Out of his daily struggle to understand and express what he felt emerged his unique style: the faces and bodies of the people he drew are strangely elongated. There is distortion in his pictures, a cunning and planned departure from the realistic which gives them a terrifying emotional impact. No one has ever painted quite the same way.

Unquestionably one of our greatest painters, El Greco was ignored and forgotten for almost three hundred years after his death. In the year 1881 a director of the Prado museum in Madrid protested against the need for hanging his "absurd caricatures." As late as 1902 there appeared a seemingly authoritative book of nearly seven hundred pages on art that failed to mention his name.

His resurrection began in Paris at the turn of the century. The art world was in a blaze of revolt against traditional painting. Cézanne, Monet and others were fighting for freedom in the use of light and form and color. These rebels discovered in El Greco a man as fresh and modern as the greatest of this school of Paris.

It was a miracle, a rising from the tomb, as this painter soared from obscurity to world renown. Art dealers and amateur collectors invaded Toledo to rummage in attics

THE ANNUNCIATION

The painting above hangs in the sanctuary of the chapel of Our Lady of Charity Hospital, built by the artist's son at Illescas, a small town between Madrid and Toledo.

ɪE BURIAL OF COUNT ORGAZ
ɛ altarpiece (left), painted for the Church of ɪnto Tomé founded by Gonzalo Ruiz, Lord of Orgaz, ɪl Greco's masterwork. It shows St. Augustine ɪ St. Stephen descending to bury the pious count.

VIEW OF TOLEDO
(Above) El Greco pictured, not what the ancient capital of Spain actually looked like, but how he saw it in his imagination. He has moved buildings, changed streets to build his fantasy.

and cellars. Small churches and private owners who had never thought much of El Greco were convinced that these breathless buyers were a trifle mad. But the owners were quite willing to take their money, selling the masterpieces for ridiculously small sums. His *Cardinal Fernando Niño de Guevara,* virtually given away, was later sold for a substantial sum—and is today almost priceless. Whetting the appetite of collectors was the fact that so many of his paintings have disappeared. There are today not quite 300 known El Grecos. But seven years after El Greco died, his son listed 241 pictures in his possession; and of this group a great many are unaccounted for. Where the missing ones are, what happened to them, nobody knows. Nor does anyone know how many others have been lost.

Torrents of books and pamphlets flowed to a public eager for information about this sixteenth-century artist who was a smash hit in the twentieth—but the man himself remained obscure. El Greco kept no diary, wrote few letters. What we know has been unearthed in widely scattered documents, a story in outline only; the basic questions are still unanswered—will always perhaps remain to frustrate our curiosity.

He was born in Candia on the Grecian island of Crete in 1541, and was christened Domenikos Theotokopoulos, later to be known as El Greco (the Greek). He went to the school of St. Catherine's Monastery, which maintained a shrine on Mount Sinai. His earliest drawings, now lost, are said to have depicted that holy place.

When he was eighteen years old, already a painter of promise, he arrived in Venice, where, according to many scholars, he worked in the studio of Titian and learned many arts, principally color. A few years later he went to Rome, where he soon got into trouble with the artist-ruler of the city, Michelangelo. The holy fathers had asked Michelangelo to clothe some of the figures in his *Last Judgment.* In the controversy that followed this request El Greco declared: "Destroy the whole thing and let me do another; I'll do one that's decent and honest and no less great." In the art world of Rome, El Greco's hopes of obtaining commissions were reduced to zero; he was practically banished.

Spring of 1577 found him in the Spanish city of Toledo—the profoundly beautiful former capital. He had obtained work painting for the new Church of Santo Domingo el Antiguo. To understand El Greco, one must appreciate the old city and the mystery of its great influence upon him as a painter. Arriving there at the age of thirty-six, El Greco was a good craftsman and not much more—in other words, a second-rate artist. In less than five years he was a great one. Toledo had performed a miracle. Floating in the ancient air was a spark which set fire to the Greek. You can see his smoldering passion for the city in his painting, *View of Toledo;* he has made of it a dream not quite real in its mortar and stone but authentic in spirit, more Toledo than Toledo itself.

In the thirty-seven years he lived there, he occupied three homes. Most of the time he lived where he was to die, in a beautiful twenty-four-room mansion. The woman in his life was Jeronima de las Cuevas, whose loveliness is apparent in her portrait, *La Dama del Armiño.* Was she his wife? No one is quite sure. One biographer suggests that the only reason he did not legitimatize the union was that he already had a wife in Italy. Jeronima bore him one son, Jorge Manuel, who was also a painter and who always worked by the side of his father. In *The Burial of the Count Orgaz,* a charming little boy stands in the foreground. In his breast pocket is a white handkerchief on which is written in Greek the painter's name, the words "I Made It" and the year of Jorge Manuel's birth.

Living also in the large house was an old housekeeper and cook, his business agent and several pupils. When the painter had money, he employed musicians to play for him at each meal. Occasionally friends would spend an evening: architects, poets, learned monks. In their company the solitary Greek would charm his guests with his wit and sophistication. Such social gatherings were rare, however. His life was the thing on the easel and the agony of translating into pigment the emotion and thought that filled his waking hours. The first important pictures he did in Spain were two great altarpieces—both so successful that he was invited to do one for the sacristy of the great Toledo cathedral. His subject was *The Disrobing of Christ.* It was a masterwork, a departure from the traditional serenity of the Italians. Its bittersweet colors cry out, its shadows bellow; a painting far too strong and original for the Church fathers, who not only did not want it but refused to pay for it.

El Greco brought suit to collect his money, and the result was a historic trial in which the witnesses on both sides were equally divided. During the trial El Greco stood by saying nothing, his head held high in pride and disdain for the comments of his critics. When the judge asked him why he had come to Toledo, he shouted his refusal to answer. At last he gave his name, but only when he was threatened with imprisonment. He settled for about one third of the price he was originally promised.

The final word in the dispute was the artist's. He copied the *Disrobing* no less than seventeen times, selling the variations to individuals and churches—making a profit out of his misfortune. Painting and selling copies of one's pictures was common practice in those days. El Greco did it often. He sold his *St. Francis in Ecstasy* eighty times. A rebel in many ways, El Greco also fought and beat the government when it sought to levy on his paintings a kind of sales tax—a victory of enormous help to other Spanish artists.

He had no illusions about his own merit. "As surely as the rate of payment is inferior to the value of my sublime work," he said, "so will my name go down to posterity as one of the great geniuses of painting." Self-praise perhaps, but time has proved him right.

In April 1614 El Greco died—a poor man, according to many. He owed three years' rent; his twenty-four rooms were bare of furniture, perhaps because he had sold most of it in order to live. His remains were moved from one church to a second, which was demolished, leaving no trace of the bones and dust of the Greek whose unique vision made him one of Spain's greatest painters.

—GEORGE KENT

SELF-PORTRAIT

·P·RVBENS·F·

PETER PAUL RUBENS

1577–1640

Ambassador of Grand Art

THREE PRETTY GIRLS were sitting by a ground-floor window spinning when a tall, redheaded, good-looking fellow in a plumed hat stopped and stared in. His gaze was cool and deliberate; he might have been examining butterflies.

Walking into the house without a knock, he said matter-of-factly, "Take off your clothes, please." One of the girls shrieked, but her older companion allayed her fears. "The gentleman doesn't seem like that kind of man."

"Nor am I," he agreed. "I am an artist. If your bodies are what I think they are, you will make much more money sitting as my models than you earn with your spindles."

The year was 1622. The place was Paris. The man was Peter Paul Rubens, master painter of the Flemish School. He had just been commissioned by France's queen mother, Marie de Médicis, to do twenty-one large murals for the Luxembourg Palace.

No one painted the female form more often than Rubens, and no one, except possibly Titian and Renoir, brought it so beautifully to life. Rubens' nudes—reclining on the grass, rollicking in the woods, coming out of the bath—hang in museums throughout the world. The figures—broad-hipped, substantial women for the most part—are symbols of abundance and fruitfulness. Whatever their posture, they wear an innocent though undeniably voluptuous air.

Nudes, however, are only a part of Rubens' incredibly large production. He painted hundreds of portraits, landscapes, hunting scenes, quiet interiors. Greatest of all are his religious paintings. Few artists have portrayed Christ more tenderly: Christ on the Cross, Christ descending, Christ pierced by the Roman lance. We feel the suffering in the texture of the flesh, in the eyes and lips, the posture of the head, the collapse of the body. But the secret of the emotion he arouses is in the movement, the rhythm of mass and color—a rhythm of religious fervor.

No man worked harder at his craft. Though the Antwerp guild of painters had officially recognized him as "Master" when he was only twenty-one, he kept on studying and learning to the end of his life. At fifty, he was still making copies of Titian and others to improve his technique. A true genius, he painted always at terrific speed, never hesitating, never correcting. One of his largest and most beloved creations, *The Adoration of the Magi,* was allegedly completed in six days.

In addition to being a prodigy at the easel, Rubens was master of a greater art: the art of living. He was supremely happy in marriage, strictly faithful to his wife in an age of widespread dissipation. His children respected and adored him. When he died at sixty-two, all the notables of Antwerp attended his magnificent funeral.

None of the waywardness that often goes with great talent affected Rubens. Never spoiled by success, he was as orderly in his habits as a filing clerk. A man of enormous vitality, he would get up at four each morning, attend early Mass, then begin work. As he painted, he listened to

RAPE OF THE DAUGHTERS OF LEUCIPPUS
For this 8-foot-high canvas, Rubens took his classical theme from a poem by Ovid, which was based on the Greek legend in which the heroes Castor and Pollux follow the Spartan custom of capturing their brides. In his lifetime Rubens painted 280 mythological pictures.

DESCENT FROM THE CROSS

Rubens became the most famous painter in Flanders when, at the age of thirty-seven, he completed the work below for the Antwerp cathedral.

THE STRAW HAT

(Bottom) Lovely Susanna Fourment poses a longstanding, popular puzzle: Why does her "straw" hat not look like straw?

a boy whose job it was to read to him from Tacitus or Plutarch. At noon he paused for a snack—mostly vegetables, for he believed that meat was bad for a creative artist. At five he quit painting. Then he would saddle a horse and ride in the outskirts of Antwerp. In the evening friends and family would gather around his hospitable table for food and conversation.

Peter Paul Rubens was born in 1577 in Siegen, Germany, where his father, an important native of Antwerp, then part of the Netherlands, was living in exile. It was not a happy household. The elder Rubens, legal adviser to the wife of the Prince of Orange, Princess Anne, had been found guilty of adultery with her and condemned to death. Only the efforts of his wife saved him and at last won his release from prison. It may well be that the bitter experience of his father gave Rubens his aversion to frivolity.

At the elder Rubens' death, the family moved back to Antwerp, where Peter Paul became a page in a noble family. There he learned the social graces and impeccable manners that were to distinguish him all his life. Painting, however, was his passion, and he became an apprentice to minor painters. When he was twenty-three, Rubens set out for Italy. In Venice, a few months later, he was sitting in the courtyard of an inn, copying a famous painting from memory, when a stranger behind him exclaimed, "Marvelous—it's better than the original! I'll take you to my friend Duke Vincenzo Gonzaga of Mantua, and your fortune will be made." In Mantua, Rubens became official painter to the court.

After some years, Rubens journeyed to Spain, where he received word that his mother was gravely ill. He returned at once to Antwerp, too late to see her. But the Archduke Albrecht and the Infanta Isabella, rulers of the Netherlands (then under Spanish influence), were enchanted with him personally, and named him court painter. For the city's town hall he did his imposing *Adoration of the Magi,* with twenty-eight life-size figures. Shortly afterward he painted the *Descent from the Cross,* generally considered his masterpiece.

At thirty-two he married Isabella Brant, daughter of a town dignitary; she was fourteen years his junior. They had three children. After seventeen years of serenely happy married life, his wife died suddenly. A heartbroken Rubens, seeking escape from his grief, took a job which few painters could have done well—that of ambassador. Highly polished, cultivated and persuasive, Rubens had occasionally undertaken assignments of state before, but now he was to become one of the ablest diplomats of his day, competing with that wiliest of statesmen, Cardinal Richelieu.

During his many tours of duty, Rubens did not cease to paint. The intimacy of a studio even helped his work as ambassador; posing is tedious and encourages confidences. Painting the Duke of Buckingham one day, Rubens was given to understand that England would not be averse to making peace with Spain. Taking the hint, Rubens moved between the courts of Philip IV of Spain and Charles I of England and after many months of effort won their signatures to a treaty ending hostilities between the two countries. Both nations honored him with knighthood.

Rubens had led a widower's life for four years when he fell deeply in love with a sixteen-year-old girl, Helena Fourment, and married her. He never tired of painting his young wife, doing more than fifteen portraits. She also posed for many of his religious and mythological pictures.

In time it became a physical impossibility to execute alone all the commissions that came his way. He established an "assembly line" of art for some of his paintings. He would make the outline of a picture and indicate the colors needed. He or a pupil would block in the painting; then one assistant would add landscapes, another horses, a third wild animals, a fourth figures, a fifth the still-life portions. Rubens' own final touches would stamp the picture with his personality. His assistants were gifted artists, among them Anthony Van Dyck, Frans Snyders and Jan Brueghel—son of the great Pieter. They were delighted to work for him, for Rubens paid them well.

He made no attempt to deceive buyers. A memorandum he sent to a British lord explained how each picture was made: "*Prometheus Bound,* an original from my own hand; the eagle done by Frans Snyders, 500 florins. *Leopards,* original picture by my own hand, except a fine landscape done by an artist clever at this sort of work, 600 florins." When one purchaser refused to pay, claiming the picture was not by his hand, Rubens retorted, "Had I done it all by myself, the price would have been double."

The serenity of Rubens' later days was marred by gout, which crippled his hands. Often the brush would fall from his rigid fingers; but never were his paintings more joyous, more riotous in light and color.

In Antwerp today, Rubens still colors the atmosphere. His statue salutes you in front of the cathedral; and as you walk the streets the name Rubens can be seen wherever you turn. In every way this is still his town. But his genius is too great to be confined to one place. Rubens created the beauty that enriched an era, raising it to enduring splendor and vitality. —GEORGE KENT

CHILDREN OF CHARLES I

All three portrayed by Van Dyck became monarchs: Charles II; his brother, James II; and Mary, Princess of Orange. The dogs also achieved fame—the breed became the King Charles spaniel.

SELF-PORTRAIT

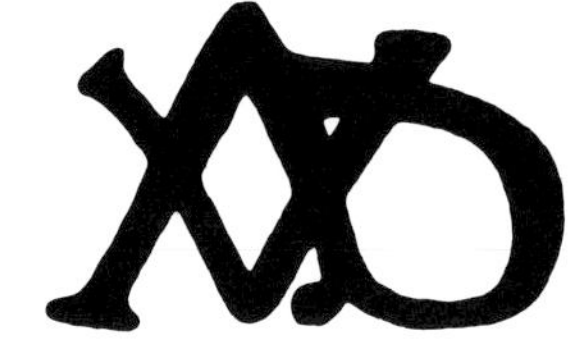

ANTHONY VAN DYCK

1599–1641

The Patrician

ONE OF THE MOST precocious of the world's great painters, Anthony Van Dyck revealed in a self-portrait at the age of sixteen the qualities that were to mark and limit his genius—grace, finesse and a soft beauty almost unbecoming to a man.

It was just like Rubens to hail and encourage the talent of the young Adonis who first began to work with him about 1617. The boy had been apprenticed to the artist Hendrik van Balen at ten; at sixteen he had pupils of his own and at nineteen he was a registered master, not so

CHARLES I OF ENGLAND

Although Van Dyck painted some thirty-eight portraits of the English monarch, the regal picture above is probably responsible for Charles' reputation as the man who "looked every inch a king."

much a pupil of Rubens as a highly valued aide. Rubens rated an early painting by Van Dyck as equal in worth to his own *Daniel* of the same year. And Van Dyck's fellow artists were happy to sit for him as an added hedge against oblivion. It was one of his many lovable qualities that he liked his rivals. These portraits suggest that in Rubens' studio there was a pleasant spirit of comradeship not always present in the realm of art.

In 1620 the Earl of Arundel received a letter from Antwerp: "Van Dyck lives with Rubens, and his works are being esteemed almost as highly as those of his master." He invited the twenty-year-old artist to England. Van Dyck went. He received a piddling pension of about five hundred dollars from James I and painted a few portraits. But, rebelling at the menial copying required of him by the king, he asked for an eight months' leave of absence and stretched it to twelve years.

After a short stay in Antwerp in 1621, where he may have provided for his mistress and her baby, the painter hurried down into Italy. There for the first time he struck his stride, and he left fine portraits at almost every stop. He pored over the great Venetians, not so much to study their color and massive scope, as Rubens had done, but to ferret out the secrets of poetic portraiture in Giorgione, Titian and Veronese. He journeyed to Bologna, Florence, Rome, even to Sicily. At Rome he stayed with Cardinal Guido Bentivoglio and repaid him with a portrait. His courtly manners were resented by the Flemish artists who were starving in Italy; they dubbed him *"il pittore cavalleresco"*—the cavalier painter. He was especially welcomed in Genoa, however, which remembered Rubens and had heard of Van Dyck's flair for ennobling nobility, making every sitter seem to be a prince. Among these aristocratic Genoese portraits are those of the Marchesa Durazzo, with sensitive face and, as always in Van Dyck, fine hands; and the Marchesa Grimaldi, proud and pregnant.

When Van Dyck returned to Antwerp in 1627, his pockets were full and his lace was exquisite. His native city had called him back from nobles to saints. To fit himself to paint these he repented of his promiscuity, willed his young fortune to two nun sisters and appears to have joined a laymen's religious organization, the Jesuit Confraternity of the Unmarried. He could not rival Rubens in painting religious themes, but he avoided the exuberant master's exaggerations and carnal effulgence, and gave to his pictures a touch of the elegance he had learned in Italy.

Van Dyck tried his hand at mythological pictures, but though he had pursued many women he was not impelled to paint nudes. His forte was always portraiture, and during his four years in Antwerp his brush rescued from oblivion Baron Philippe Le Roy and a devoted dog; General Francisco de Moncada and his horse; Count Rhodokanakis; Jean de Montfort, looking like Falstaff; and—most beautiful of these Van Dycks—young Rupert, "Prince Charming" of the Palatine. Alluring, too, is the portrait of Maria Luisa of Tassis, lost in her swelling robes of black satin and white silk. And as good as any of these is Van Dyck's etching of the famous Brueghel's son Pieter, an old man still seething with the unspent sap of an amazing dynasty of painters (see page 82).

Some of these portraits he took with him when Charles I invited him to try England again. Charles, unlike his father, had a sure taste in art. He surmised that this handsome Fleming was just the man to do for him what Velázquez was doing for Philip IV. Van Dyck came and transmitted the king, Queen Henrietta Maria and their children to canvas for posterity, indelibly marked with the Van Dyck elegance.

Most famous of his royal portraits is the one in the Louvre, the proud king posing in riding costume, one arm akimbo, sword prominent, jaunty hat and Van Dyck beard; the tired horse, champing the bit between hunts, can be more easily loved.

In Dresden and Turin are rival paintings of Charles' children, as yet harmless and innocent. Charles was more human than he pretended; his capacity for warm affection showed in his fondness for Van Dyck; he knighted him, gave him expensive homes in London and in the country, a yearly pension of ten thousand dollars, additional payment for each picture and every welcome at the court.

The happy artist lived up to his income, loved fine clothing, had his coach-and-four, his thoroughbreds and his mistresses, and filled his homes with music and art. He bettered Rubens' instruction in delegating work—left the painting of costumes to assistants, painted a portrait in an hour from a sketch made at one sitting and made hay while the sun played hide-and-seek. Once, the story goes, Charles I, suffering from parliamentary parsimony, asked the extravagant artist if he knew what it meant to be short of funds. "Yes, Sire," answered Van Dyck blandly. "When one keeps an open table for his friends and an open purse for his mistresses, he soon reaches the bottom of his money chest."

If at times he sank into debt, it was not for lack of patronage. Half the English aristocracy waited in turn to receive his imprimatur: James Stuart, Duke of Lennox;

Robert Rich, Earl of Warwick; Lord Derby and his family; Thomas Wentworth, Earl of Strafford. Poets too had their hour—Carew, Killigrew, Suckling. And finally there was Old Parr, claiming to be 150 years old and looking it. Van Dyck painted three hundred portraits in England, almost all distinguished by the grace and dignity that he saw in a lord even when they were not there.

His mistress, Margaret Lemon, competed expensively with the aristocracy for his time. The king suggested that marriage would be cheaper, and about 1640 he helped Van Dyck to secure the hand of Lady Mary Ruthven, of a family famous in Scottish history. The artist painted a lovely picture of his bride, but it could not compare with the handsome face he gave himself in the *Self-Portrait* that all the world knows—the elegant with rich wavy hair, sharp eyes, refined features, scissored beard, gold chain proclaiming his knighthood.

Did Van Dyck flatter Sir Anthony? If so it was of no use, for his health, consumed too lavishly, had already begun to fail. Loath to be remembered only for portraits, he asked Charles to let him paint historic scenes on the walls of the banqueting hall at Whitehall, but Charles was by now living from an empty purse.

In 1640 Van Dyck crossed to Paris, hoping for the commission to paint the Grande Galerie of the Louvre. Louis XIII had already chosen Nicolas Poussin, and when Poussin relinquished the assignment it was too late for Van Dyck. He fell ill, rushed back to London to his lying-in wife. He died in 1641, eight days after she gave birth to a daughter. He was not yet forty-two.

He founded no school and left no mark upon Continental art, but in England his influence was overwhelming. Local painters made haste to copy his flattering, lucrative style. And when a great burst of portraiture came later with Reynolds and Gainsborough, it was the Van Dyck legacy that gave these masters their schooling and stimulus.

Van Dyck was too hurried to search for the soul, and sometimes he stopped at the face or the beard. The Cavaliers who surrounded Charles I were known for their fine manners, but it is unlikely that so many of them looked like poets. And some of the romance that we find in their brave stand for their king may have come to us from seeing them through Van Dyck's eyes.

If the frail and fortunate youth did not have the robust vitality of Rubens or the profundity of Rembrandt, we nevertheless cherish these famed cavalier portraits as a bright and precious heritage. —WILL AND ARIEL DURANT

SELF-PORTRAIT

DIEGO VELAZQUEZ

1599–1660

Perfect Courtier

THE BLACK-EYED, black-haired young man rode up to the capital in 1623, was made court painter and took the fancy of King Philip IV by picturing him as an intrepid horseman on a prancing charger. Philip himself not only posed for Velázquez many times, but he encouraged the royal family—brothers, wives, children—and the court—ministers, generals, poets, jesters, dwarfs—to take their turn before that immortalizing brush.

Velázquez was given a studio in the royal palace and there, or near it, he spent most of the remaining thirty-seven years of his life. It was a magnificent opportunity and a narrowing imprisonment.

He was born in southern Spain in the same year (1599) as Van Dyck. He received a good education, learned some Latin and philosophy and for a while tried science; then he turned to painting. He studied briefly with Francisco Herrera the Elder, longer with Francisco Pacheco. "I married him to my daughter," Pacheco tells us, "induced by his youth, integrity and good qualities, and the prospects of his great natural genius."

Velázquez set up his own studio, and soon attracted attention by his fondness for profane subjects. He mingled with the lowly, and delighted to put their thoughts and biographies into their faces. When he was still a lad of twenty he painted a superb picture, *The Water Carrier of Seville;* here, in rags and patience, is the dignity of honest poverty. And at twenty-three he portrayed with already mature insight the poet Luis de Góngora—eyes and nose piercing the world.

Two major influences broadened him. Rubens, then the most famous artist in the world, visited Madrid in 1628—a master of light and shade, a reckless painter of pagan deities and voluptuous nudes; Velázquez was stirred. Rubens advised him to go to Italy and study those geniuses of coloring. Velázquez pleaded with Philip and was granted permission and 300 precious ducats (1500 dollars) for the trip. He reached Genoa August 20, 1629, crossed Italy to Venice and sat for days before the great canvases of Tintoretto and Veronese and the portraits and the mythologies of Titian. He passed on to Ferrara and Rome, copied the ancient marbles in the Forum and envied the drawing in the frescoes of Michelangelo on the Sistine Chapel ceiling. From Naples he sailed back to Spain in January 1631, to resume his work at court.

Between the king's pictures came Queen Isabel, then Queen Mariana, and Philip's sister Queen Maria of Hungary (sitting to no great result), as well as others, royal or servant. The most pleasing of these court portraits are those of the young prince Don Baltasar Carlos, in whom all the hopes of the dynasty rested. Velázquez painted this lovely child again and again, with transparent delight. So the series progressed from Carlos' second to his sixteenth year, when the beloved lad fell into a fever and died. One of these pictures shows him with a dwarf, a member of the group who gave the failures at Philip's court a comforting sense of superiority and magnitude. The custom had come down from Imperial Rome and the even more ancient East. For their own satisfaction, and the general amusement, Philip IV's dwarfs were dressed in sumptuous raiment flashing jewelry and gold. Velázquez painted them with sympathy and humor.

In 1649, as reward for twenty-six years of work, Philip financed Velázquez's second visit to Italy and commissioned the artist to secure castings of classic statuary and to purchase paintings by Italian masters. Velázquez found prices already awesome; hardly any major work by the great Venetians could be bought at any price. For five pictures he had to pay 12,000 crowns (150,000 dollars). Were millionaires and others already using art as insurance against inflation?

The best painting done in Italy that following year was his portrait of Innocent X. When the Pope consented to sit for him, the artist, feeling out of practice, prepared his hand and eye by making a portrait of his mulatto assistant, Juan de Pareja. This picture met with universal acclaim among the artists of Rome, who at once elected Velázquez to their Academy of St. Luke. The Pope gave him only a few sittings; Velázquez made preliminary studies of the head, and one of these is almost indistinguishable from the finished portrait that passed down as an heirloom in

VENUS AND CUPID

This was the first female nude in Spanish painting, as the subject was forbidden. Protected by the king, Velázquez escaped penalty. No other nude was painted in Spain until Goya's Nude Maja, *whose supposed model, the Duchess of Alba, once owned this work.*

PHILIP IV
PRINCE BALTASAR CARLOS
INFANTA DONA MARGARITA

When Velázquez joined the royal household as court painter, he was twenty-four and Philip IV, a Hapsburg, was eighteen. In the following forty years the artist painted his king forty times. The portrait below was the second. Philip, known as the finest horseman of Spain, was proud of the riding ability of his son, Prince Baltasar Carlos. Shown here at five years of age, Carlos was the artist's favorite subject. The Infanta Margarita, also often painted by Velázquez, was the subject of one of the last, and perhaps the most brilliant, of all the royal portraits.

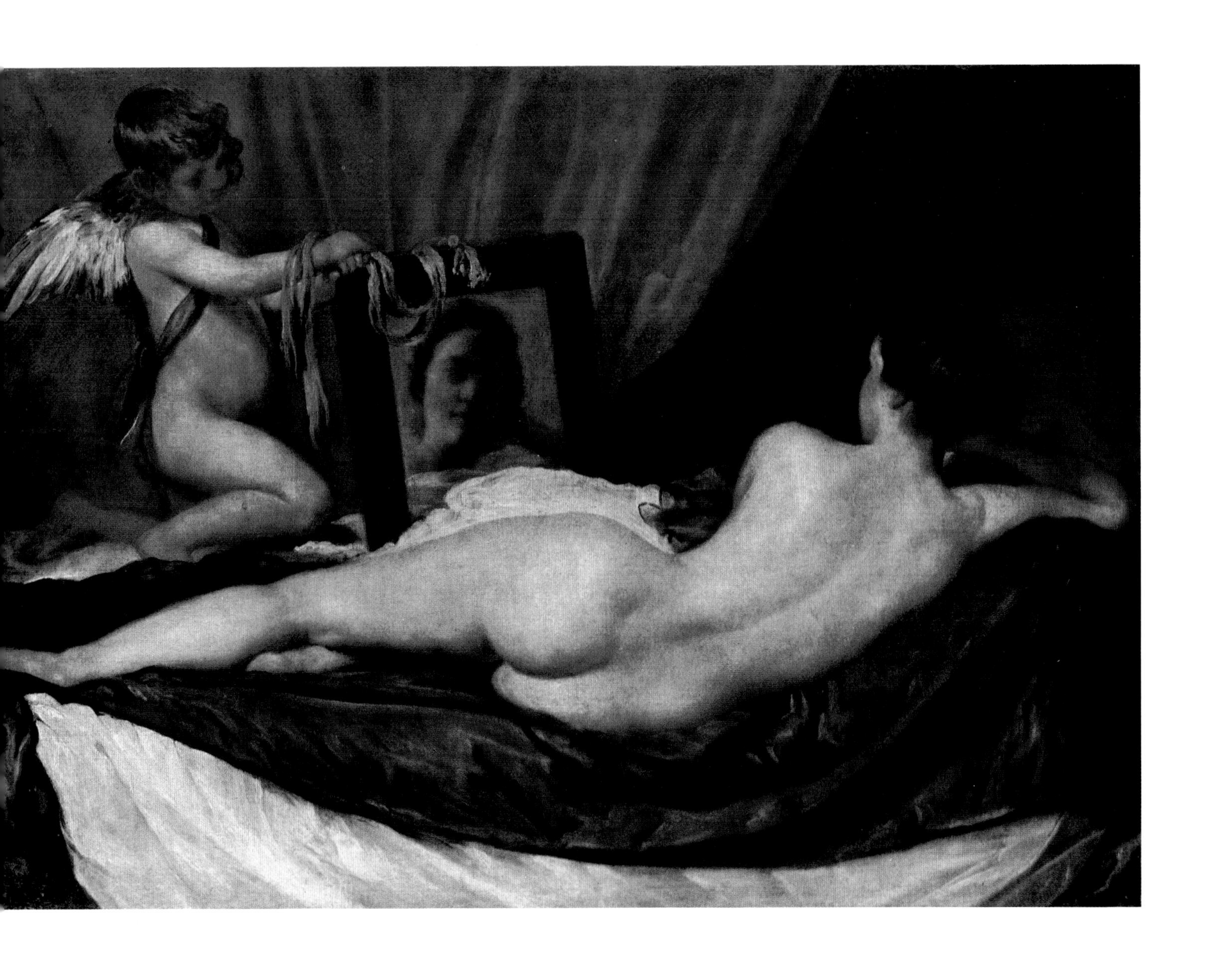

the Doria family to which the Pope belonged. The great English painter of portraits, Joshua Reynolds, viewing it a century later, judged it "the most beautiful picture in Rome." Coming upon it there today, one feels in it a power, both of character and of art, that places it among the most impressive portraits of all time.

Innocent X was seventy-six when he posed for this picture. But for his pontifical dress and ring, one could mistake him for one of the bandit leaders who had troubled so many popes; but then, studying those hard and resolute features, we realize that Innocent was what he had to be—a ruler guiding a Church that reached from Rome to the Philippines. He had to have iron in his blood, steel in his eyes, mastery in his face; and Velázquez saw and placed them there. The Pope made one wry comment about the portrait: "Too true!" When Velázquez left Italy (June 1651), it was not as a pupil seeking old masters, but as himself the acknowledged master of the age.

Back in Madrid, Velázquez made the outstanding blunder of his life: he applied for and obtained appointment as *aposentador del rey*—manager of the royal palace. Perhaps he was tired of painting, or felt that he had reached the limit of his possibilities in that field. The post involved personal supervision of the palace, of its furniture and decoration, heating and sanitation. Velázquez was also expected to make arrangements for court plays, balls and tournaments, to provide quarters for the court on royal tours and to accompany the king on major trips.

In the eight years that remained to him he gave to painting only such time as could be spared from his official chores. He resumed the portrayal of the royal family, of distinguished courtiers and of the king himself. He made three lovely pictures of the Infanta Margarita, and painted her again as the center of one of his masterpieces, *Las Meninas—The Maids of Honor;* servants, dwarf and dog gather around the princess, and Velázquez himself is seen in the background, putting them all on canvas. We see him as he saw himself in his final years—hair abounding, proud mustache, slightly somber eyes.

His death resulted from his office. In the spring of 1660 he arranged the complex ceremonies and festivities that were to accompany the betrothal of the Infanta Maria Teresa to Louis XIV. Lost in official duties, he returned to the capital "tired with traveling by night and working by day," as he reported to a friend. On July thirty-first he was put to bed with tertian fever. On August sixth, or, in the words of a biographer, "on the Feast of the Lord's Transfiguration . . . he resigned his soul to God." A week later his wife died and was laid beside him in the earth.

Always honored in Spain as her greatest painter, Velázquez was hardly known north of the Pyrenees. Manet and the Impressionists hailed him as their precursor in the study and representation of light and atmosphere; and for half a century Velázquez was ranked with the highest. Whistler called him "the painter's painter," as the teacher of them all; the critic Ruskin declared that "everything that Velázquez does may be regarded as absolutely right." Then Julius Meier-Graefe, another critic, went to Spain, found El Greco in Toledo and announced that Velázquez "stopped where El Greco began." Suddenly half the world believed Velázquez to be second-rate.

Fame is a fashion. There is no telling how great Velázquez will seem when the vanes of taste veer again.

—WILL AND ARIEL DURANT

SELF-PORTRAIT

FRANS HALS

1581?–1666

Hearty Dutchman

IF FRANS HALS HAD A DOLLAR he spent it. If he was broke, he borrowed and relaxed in a beer hall, cheerful as a cricket. The butcher, the baker, the landlord were always extending him credit—and often had to haul him into court to get their money. People shook their heads and said jolly Frans ought to discipline himself. But they liked him. And they knew he was a great artist—who turned out, by present-day judgment, the heartiest, most buoyant portraits in the history of painting.

No matter how hard up he was, Hals never lowered his standards of art. The year he painted *The Merry Lute Player*—one of his happiest inspirations, connoisseurs call it—his dairyman was continually dunning him for thirty-five dollars for butter and cheese. When he hadn't a dime to his name his step continued jaunty, his lean face expressive and alert, his blue eyes a-sparkle.

THE JESTER
(Above) Hals' love for music is shown in his many portraits of players—most of them youthful musicians who are thought to have been his own children.

THE BOHEMIAN GIRL
(Upper right) She may have been a girl who merely glanced at Hals in a tavern. His camera-like eye needed only such an inspiration to bring a great portrait to life.

THE LAUGHING CAVALIER
(Lower right) Far from laughing, the officer indulges in no more than a faint smile, as though at some irony. The portrait was sold in 1865 for ten thousand dollars. Today it would probably bring more than a million.

To be sure, Hals lived in exhilarating times. Tiny Holland had wrested her independence from the mighty grip of Spain and the rugged Dutch then built up a navy which became, in Hals' day, the foremost sea power in the world. The energies released by national freedom brimmed over into lusty living. Taverns were crowded, lively, festive. Good talk was sprinkled with laughter, pranksters' capers, rollicking music from roving minstrels.

Although legend says that Hals was an alcoholic, scholars today tell us he drank no more than the average fellow of his time. Many another in his thorny circumstances might well have tippled. For his "shotgun wedding" bound him to an illiterate wife who could offer him no deep understanding; his small house teemed with boisterous children (he had at least ten); and with several of the children he suffered serious trouble (one of the boys was mentally retarded, one of the girls a trollop).

That Hals didn't drink enough to be a muddlehead is confirmed by the chain of masterpieces he painted across the years: powerful portraits of scholars, clergymen, officials and other prominent Dutch citizens. Furthermore, the administrators of Haarlem, the city where he spent most of his life, held him in high regard, calling on him to appraise pictures and restore old paintings, and to serve on a jury trying another artist for faking old masters. At his guild Hals was on the board of directors and, in 1644, became its dean. He was a sergeant in a volunteer national-guard unit. And he was abstemious enough to teach a whole troop of pupils how to paint extremely well. Several went on to make names for themselves, and one, Judith Leyster, became foremost among the women painters of the day.

The grinning *Jester* is but one of jolly Frans' lighthearted masterworks. No other artist has given us so many men, women and children who smile or laugh, who show hearty good humor and vigorous spirits.

Frans Hals didn't paint often and, because he painted swiftly, he may not have put in many actual working hours. His three hundred portraits and figure pieces that have come down to us were painted over a period of fifty-five years. Long working hours, including travel from Haarlem, may well have caused the wrangle Hals got into with a civic club of Amsterdam. And possibly the members were not as fun-loving as his home-town people. But one day he simply stopped working on the group portrait they had paid him to do. After quarrels and a near-lawsuit, the job was finished by another artist.

The years were harsh to Frans Hals. At fifty he had to pawn his paintings to pay the baker. At sixty he was sued for canvas he'd painted on but hadn't paid for. At seventy his paintings and furniture were seized by a creditor. To the list of Frans Hals' frailties, add extravagance. Money not only burned a hole in his pockets, but the pockets were often in very expensive clothing. In a double portrait of himself and his wife we find them decked out in brocades fit for royalty. He probably had just collected a fat fee.

Finally, when he was nearly eighty and destitute, the city fathers made their great artist a gift of 250 dollars plus a pension of a thousand dollars a year. To this they added three carloads of peat for heating his house. He died two years later in 1666 and was buried at city expense in the principal Church of Haarlem.

His last pictures were two imposing, monumental group portraits: *The Governors of the Old Men's Almshouse* and *The Lady Governors of the Old Men's Almshouse.* Of these two paintings, the authority on Dutch art, Dr. W. R. Valentiner, has written: "With their indescribably bold and easy technique, they belong to the greatest creations in painting of all time." —MALCOLM VAUGHAN

REMBRANDT VAN RIJN

1606–1669

The Incomparable

FROM RUBENS TO REMBRANDT, what a gamut and chasm! Between joyous light and somber shadow, between the abyss and the Court, between the happy sensuality of the Flemish noble, Rubens, at home with palaces and kings, and the Dutch bankrupt, Rembrandt, who knew the lower depths and was acquainted with grief.

Rembrandt Harmensz van Rijn was born at Leiden, the son of a prosperous miller, Harmen Gerritsz, who added "van Rijn" to his name, probably because his house overlooked the Rhine. The artist must have loved his father, for he painted him eleven times or more. His mother too he pictured a dozen times, most memorably in the *Old Woman Seated* of the Vienna Gallery, worried and worn.

At fourteen he entered the University of Leiden, but a year later he withdrew and persuaded his father to let him study art. In 1625 he was sent to Amsterdam as pupil to Pieter Lastman, who put a classic emphasis on correct

SELF-PORTRAITS

Possibly the first portrait Rembrandt ever painted was of his own face. Through his long career he did scores of self-studies (see the eight examples above). No two are alike in expression and composition. They comprise an amazing record of a man's life—executed as only such a master artist could.

drawing. But after six months in Amsterdam the restless youth hurried back to Leiden, eager to paint after his own fashion. He drew or painted almost everything that he saw, including hilarious absurdities and shameless obscenities. He improved his art with fond experiments; the mirror became his model, and he left us more self-portraits (at least sixty-two) than many great painters have left paintings. Among them is a charming head now in The Hague: Rembrandt at twenty-three, handsome, hair carelessly tossed about with young superiority to conventions, eyes alert and proud with the confidence of proved ability.

In fact, he had already established himself. It was said that in 1629 a connoisseur paid him five hundred dollars for a picture—quite a fee for a young competitor in a land where painters were as numerous as bakers, and not so amply fed. His first themes, after himself and his parents, were Biblical. So many commissions came from Amsterdam that Rembrandt went back in 1631 and lived there the rest of his life.

Within a year he was to paint one of the world's masterpieces, *The Anatomy Lesson of Professor Nicolaes Tulp.* The distinguished surgeon asked Rembrandt to picture him giving a demonstration in anatomy in the Hall of the Surgeons' Guild. It was probably Dr. Tulp who chose the seven "students" to share the picture with him—obviously not pupils but friends of maturity and standing. Rembrandt made full use of the chance to show faces illuminated with character and intelligence; and the play of light upon flesh and ruffs announces his specialty.

Commissions now flowed in—forty in two years. With money in his pocket and hunger in his blood, the artist was ripe for marriage (1634). Saskia van Uylenborch had a lovely face, dancing eyes, hair of silk and gold, a comfortable figure and fortune. She was the orphaned daughter of a wealthy lawyer and magistrate. It seems her cousin, an art dealer, had induced her to sit for Rembrandt for a portrait. Two sittings sufficed for a proposal. Saskia brought a dowry of ten thousand dollars which made a rich man of Rembrandt, the future bankrupt. She became a good wife despite her money. She bore patiently with her mate's absorbed genius and sat for many pictures. We see his happiness in a painting where he holds her on his knee, irradiates the canvas with his smile and raises a tall tumbler to his physical and financial ecstasy.

In these grateful years (1634–1642) Rembrandt turned out one masterpiece after another. He continued to picture himself: once as handsome and jolly, with jewels in his hat and a gold chain on his chest; again as an officer, magnificent, world-conquering; and still another time he appears wearing a gorgeous hat whose plume tickles the sky. Looking for character rather than beauty, he painted the *Old Lady,* her face corrugated by the years. And among the human ruins of Amsterdam he found an octogenarian whom he dressed in turbans and robes and pictured in *The Oriental.*

Now, too, he painted timeworn religious subjects with a fresh sincerity, taking his models from the old men and young women whom he met in the streets—each picture so remarkable in technique, so striking in its manipulation of light, and so moving in the intensity of its feeling, that any one of them might be defended as the artist's best; let *Abraham's Sacrifice* and *The Angel Leaving the Family of Tobias* serve as examples. And from these blessed years came also some famous portraits, like *The Lady with a Fan* and *A Man with Gloves*—both defying words.

The last achievement of this period was the immense canvas (14 by 12 feet) known as *The Night Watch,* but more properly named *Captain Cocq's Company of Harquebusiers* (1642). No detail is unfinished in that vast expanse, no shade of darkness or incidence of light is uncalculated, no contrast of color is unexplored. In the center the proud captain stands in brown and white and red; at his left a lieutenant in golden-yellow boots; swords gleam, pikes flash, pennants wave; at the right the fife-and-drum corps; the company emerges from its headquarters, apparently for some festival parade. Rembrandt had signed a contract with each of the sixteen persons to be painted, each paying one hundred florins (five hundred dollars). Many felt that equal pay had not been rewarded with equal prominence in the picture; some complained that he had put them too deeply in shadows, or had neglected to make them recognizable to their friends. Few further group commissions came to his studio, and his prosperity began to wane.

It must have been high, however, in 1639, for in that year he bought a spacious house in the Joden-Breedstraet. It cost him sixty-five thousand dollars, which he never succeeded in paying off. Probably it was intended to shelter not only his family but his pupils, his studio and his growing collection of antiquities, curiosities, and art. (He had a penchant for collecting costumes, jewelry, swords, fancy hats and shoes.) After meeting half the purchase price in the first year of occupancy, Rembrandt let the rest remain as a debt, on which the unpaid interest rose to a point that eventually drove him to bankruptcy.

Meanwhile his beloved Saskia was declining in health.

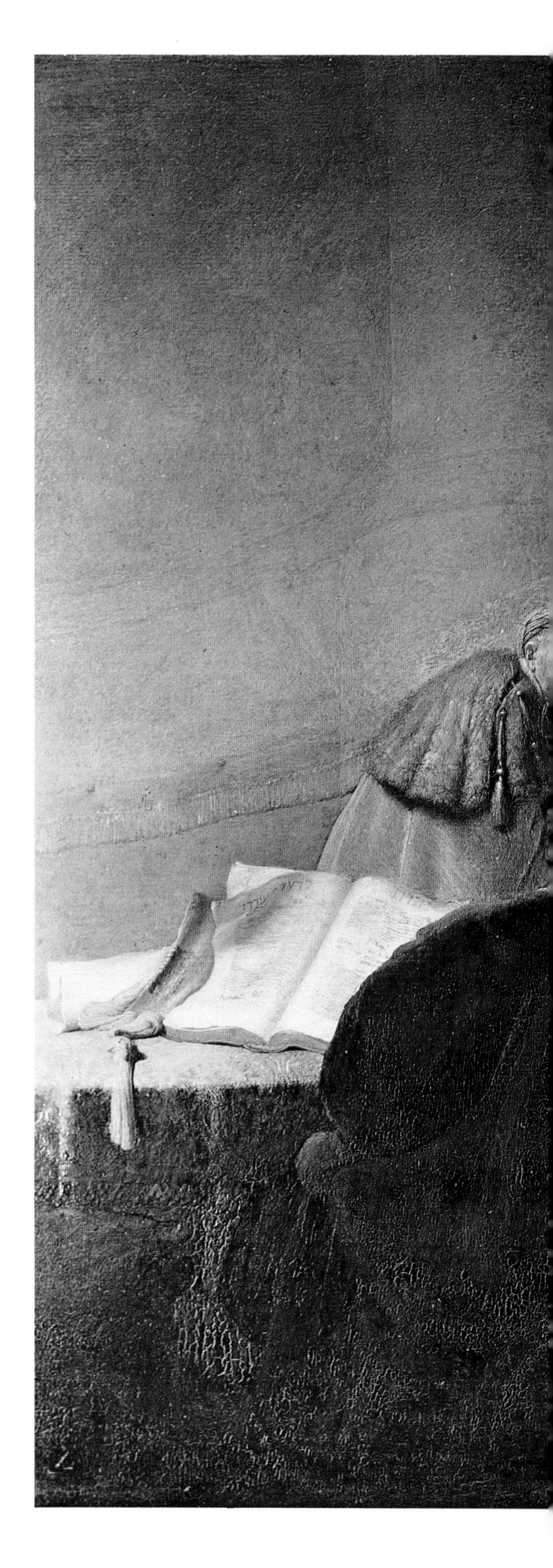

JUDAS RETURNING THE THIRTY PIECES OF SILVER
Before Christ was put on trial, Judas repented. He cast down the thirty pieces of silver, then he "went and hanged himself." Rembrandt's outpouring of religious works—over eight hundred paintings, etchings and drawings—surpassed his portraits in number.

YOUNG GIRL AT AN OPEN HALF-DO

The model for the portrait above, painted in 1645, is unknown. She appears in other portraits and bears a family resemblance to Hendrikje Stoffels, the artist's housekeeper.

THE ARTIST'S SON TITUS

Young Titus (upper left) posed in many roles for his father—as an angel, as a saint, as the young Christ. He took painting lessons, but grew up to become an art dealer.

THE NIGHT WATCH

Among Rembrandt's most famous paintings, the group portrait of Captain Cocq's civil guards was later callously cut to fit a space between doors in the Amsterdam town hall.

She had borne him three children, but each died in childhood, and their painful birth and tragic end weakened her. In 1641 she gave birth to a son, Titus, who survived; but in 1642 she passed away. Her will left all her possessions to Rembrandt, with the proviso that on his remarriage the remainder of her legacy should be transferred to her son. A year after her death Rembrandt painted her from loving memory.

Thenceforth he seemed obsessed with thoughts of death. Though deeply affectionate within his family, he had always preferred privacy to company; now he courted a somber solitude. He was not a cultured man of the world, like Rubens. He read little—hardly anything but the Bible. Living in a wordless realm of color, shadow and light, he had difficulty in donning the social graces when sitters came, and in making small talk to keep them amused and still. They came in fewer numbers when they found that Rembrandt was not content to make a sketch from a sitting or two and then paint from the sketch, but preferred to paint directly on the canvas, which required many sittings. Moreover, he had an impressionistic way of painting what he thought or felt, rather than merely what he saw, and the result was not always flattering.

In 1649 we find him painting *Hendrikje Stoffels in Bed,* and we perceive that he has taken a mistress. She had been Saskia's maid; she stayed with the widowed artist, took faithful care of him and soon consoled him with the warmth of her body. He did not marry her, for he was loath to relinquish Saskia's legacy to Titus, still a boy of eight. As he painted Hendrikje in 1652, she was tolerably fair, with eyes of haunting wistfulness. In October 1654 she bore him a child; Rembrandt acknowledged it as his and managed to get it safely baptized. He learned to love his mistress as deeply as he had loved his wife; how else could he have put such tenderness in her face when he painted her in 1658 in the red robe that matched her hair? She was a good stepmother to Titus, who was growing up into a bewitching lad.

Rembrandt was fifty when disaster came. He had recklessly bought house and art, even shares in the Dutch East India Company. Now, as patronage lagged far behind maintenance, he found himself hopelessly in debt. In 1656 the Orphans' Chamber of Amsterdam, to protect Titus, transferred the house and grounds to the son. In July Rembrandt was declared bankrupt. His furniture, paintings and collections were sold in costly haste but the proceeds fell far short of his obligations. Out of the wreck some thirty-five thousand dollars were salvaged for Titus. He and Hendrikje, to save Rembrandt, formed a partnership by which they could sell his remaining works without letting them go to his creditors.

Amid these tribulations he continued to create masterpieces—some of which were *The Man on Horseback,* sold to the National Gallery of London in 1959 for 400,000 dollars; the wonderful *Head of an Old Man* and the astonishingly natural *Woman Cutting Her Nails.*

In his final decade (1660–1669) Rembrandt was lovingly kept alive by his mistress and his son, but his quarters were cramped, his studio was badly lighted, his hand must have lost some of its decisiveness. *St. Matthew and the Angel* is coarse in its texture, but the angel whispering in his ear is none other than Titus, now twenty and still as fair as a bride. And then, in 1661, came the master's last triumph, *The Syndics of the Drapers' Guild.* The *staelmeesters*—examiners and controllers of cloth—commissioned the old artist to commemorate them in a group picture to be hung in the hall of their corporation. The subdued foreground and background make the five main figures leap to the eye, each of them "a single and separate person," but all caught in the living moment of their common thought. This is wondrous fruit to come from a dying tree.

But we have said nothing of his landscapes, his drawings and his etchings. Only a few of the landscapes stand out, but the drawings are at the top of their kind and the etchings prized as highly as any in the history of that painstaking art. One of them, *Christ Healing the Sick,* came to be known as "The Hundred-Guilder Piece" because it was bought for that unprecedented price (1250 dollars). Three hundred etchings, 2000 drawings, 650 paintings—this is the surviving work of Rembrandt, almost as widely known as Shakespeare's plays and almost as varied, original and profound.

More and more, as he grew older, he loved the simple people around him rather than men dehumanized by the pursuit of gain. Where artists like Rubens sought their subjects among the beautiful, the happy or the powerful, Rembrandt lavished his sympathetic art on the outcasts, the sick, the miserable, even the deformed. We take a last look at him in the self-portraits of his old age—the autobiography of defeat. As he pictured himself in 1660, he was still facing life with a blend of courage and resignation; the pudgy, unshaved face was quizzical but not sad; he was still moving forward. In another portrait of the same year a worried look darkens and ridges the face. A year later he saw himself as baffled, but philosophically shrugged away his wrinkles. And in his last year he pictured himself as having found peace in accepting the limits and the wry humor of life.

Hendrikje died in 1662, but Titus still blessed him with the sight of youth; and in 1668 the old man rejoiced in the marriage of his son. When in that same year the son followed the mistress in death, the artist began to lose his hold on life. On October 8, 1669, his passing was recorded in the register of the Westerkerk: "Rembrandt van Rijn, painter . . ."

His contemporaries hardly noticed his passing. None of them dreamed of ranking him with Rubens, or even with Van Dyck. Joachim von Sandrart, the German painter, wrote: "His art suffered from his predilection for the society of the vulgar." John Ruskin, the nineteenth-century critic, agreed with him: "It is the aim of the best painters to paint the noblest things they can see by sunlight. It was the aim of Rembrandt to paint the foulest things he could see—by rushlight." But Eugène Delacroix, reflected a later democratic trend: "Perhaps we shall one day find that Rembrandt is a greater painter than Raphael. I write down—without taking sides—this blasphemy, which will cause the hair of the Academicians to stand on end." Art critics today tend to rate Rembrandt above Raphael and Velázquez, equaled only by El Greco. Truth, we perceive, is a vassal of time.

—WILL AND ARIEL DURANT

THE LACE-MAKER
Half of Vermeer's forty known paintings show a solitary woman. This picture Renoir called one of the world's most beautiful.

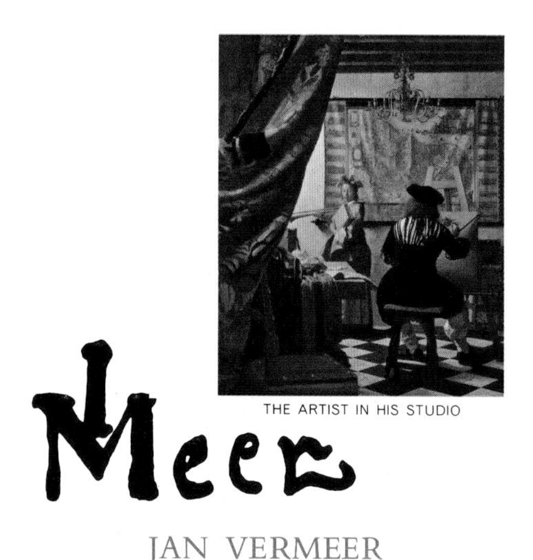

THE ARTIST IN HIS STUDIO

JAN VERMEER
1632–1675
Exquisite Craftsman

JAN VERMEER, remembered as Vermeer of Delft, after his birthplace, is one of the most coveted of painters. No other canvases are quite like his—quite so perfect in their way.

Of his life the records are scant in the extreme. There is no indication that he ever left his native town, which he paid an immortal compliment with his crystalline

THE LITTLE STREET
*For decades only one Vermeer landscape—*View of Delft*—was believed to exist. Then this view from the rear window of his house was discovered. There is evidence of a third, not yet found.*

THE MUSIC LESSON

Vermeer used so many colors in "tonal chords" that his pictures were described as visual music. The largeness of objects in the foreground indicates that he probably used a reflecting machine, the "camera obscura," to achieve depth.

landscape, *View of Delft.* In April 1653, at twenty, he married young Catherine Bolens. Later that year he was admitted to the painters' guild, of which he was to be headman for three years. His teacher was Carel Fabritius, who had been a pupil of Rembrandt. In 1654 Fabritius was killed at Delft and many of his paintings destroyed when a powder magazine exploded. A poem written about the tragedy called the twenty-two-year old Vermeer "the phoenix" in whom Fabritius' talent would live on.

The younger man's paintings brought comparatively high prices but, owing to his slow method of work, the size of his family and his habit of buying art himself, he was always on the ragged edge. He died in bankruptcy in 1675, leaving his widow and ten children.

The secret of Vermeer's fame—and it is hardly a secret—may be found in a remark by Michelangelo, who said that little things, or trifles, done to perfection, build up into great things, or art. Jan Vermeer knew exactly what he could do and how to do it.

So seductive is Vermeer's craftsmanship that within recent years his works have been appraised in terms of the greatest masters. His paintings are among the rarest treasures in art: only forty have come to light, and should a new one be discovered, it would make a bedlam of the auction market. A few years ago a Dutch painter, soured by failures and longing for money, took vengeance on the collectors who had rejected his work. After fifteen years of the most painstaking preparations, he forged a number of Vermeer pictures—forged them so convincingly that before he was jailed he had sold the canvases for more than two million dollars!

But scarce as his works are, Vermeer is even rarer in that property of paint known as *quality*. Technically speaking, Vermeer painted by concentrated observation. He looked at his model, examined the fall of light and dark on the face and figure, apprehended the gradation in atmospheric density from the highest light to the deepest dark; and then, with brushes and paint, translated the array of appearances into an equivalent scale of colors. A thousand other Dutchmen did the same thing; and so did Velázquez, on a larger scale and with more imposing models and a broad stroking. But all of these artists made naturalistic appearances more grandiose and aristocratic than Vermeer's.

Vermeer worked closely, weaving his pigments and blending his tones into a harmony of blues and yellows, into a surface which has the luster of ivory, the texture of enamel, the virginal purity of cool water. So delicately fused are his pigments that all evidence of the human touch has disappeared, as if nature herself, in some subtle mood, had crystallized her colors in glazed patterns. Thus his *Milkmaid,* a study of Dutch life, has an indefinable quality that charms the eye, and a richness of surface and of texture suggesting a precious object.

Vermeer did not look on art as some vast philosophical system, in Michelangelo's way, but as one small job done beautifully. Master of natural tones, Vermeer raised little pictures to monumental stature. His subjects are small interiors: In his earlier works, a room with a tiled floor, a gray wall hung with a map or a picture—one that he had purchased at the expense of the family larder. To the left a window, and in the middle a woman standing at a table, pouring milk or reading a letter. A flawless example of his work with two figures is *The Letter*—an interior seen through a vestibule, as the maid delivers what is possibly a love letter, but may be a note from a suspecting spouse—or a sheriff's warning. In the fastidious adjustment of tones Velázquez alone is Vermeer's equal, but in the projection of forms in serene space the Spaniard comes off second best.

How long Vermeer worked on a painting will never be known, but it must have been the labor of months to effect the distribution of light which made it possible for him to separate a head—no larger in area than a postage stamp—from the background of the wall.

His ingenuity defies analysis, one writer having advanced the theory that he used a system of mirrors in order to observe from a single point of view the reflections and intensities of light in every part of the room. His textures are such perfect replicas of surfaces that his table covers and stuffs strike the eye, not as painted illusions, but as actual materials preserved in amber glazes.

Like a diamond cutter in his manner of working and in his handicraft, Vermeer added globule to globule of paint to fashion a jeweled object, just as the lapidary, with infinite skill, adds facet to facet to bring out the splendor of an expensive substance.

Vermeer's art makes small claims on the imagination; nor has it exerted perceptible influence on the larger developments of painting. It would seem, in its decorative color and beautiful compactness, to have been aloof and isolated—yet it was part of a natural tendency, and it contains the quintessence of a period. His *Girl with a Flute* is the last word in craftsmanship and in the glorification of materiality—a golden note in the Dutch chorus of honest rejoicing in their possessions.

—THOMAS CRAVEN

THE NEW TRADITION

A storyteller in art, Hogarth, as early as 1735, was painting the robust and brash life of London. British aristocrats still looked to Italy (the only proper and "acceptable" source) for any pictures they wished to purchase. After Hogarth, another fifty years passed before an Englishman, Reynolds, one of the founders of the Royal Academy, could break into the fashionable world as a portraitist of the rich. Soon he was rivaled by Gainsborough, who chafed under the demand for handsome portraits but could find no buyers for his beloved landscapes. Influential in breaking the fixation on portraits was the untaught American genius, Copley, who even in the days of the American Revolution painted England's most exciting historical scenes. In Spain, Goya, a court painter in the tradition of Velázquez, created royal portraits but, with his terrifying attacks on war and social degradation, became a raging satirist, like Hogarth. Finally, in the early decades of the 1800's, a new popular market for landscapes was roused by the persistent genius of English painters. Constable's true-to-nature colors and Turner's dazzling use of light brought landscape painting to its greatest peak.

SELF-PORTRAIT

Wm Hogarth

WILLIAM HOGARTH

1697–1764

Satirist Extraordinary

HOGARTH HOUSE AND PALETTE

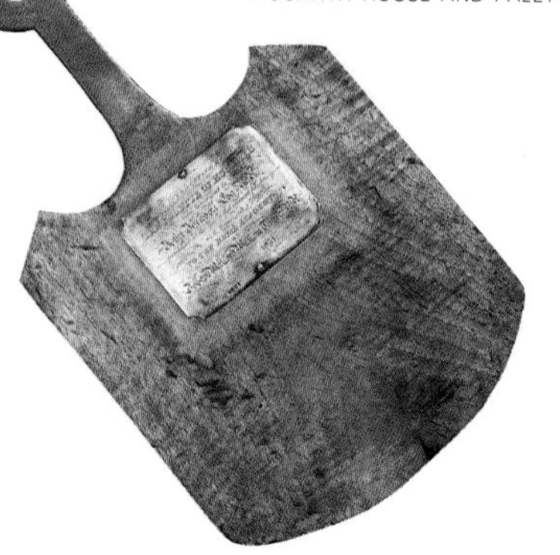

IN ONE OF HIS SELF-PORTRAITS, Hogarth was at pains to include three books bearing the respective names of Shakespeare, Milton and Swift. He rightly felt that he belonged in the company of the great men of England, and was not too modest to remind the bigwigs of his time that he was more than a plebeian storyteller with a sense of humor. He was Shakespearean in his conception of painting as a dramatic art: "My picture is my stage," he wrote, "my men and women my players." Like Milton he was constantly occupied with esthetic speculations, which, being expressed without cant or classical humbug, were not taken seriously by his contemporaries. As a satirist of a bawdy, gin-drinking age, he joined hands with the author of *Gulliver's Travels.*

Hogarth was born in London in 1697, the son of a poor schoolmaster who had come up from the country in search of a better living and had failed to find it. His education, if it may be so dignified, was scant and irregular, but the lack of academic training was no disadvantage to one suspicious from infancy of conventional schemes for improving the mind. He educated himself.

He was apprenticed to a silver-plate engraver, and in his twentieth year, on the death of his father, struck out on his own hook as a commercial artist, designing arms, shopkeepers' signs, tradesmen's cards and formal invitations to sprees and funerals.

The age was a rough-and-tumble one. The crowds were preyed upon by political sharpers, exotics and quacks of all kinds. At night nobody was safe; leaky oil lamps flared dimly in the fog, and bullies lurked in the shadows, ready to waylay straggling revelers and beat them to death for the sheer pleasure of hearing their bones crack.

For fifteen summers the prosperous Hogarth lived and worked in Chiswick Gardens, a red-brick Georgian villa (top of page), in Middlesex, just outside London. In nearby Chiswick churchyard, the great chronicler of his time was laid to rest. Hogarth's palette is pictured above.

I THE MARRIAGE CONTRACT

II DISAFFECTION

III THE EARL AND HIS MISTRESS

IV THE COUNTESS ATTRACTS A LOVER

V THE LOVER KILLS THE EARL

VI SUICIDE OF THE COUNTESS

HE SHRIMP GIRL

eft) This vivid sketch, made from memory, of a ung street hawker is believed to be the only such free pression the English satirist ever did. inted in little more than half an hour, the canvas nained in the artist's possession until his death.

MARRIAGE A LA MODE

To Hogarth's satirical brush, the "fashionable" marriage of his day was motivated by the craving for money and position. This series dramatized a tragic love quartet. In six carefully detailed scenes, he unfolded the scandals of a titled pair as well as various vanities of "high society."

But in this rugged world were groups of intelligent men. Hard drinkers they were, and hard fighters, justly appreciative of one another's talents and often joining forces in the interests of good work. Most of them were writers, but one—a short, stocky, blue-eyed man with the keenest wit and tenderest heart in the entire company—was Hogarth, painter and engraver.

From his twentieth to his thirtieth year Hogarth diligently pursued his trade, training himself for the great works which were shortly to astonish his friends and expose his enemies. He went about his tasks in a thoroughly businesslike manner, made a fair living and very early brought himself into public notice. He knew his London; he loved Englishwomen and the beefy men whom he drew and painted with the bulk strength of sculpture. He frequented fairs and taverns, sideshows and cockfights, dances and all-night supper parties; watched parading Redcoats and election riots, and followed the crowd to executions. He observed the comedy of English life as a man, a commoner who was part of it, studying its significance and the character, expressions and behavior of the players composing it.

During these years of experiment he undertook book illustrations, but with indifferent results. Between jobs he taught himself to paint, and from his small paintings he made engravings, which could be sold easily and which became quite popular. Their success led him to the drawing classes of Sir James Thornhill. Here he was disappointed, as he was with book illustration: it was mere drawing.

The venture ended happily, however. Hogarth won the love of Jane Thornhill, his master's only daughter, twenty and very lovely, and he proposed marriage. Thornhill frowned on the match, skeptical of the engraver's ability to support the girl. The young couple immediately eloped and had no cause to regret it. Nor had the father, after the enormous popularity of Hogarth's first important work, which he began soon after his marriage.

Impatient to put to a practical test his ideas of "composing pictures on canvas similar to representations on the stage," he took a house in Leicester Fields—which he occupied till his death—and bent all his wits to a study of the career of a loose woman. In 1732, *The Harlot's Progress* burst upon London. This, the first of his social dramas, relates in a sequence of paintings the story of Moll Hackabout, a pretty country girl of easy virtue: she arrives in London; she becomes a kept woman; she quarrels with her rich lover; she is apprehended by a magistrate; she beats hemp in Bridewell Prison; she dies; she is buried. In the funeral scene her little son is perched on the coffin winding his top.

The Harlot's Progress was received with instantaneous and universal applause, netting the author, by the sale of engravings, five thousand dollars, a snug fortune in those days, and reinstating him in the goodwill of his wife's father. The plates were freely pirated, and Hogarth, tired of this evil, petitioned Parliament for protection. A bill granting the privileges of copyright to engravers and designers was passed and piracy was gradually extinguished. Poor Moll Hackabout was the rage of London. She was put into pantomime and opera, sung in street ballads, painted on fans and tea services. Her only detractors were the highbrow painters of the grand style and the auctioneers, who grudgingly allowed that she was an appealing wench, but said she was not art. The public did not pause to consider her artistic pretensions. They recognized her as one of their own kind. They were delighted with Hogarth's unsparing realism. The truth is that he revived the oldest and most appealing form of art—storytelling, which had been lost to the world since the era of Giotto and his religious fables.

Hogarth did not rest on his laurels. His next satire was *The Rake's Progress,* a play in eight scenes picturing the career of a spendthrift: the miserly father is dead, and the young heir, Tom Rakewell, takes possession; he is surrounded by fashionable parasites; he revels; he is arrested for debt; he marries an old maid for her money; he gambles and loses; he is sent to prison; he dies in Bedlam. A better work in every respect than its predecessor—in characterization, draftsmanship and color—*The Rake's Progress,* though greeted with enthusiasm, did not set London on fire as did the story of the lowly Moll Hackabout. The picture-drama was no longer a novelty.

But Hogarth did not grieve over fluctuating public tastes. He had been well repaid for his efforts, and if he was snubbed in certain art circles as a bourgeois anecdotist, he was everywhere recognized as a man with whom one would not care to quarrel.

When his father-in-law died, Hogarth assumed control of the art school, endowed it and supervised the curriculum, hoping against his suspicions that he might discover a method other than his own "whereby talent might be developed freely and not shaped to copy the dead for the dealers." The dealers were his special abomination. "The connoisseurs and I are at war," he said.

His other abomination was the French, whom he eviscerated at the smallest provocation—sometimes with more passion than judgment. Hogarth was not much of a traveler, but in his fiftieth year he crossed the Channel and was unjustifiably arrested as he sat sketching at the gate of Calais. The outrage stung his pride and his British sense of justice; and, happily for posterity, led to the painting of *Calais Gate,* one of his unquestioned masterpieces. But it was through portraiture that he showed up his enemies in their own sphere, even though his returns from portraiture were small. He was not a flatterer and he would not paint, for any consideration, a person who did not appeal to him. He portrayed a decrepit lord so truthfully the picture was rejected. "If his lordship does not send for the canvas in three days," Hogarth wrote, "it will be disposed of, with the addition of a tail, to Mr. Hare, the wild beast man." The gentleman sent for the picture.

In 1743 he announced a third dramatic performance, a study of high life in six scenes, entitled *Marriage à la Mode.* It is a brilliant achievement, the high-water mark in his work of this type. However, the patrons of art did not rush forward to bid for it. What, besides shame and resentment, could they have got from paintings that not only disclosed the seamy side of high life but which, in the absurd classic nudes disfiguring the backgrounds of *Marriage à la Mode,* had burlesqued the tastes of would-be connoisseurs? Hogarth kept the six paintings in his studio for five years rather than entrust them to the dealers, finally disposing of them at public auction. The whole set brought the insignificant sum of five hundred dollars!

The last decade of his life was enlivened by controversies, some of which caused him more trouble than they were worth. *Sigismonda,* his last work in the ideal style, was rejected by the patron, hooted by the critics, hated by the dealers. Hogarth was hurt. He knew that the picture was a creditable job—better, to tell the truth, than anything manufactured by the bigoted guardians of the great style. And he knew that, in attacking it, his adversaries were indirectly attacking the character of the man who had painted it. But the hurt did not stop him. He pitched into his foes with redoubled vigor, matched his engravings against the pen of a political rogue in a heated duel, defeated him and called for more battles.

In his last years he wrote *The Analysis of Beauty,* the first treatise on the esthetics of painting to appear in the English language. He died in his sixty-sixth year.

Hogarth is called a moralist, a creator of epics. But above all, he was a man who purified the gloomy house of art with his blasting laughter. —THOMAS CRAVEN

SELF-PORTRAIT

Joshua Reynolds

JOSHUA REYNOLDS

1723–1792

Self-Made Aristocrat

HIS FATHER, a poor clergyman in a village near the eighteenth-century town of Plymouth, England, whitewashed the hallways in the house from time to time and let the children scribble and draw on the walls with bits of charcoal. Joshua, one of the younger boys, drew so well that neighbors came in to look at what he had done.

The parents had proposed to apprentice him to an apothecary. But at seventeen Joshua got hold of an artist's kit and turned out his first painting in oils—a portrait. This picture so impressed his parents that they agreed to let him take up painting as a career. The youngster told them, "I'd rather be an apothecary than an *ordinary* painter."

Fifteen years later Joshua Reynolds was the most remarkable painter in England. Beautiful women, eminent men and the lordliest lords and ladies in the land flocked to his studio for their portraits, paying him fabulous prices. In the midst of his career the Royal Academy was founded and he was chosen its first president. George III knighted him and appointed him court painter.

Of middle height, plumpish, with gray-blue eyes and a ruddy complexion, Reynolds' good looks were scotched by pockmarks and a scarred upper lip; he had been cut when a horse he was riding fell down a cliff. He also suffered from deafness and had to carry an ear trumpet, which he poked into everyone's face to hear what was said. Yet people bore this nuisance because his manner was so attractive.

The most amazing thing about his great success was that he accomplished it by pulling himself up by his own bootstraps. He had no more education than the average schoolboy. His training as an artist was only so-so (he was apprenticed in London for a while to a mediocre por-

COLONEL TARLETON
The subject of the portrait above had a colorful career as a British officer during the American Revolution. After fighting in many battles, he was finally taken prisoner following Cornwallis' surrender at Yorktown. Paroled, he returned home to serve as a member of Parliament.

MRS. SIDDONS AS THE TRAGIC MUSE
One of the great English actresses, famed for her role of Lady Macbeth, Mrs. Siddons (opposite page) was also renowned for her breathtaking beauty. George IV is said to have remarked, "She is the only real queen—all others are counterfeits!"

trait painter). His drawing was often hit-or-miss; his colors were likely to fade because he lacked enough technical knowledge to know what painting materials to use. But Joshua Reynolds succeeded, by dint of ambition, in what Aristotle called "art through reasoning." Unassisted, he made a careful study of the great masters. "I had an inordinate desire," he said, "to possess every excellence I saw in the work of others."

In his youth he had a stroke of luck. England's hero of those days, Commodore Augustus Keppel, put into Plymouth for repairs to his ship. The young painter, happening to hear the commodore say the ship was headed for the Mediterranean, told him that the dream of his life was to go to Italy—treasure land of art. Keppel offered a cabin, free. Joshua borrowed what money he could, then added to his nest egg by painting portraits of officers aboard and at the various garrisons they visited en route. By living cheaply, the young artist was able to study in Europe for more than two years, visiting Rome, Florence, Venice and Paris. Often he copied or made diagrams of museum masterpieces to learn how they had been created. All this labor was self-imposed, but no teacher could have kept him more eagerly at it.

When he returned to England, he soon set up a studio in London. He produced and exhibited an effective full-length portrait of his benefactor, now Admiral Keppel. From that moment, the hitherto unknown artist had to work furiously to keep up with the flood of portrait orders that poured in upon him. Within five years he had painted a total of 677 portraits. Success swept him upward. He moved to a bigger and then a bigger house, and spent huge sums for pictures by the masters to hang on his walls—Rembrandt, Titian, Van Dyck, Rubens.

Joshua Reynolds' deepest care was to make his every portrait the best he had ever painted. Borrowing a thousand motifs from the great artists whose works he had studied, he *compiled* a style, and it was endlessly diverse. Everyone marveled how seldom Joshua Reynolds repeated himself. His rival as a portrait painter, Gainsborough, exclaimed: "Curse him, how various he is!"

Although he did borrow from other artists, his nearly three thousand canvases nevertheless bring forth an art of his own—for he was a master of consummate good taste.

When Joshua Reynolds began his career, English portraiture was scarcely more than provincial "face-painting." The poor boy who didn't want to be an "ordinary" painter lifted the stodgy tradition of English painting to world significance.

—MALCOLM VAUGHAN

SELF-PORTRAIT

Tho Gainsborough

THOMAS GAINSBOROUGH

1727–1788

Captive of Fame

GAINSBOROUGH WAS NOT the calm and meticulous man of society that Reynolds had been, but there can be little doubt that he became by far the greater painter. From him stemmed the entire Romantic school of landscape painting in England and, to a certain extent, that in France as well. To look at the masterful elegance of some of Gainsborough's portraits, in which he completely captured the silky smoothness of Van Dyck's aristocratic figures, it is difficult indeed to imagine that he himself was certainly no aristocrat.

Thomas Gainsborough was born at Sudbury, in Suffolk, the son of a clothier. At thirteen he was sent to London, where he studied with Francis Hayman, a somewhat questionable master from whom Gainsborough's later inelegant behavior may have derived. "He sometimes used oaths," a chronicler said of Gainsborough, "and strayed occasionally from the path of sobriety."

The young man soon set himself up in Hatton Garden as a portrait painter, since this was the only way to make a living as an artist. From the beginning, he painted landscapes as a diversion. Several years after marrying a young woman blessed with an annuity of 200 pounds (1000 dollars), he moved off to Ipswich. Here he attempted to adjust himself to the life of the place, please his patrons and obtain as many commissions as possible. He was shy in the extreme, apt to blush when spoken to and sometimes surprisingly naïve. We are told that he belonged to a musical club at Ipswich, of which he was the good-natured butt. When the musician Felice di Giardini played the violin, Gainsborough was so much attracted by the music —thinking the instrument was the sole cause thereof— that he made frantic attempts to obtain the violin. He was

MASTER NICHOLLS

Often referred to as the Pink Boy *because of the artist's famous* Blue Boy, *which had been painted twelve years earlier, the picture above also displays Gainsborough's elegance of form and texture. During his forty-three-year career, an avalanche of some twelve hundred pictures came from his brush.*

THE HON. MRS. THOMAS GRAHAM

The portrait at the left was first exhibited in 1777. When the beautiful Mrs. Graham died fifteen years later, her devoted husband, unable to look at her portrait again, had the picture put away. It was finally recovered after fifty years in a London warehouse.

ROBERT ANDREWS AND HIS WIFE

Gainsborough, while investing his sitters with a frail, inbred quality, could not refrain from showing his dislike for some of them. Note the sour expression of Mrs. Andrews. The remarkably fine background, however, reveals the painter's love for the English countryside.

shocked to find out, upon acquiring it, that the lovely music remained with Giardini.

About 1759 Gainsborough settled in Bath, a fashionable watering place, where he began his career as a society painter. He spent several years there, occasionally sending pictures to London. Although he was not well educated, he gained by his wit and charm the friendship of many in the literary world. When the Royal Academy was established, he was among the founding members.

During this period, Gainsborough rose to full maturity. A typical example is *The Hon. Mrs. Thomas Graham*. From Van Dyck are derived elongated proportions and handling of cloth. But while Van Dyck conveys the air of a court pageant and most of the English portraitists give a sense of worldly riches and even smugness, Gainsborough imparts a feeling of refinement and delicate breeding. It is amazing that he could lend such distinction to so many of his sitters.

Describing his working method, Gainsborough said he would ignore the sitter for a long time and, instead of trying to get her likeness, would paint the most beautiful creature he could imagine while his client sat in the room with him. He would then begin to depart from this idealization to a point resembling the lady sitting before him, and when she saw a resemblance he stopped working. Although this is probably an exaggeration, one may suppose that many ladies came off better than they deserved.

In 1774 Gainsborough left Bath and settled in London. Already famous, he was a bit arrogant and capricious as well. While the eminently proper Reynolds felt himself bound to pay Gainsborough a call, the latter took not the least notice of that great man for a number of years. Finally Gainsborough returned the visit and asked Reynolds to sit for his portrait. Sir Joshua immediately complied, but the sittings were interrupted by illness that forced him to leave the city. When he came back to London, he sent word to Gainsborough, whose only reply was that he was glad Sir Joshua was well—but no word about the painting. It was only later, when Gainsborough was dying, that he sent for Reynolds and thanked him for his liberal attitude and comments.

Weary of the rigorous code of the society painter of the day, Gainsborough said: "I'm sick of portraits and wish very much to take my viol-da-gamba and walk off to some sweet village, where I can paint landscapes and enjoy the fag end of life in quietness and ease. But these fine ladies and their tea-drinkings, dancings, husband-huntings, et cetera, will fob me out of the last ten years."

In addition to his love for music and his appreciation of a pretty woman and a good bottle of wine, Gainsborough was devoted to landscape painting. Here he was apparently able to express in an intimate way the delicate and sensitive moods of his extremely volatile temperament. His efforts in this field almost invariably tend toward the sweet and the sentimental, but it is the sort of sentiment that does not offend. Rather it makes us feel the same love of nature that affected the painter himself. In the simple and sweet *Child in a Forest* and in the well-known *Market Cart* we encounter the artist's interest in a homely sort of peasant subject.

The great phase of Gainsborough's treatment of rural scenes, however, is to be found in such a work as *English Landscape*. It brings a feeling of unworldliness, of evening quiet, as the little figures move diagonally across the picture, some coming from the small church, others going toward it. A series of broad, sweeping curves and generalized hills, and a shimmering cool color unite the luminous background of Titian and the great feeling for nature of Rubens. But the color quality and the particular mood are Gainsborough's: all the nuances of the Englishman's love of nature are conveyed to us. —BERNARD S. MYERS

SELF-PORTRAIT

John Singleton Copley

JOHN SINGLETON COPLEY

1738–1815

Colonial Wonder

HAD YOU BEEN BORN in a colonial land and wanted to become a painter, the chances against you would be heavy. If, added to these odds, you had never had a formal art lesson, how could you scale the heights of international success? It has been done—an American, John Singleton Copley, did it.

He was one of the first native American painters. Self-schooled in early Boston, he had never seen a European masterpiece; he had no way of measuring his merit. To find out whether his work was worthless or not, he asked

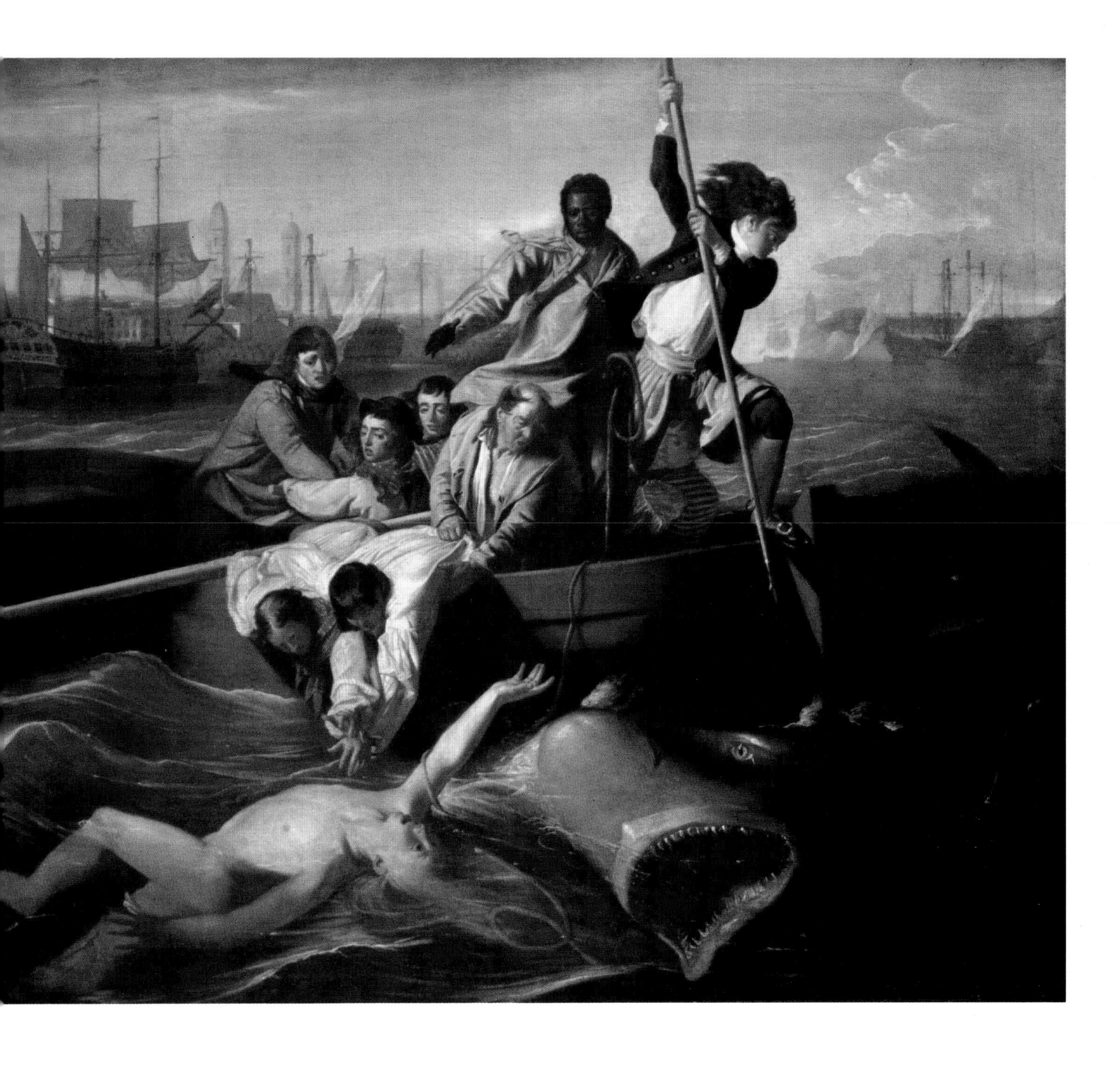

BROOK WATSON AND THE SHARK
Most dramatic narrative painting of its time, the picture above was a turning point in the career of the American Copley. It was a striking success, capturing the attention of all England. The subject, Brook Watson, survived his ordeal and ultimately became the Lord Mayor of London.

BOY WITH A SQUIRREL
After painting this portrait of his half brother, Copley prospered as an artist in colonial Boston. He painted Paul Revere, John Hancock and many other pre-Revolutionary-War Americans, before settling in England for the rest of his life.

a sea captain to take one of his pictures abroad to the spring exhibition of the Society of Artists of Great Britain —an event at which a new painter might make his name.

Into the captain's hands Copley put a portrait of a boy seated leaning over a table, playing with a pet squirrel. The captain carried the picture overseas, addressed to Benjamin West, the leading American painter in England. The most fashionable British artist then alive, Sir Joshua Reynolds, couldn't accept the story that this was the work of a man who lived "out there" in rude eighteenth-century Boston, a colonial settlement that he visualized lying between the ocean and primeval forest. Reynolds sent for the captain and listened, amazed, while the old sailor testified that *Boy with a Squirrel* had been painted by a twenty-eight-year-old, self-taught American who had never seen anything but second-rate paintings in his life and who had, in fact, sent the picture abroad by way of inquiring if his work was any good.

The great Sir Joshua promptly directed a message to Copley, saying that the picture was "a very wonderful performance." He joined Copley's countryman West in urging the painter to study in Europe. "If you are capable of producing such a piece by the mere efforts of your own genius," Sir Joshua wrote, "with the advantage of example and instruction you would have in Europe, you would be a valuable acquisition to the art and one of the first painters in the world." But he cautioned the new wonder from the colonies to "receive these aids before it is too late in life—before your manner and taste are corrupted . . . by working in your little way in Boston."

Shortly there was further news: the display of the picture in the exhibition caused sophisticated London to marvel how such an artist could have sprung up in primitive America.

The success of *Boy with a Squirrel* spread the painter's reputation at home in America and whipped up his desire to cross the Atlantic and meet the renowned Sir Joshua, to see and study the masterpieces of European painting. Now so many colonists wanted a portrait from his brush that he was able to raise his prices to the point where he was earning a handsome income. Copley postponed sailing for eight years, until he felt he had made enough money to keep his wife and children comfortable and at the same time to establish himself in England while he carried on his studies. It proved fortunate that he had savings to fall back on, for, shortly after he had hung out his shingle in London, the United States proclaimed her independence. His family arrived on the last English ship to leave before fighting began. War swept art into the background, and the next few years were lean.

Then Copley's genius rose to a challenge posed by a London merchant. In his youth this man had fallen into the sea off the Cuban coast and had lost a leg in a struggle with a shark. He asked the painter for a portrait illustrating his terrifying adventure.

The result of this commission was the first raw-life picture of modern times. It portrayed a man underwater, his clothes ripped from him and one leg half torn off. We see him struggling with the shark while men in a rowboat frantically try to save him. At the Royal Academy exhibition the canvas was a tremendous success. Copley followed up this picture with another that was loaded with emotion —the death of Chatham, Prime Minister of England, seized by a fatal stroke of apoplexy while addressing the House of Lords. The picture shows him falling backward while peers in scarlet and ermine leap to their feet in dismay. When Copley exhibited *Death of Chatham* in a private gallery, charging admission, he took in more than twenty thousand dollars. This proved but the prelude to financial ease. Over sixty thousand persons paid to see another historical picture by him. Meanwhile, wealthy men and women sought to have him paint their portraits, and, as word of his talent spread far and wide, for years Copley had more work than he could do.

Fame and fortune were not enough to give Copley and his wife happiness. They longed for home in Boston; they felt like aliens in their elegant English house. But it seemed unwise for Copley to give up the place he had won for himself in England. Also, they hesitated to uproot their children, the eldest of whom, John Jr., was already showing that extraordinary promise which was to make him Lord Chancellor of England.

Copley had no way of knowing that he would have done well to return to America as soon as the Revolution was over. Massachusetts had become a vital state; Boston was swiftly expanding into a flourishing city. Copley's old 20-acre farm lay at the top of Beacon Hill and was shortly to be worth hundreds of thousands of dollars. He sold it for comparatively little and was shocked to learn a few months later that the new State House was being built in the area. Had Copley returned to Boston, the renown he had won abroad would doubtless have made him one of the most sought-after artists in America—far more so than in his youth when Sir Joshua Reynolds had hailed his *Boy with a Squirrel* as "a very wonderful performance."

—MALCOLM VAUGHAN

SELF-PORTRAIT

Goya,

FRANCISCO GOYA

1746–1828

The Savage Eye

SPAIN WAS ROTTEN in body and soul, a shattered civilization, bankrupt mentally and physically, and degraded in aristocratic circles by the imitation of French frivolity. Spanish art was dead. Since Velázquez there had not been a name worth mentioning. The morbid Hapsburgs had disappeared, and in their places ruled the more vicious Bourbons. The rabid Ferdinand VII brought to the land new shedding of blood in the Inquisition. "Every heretic," announced this despicable boor, "shall have his tongue bored through with a red-hot iron." Spies herded in their victims; the Holy Office worked night and day; and Spain sank into lethargy and ruin.

Goya was part of all this, and a very conspicuous part: Goya of the bull neck, the sensual lips and devastating eye; the father of some twenty legitimate children. This virile man of the soil had an intellect—the only artist's intellect in Spain. And when that intellect was finally silenced by a stroke of apoplexy, it had created the most comprehensive history of a period that has ever been written in graphic form, an inhuman comedy. The painter ransacked the soul of Spain of its mysteries and ignoble terrors, turning his experiences into works of art.

Coming from the humblest level of society, Goya climbed to the top of his profession by brute strength and the audacity of genius. His struggle was long and hard, and if he portrayed the woes of the downtrodden in horrible symbols—fetuses, apes, cats and corpses—it was a truthful symbolism, truthful because he had been an underdog himself in Spain and had found the life abominable. He was born in 1746 in Fuendetodos, a wretched mountain village of a hundred inhabitants, in a stone hut which is now a public museum. As a child he worked in

DONA ISABEL COBOS DE PORCEL

A fast and impatient painter, Goya liked to complete a portrait in one sitting. He also had a realistic scale of prices, increasing his rate if the hands were to be shown. The woman portrayed here was the wife of a friend, Antonio de Porcel.

the fields with his two brothers and his sister until his talent for drawing gave him a way out of his misery.

At fourteen, brought to the attention of a wealthy man who came to his aid, he was sent to Saragossa to study with a court painter. Here, in the capital of Aragon, footloose and free, he began his picaresque journey through a disordered world. Confident from the first, he rushed to one art medium after another. Not less boldly did he enter into the affairs of the crowded town. Goya had a fine singing voice, was an excellent swordsman, boxer and dancer. He was also a gang leader, and in a fight between his men and a rival faction, several combatants were murdered; warned that the Holy Office was moved to take action, the nineteen-year-old Goya fled to Madrid, where he stayed for several years. He frequented the bull-ring and again consorted with thieves. One morning he was picked up out of the gutter with a dagger sticking in his back. A company of bullfighters spirited him away to the coast and he took ship for Rome.

He painted only for profit in Italy and had no particular reverence for Italian art. But the life of Rome—the processions, the carnival, the prostitutes, the gay and dangerous underworld—all of these were a constant lash to his impulsive animalism.

Nevertheless he was a Spaniard and a man of strong family affections, and two years later he was home again, faced with the necessity of making a living and relieving the poverty of his father and mother. He sought work immediately, submitting designs for the decoration of a church at Saragossa, received the commission and executed it in six months.

He was nearing thirty when, with a little money in hand, he married Josefa Bayeu, sister of a well-known painter. His wife remained at home, after the Spanish custom, in a state of chronic pregnancy, while Goya continued his old life among the bohemians of Saragossa, as the favorite of gypsies, dancing girls, musicians and matadors. Sad and exhausted, his wife bore a sickly brood of children, only one of the twenty reaching maturity.

Shortly after his marriage, having been recommended to the king by Anton Raphael Mengs, the principal court painter, he was attached to the royal tapestry factory, and in the next four years made forty designs for the king's weavers. With these he leaped into fame. Instead of falling back on the artificial languors of mythology, like the French imitators of Rubens, he boldly chose Spanish subjects—stilt-walkers, boys climbing trees and playing the game of *pelota*, gallants and their wantons dining and

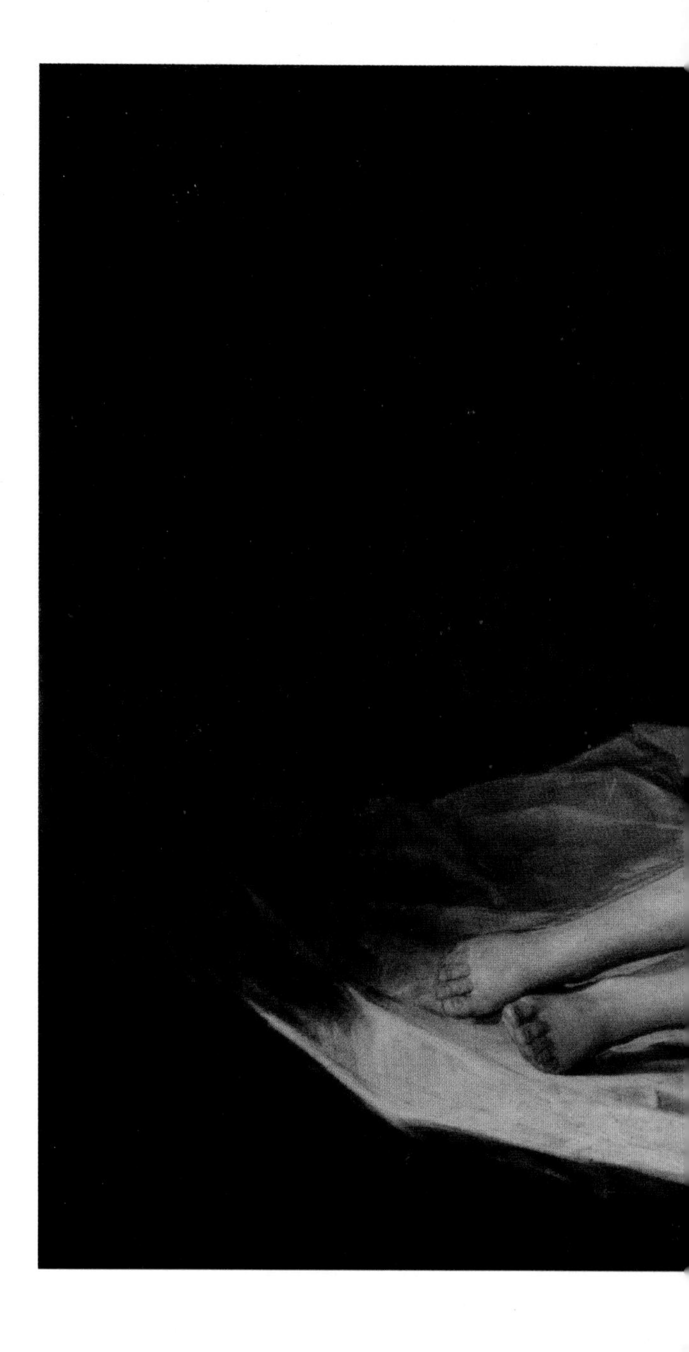

THE NUDE MAJA *and* THE CLOTHED MA
If the Duchess of Alba posed for these two paintings, as tradition claims, Goya must have deliberately concealed the fact, for the faces in the paintings bear little or no resemblance to the famed Castilian beauty. The clothed version may have been painted because of the Spaniards' objection to the nude in art at that time. When Goya died in 1828, he owned only two of the hundreds of paintings he had made during his long career. One, which he dared not exhibit, was the Nude Maja.

drinking—things snatched out of his own experiences. His choice may seem the obvious one, but in his own generation it was an innovation that would have occurred to none but a newcomer—and a genius—like Goya. The originality of his subjects irritated his envious competitors. So did the unheralded decorative quality of his designs, and his superb mixing of mass and silhouette into strangely Oriental compositions.

Being famous, he made enemies. His tactlessness and insulting candor tried the patience of his closest friends. But neither whispered slurs on his character nor the political maneuvering of his rivals could check the momentum of his fame. He became a boon companion of the king's brother, yet his petition for a court job was twice refused. When he was thirty-nine years old, he was made President of the Academy, and as soon as Charles IV ascended his father's throne, Goya was without delay named as one of the king's painters.

Up to his thirty-seventh year Goya painted nothing of any significance. His court appointment, however, was followed by a decade of ceaseless activity—years of painting and scandal, despite periods of bad health.

Duchesses quarreled over his favors. The Duchess of Alba, in all probability, was the woman who posed for the two *Majas* now in the Prado museum—*Maja* meaning gay lady, harlot or duchess, or all three, there being little difference in Goya's time. One pose is in the nude; in the other she is even more seductive in her thin, skintight breeches.

Determined to monopolize the painter, Alba comported herself so brazenly that she was obliged, at the queen's suggestion, to retire temporarily to her estate in Andalusia. Goya applied at once to the king for leave of absence, and the king willingly granted the request. The pair set out together for the South, but on a rough mountain road the carriage broke down with a sprung axle. Goya kindled a fire and with great strength forged the steel into shape again, but the heat and exertion brought on a chill which eventually led to total deafness.

Life in Madrid was dull without Goya. The king needed him, and at the end of a year the duchess and Goya were recalled. In appreciation of royal favors, Goya decorated the church of San Antonio de la Florida, situated on royal property. The decorations, however, were more suitable to a high-class brothel than to a place of worship. For angels he painted the comely strumpets of the court—his favorite duchess among them—insidiously rouged; he painted naked children climbing over railings, ballet dancers, recognizable beauties, and alluring women ogled by dandified men. But in sheer liveliness, in spontaneous agility and careless animation, there is nothing in Italy or in any other land to compare with them. They are among the gayest church decorations in art. Returning the compliment, the king rewarded Goya with the coveted post of first court painter.

In 1799 Goya executed the first of his wonderful groups of etchings, *Los Caprichos* ("Caprices"), in which the throne, the Church, the law and the army are held up to ridicule and satirized with contemptuous ferocity. When he leveled his satire at the impostures of priests, however, the Church decided to call a halt, and the king, getting wind of ecclesiastical vengeance, suppressed, or pretended to suppress, the etchings—which, he said, had been done at his command—thus saving the artist from the Inquisition.

The Duchess of Alba died in 1802; the artist's wife died in 1812, exhausted and forlorn; his one surviving son was a weakling. Surly and unmanageable, Goya lived on, alone as much as possible, self-absorbed, painting because there was nothing better to do. But his work suffered no decline. In fact, it became better with the advancing years. Napoleon's army came and slaughtered the populace at the city gate. Goya painted the massacre—with a spoon, it is said—and bequeathed to mankind the most frightening curse ever uttered against the horrors of war: ragged, cowardly people frozen with fears of death; men with their hands sticking up; men hiding their faces and clenching their fists, impotent before a firing squad.

Yet Goya—with that curious turncoat soul of his, caring not whom he painted so long as he was free to paint—welcomed the Bonapartes and clung to his office at the court. When the scene shifted again, restoring the Bourbons and all the tortures of the Inquisition, he took the oath of allegiance to the new king without a qualm. "You deserve hanging," Ferdinand told him. "But you are an artist, and I will forget everything." In his seventy-eighth year, the volatile painter obtained permission from the king to visit France, a sojourn that lasted till his death four years later.

Goya was more than an egoist riding roughshod over the world. He was receptive to all shades of feeling, and it was his extreme sensitivity as well as his muscular strength that made him assault the outrageous society of Spain. In his portraits we read not only the soul of Spain but the unconsenting, scornful soul of Goya himself. He scours every layer of society for his faces, and yet they all belong to the same family. They haunt him and turn upon him, and he begins to visualize Spain as his own nightmare.

In his old age, the medium of paint infuriates him: his hand and eye can no longer obey the unbroken will. Monstrous forms inhabit his black-and-white world: fiends with bat's wings; great birds croaking and flapping over the earth; a colossus sitting on a mountain top; animals performing like silly humans; shriveled, naked idiots huddled among bags of gold; grinning giants dancing ponderously. A corpse rising out of a grave leans on its elbow and writes, with a bony finger on a piece of paper, the artist's black godlessness in one word—*Nada*—or nothingness.

But Goya's genius attains its highest point in his etchings on the horrors of war. Nowhere else does he display such mastery of form and movement, such dramatic gestures and appalling effects of light and darkness. Even with the evidence before us, it does not seem possible that an artist can call to life such vivid characters and such dreadful condensations of human misery. —THOMAS CRAVEN

SELF-PORTRAIT

WILLIAM TURNER

1775–1851

Magician of Light

HE WAS BORN in 1775 in a shabby street near the sheds and pushcarts of London's Convent Garden. His father was a barber; his mother died in an insane asylum. He grew up to be a short, fat man with a beak nose and a receding chin. Some place him above Constable as England's finest painter, even ranking him as the greatest landscape artist the world has ever known.

For sixty-odd years, Joseph Mallord William Turner lived almost all his daylight hours with either a pencil or a brush in his hand. He produced 25,000 oils, watercolors, etchings and drawings. When he died in 1851, aged seventy-six, he left behind 630,000 dollars in bonds, two houses in London and a gallery of his own paintings for which he had turned down 500,000 dollars. He was a paradox who produced immortal beauty while he often seemed to live only for money, as though haunted by his youth.

Undersized, uneducated and slovenly, he could do only one thing well: paint. Into this solitary talent he put all his enormous energy, as a way of making up for his shortcomings. Even that was not easy. One teacher gave him up as hopeless. "Better make him a tinker or a cobbler," he told Turner's father. "He will never be an artist."

As a boy William copied pictures out of magazines which his father hung in the doorway of his shop to sell for a few shillings. They found buyers and so, at the age of twelve, the boy learned that art had a cash value. Entering art school at fourteen, he was an accomplished draftsman within a year. At seventeen, the unhandsome young man painted a curly-haired self-portrait in watercolor (at left). In those prephotography days there was an enormous demand for drawings, and Turner set about supplying it. With knapsack on his back, he slogged for miles into the country, sketching abbeys, castles and historic manors.

Out of these excursions into the country, the city boy who had known only the pavements of London became a master of trees and high skies and rolling hills; above all a master of the scene he loved more than any other—water, and the ships that sailed on it. His seascapes are among the finest ever painted.

Owners of estates hired him to draw their homes. Architects paid him to wash their designs with color. Once, instead of doing the windows in plain gray, as was the custom, he painted them as if light were shining on them. The architect wasn't impressed, but Turner had demonstrated his awareness of what was to dominate his style—light in all its myriad variations.

He got a job copying paintings at seventy-five cents an evening; he gave lessons for about two dollars apiece. With his habit of mumbling and his limited vocabulary, he wasn't much of a teacher. But driven by his two passions, money and art, Turner worked from sunrise until late at night. Soon he had more orders than he could fill. Almost to the end he went on drawing for the engravers, illustrating, among others, the works of Byron and Scott. Often his engravings were sold as separate items. Millions of them found a market in every country of the world and there was a time when no parlor, inn or public building was complete without at least one Turner on the wall. They were the basis of his fortune.

Of the private life of William Turner little is known. One story is that as a youth he fell in love with the sister of a friend and became engaged to marry her. Then he set out for a long trip into the countryside. But the girl's stepmother, disapproving of the unprepossessing youth, intercepted his letters. When he came back, the girl was betrothed to a richer man. Turner, heartbroken, never again thought of marriage.

When he was twenty-one, he successfully exhibited his first oil painting, *Fishermen at Sea*, at the Royal Academy. At twenty-six he became a full member of the Academy, one of the youngest ever elected. Despite such rivals as Constable, he was, at thirty-five, acknowledged as England's most celebrated landscape painter.

If his capacity for work appalled other artists, they were even more dismayed by his fantastic visual memory. One day he stood with a friend watching a thunderstorm. "Isn't it wonderful!" shouted Turner. Two years later he painted the dark clouds, the tossing trees, the lightning in exquisite detail. He had forgotten nothing, the friend agreed.

The critic Sir Kenneth Clark tells of a woman who rode on a train with Turner once. She was amazed to see him suddenly stick his head out of the window. It was raining hard, but he kept his position for several minutes, finally withdrawing dripping wet to sit with eyes closed for a quarter of an hour. The woman, in curiosity, also put her head out. A few months later she attended the Royal Academy show where she was startled to find the sight they had both seen from the window beautifully painted in *Rain, Steam, Speed.* "Did you ever see anything quite so absurd?" said someone behind her. The woman smiled. "Yes," she said, "I *did.*"

By the time he was forty, Turner was ready to paint only what suited him. His pictures became lighter and more vivid. Instead of detailing every object in a landscape, he simply indicated them in a kind of stormy, colorful shorthand. He delighted in fire for its swirling scarlets; in bursting clouds and tormented seas for their high drama. Some of the pictures were so amorphous he had to distinguish top from bottom so they could be hung properly. As the critic William Hazlitt said, he painted the chaos that existed before God parted the waters and created man.

Now, where once his paintings had been greeted with paeans of praise, there was violent criticism. "Soapsuds and whitewash," said one critic of his lovely *Snowstorm.* The comment embittered the little man. Lashed to the mast of a ship, he had seen the storm and set it down accurately. "I wish they had been there," he said. Of another picture, a viewer remarked, "It looks as if he has been throwing eggs at the canvas." An Italian critic, having seen an exhibition of Turner's in Rome, said, "Just a lot of salami and mustard." And even Mark Twain joined the

THE SHIPWRECK

Not until the time of Turner had the wild look of the sea been caught so powerfully on canvas. Since early boyhood the great English watercolorist had been fascinated by the ever-changing face of the ocean. "I know what waves do to ships," he once observed, "and what storms and ships do to men."

anvil chorus commenting on *The Slavers:* "It looks like a tabby cat having a fit in stewed tomatoes."

But Turner went on painting as he wished. He knew exactly what he was doing and what he wanted to do. "He took England out of the dark brown period into white—revolutionizing not only landscape but portraiture and figure painting," wrote A. J. Finberg, a biographer.

Though he grew more gruff and rude as the years passed, Turner revealed toward his friends a soft heart. "I never heard him say an unkind thing of a brother artist," said John Ruskin, "or find fault with another man's work."

At one exhibition two sedate paintings by his good friend Sir Thomas Lawrence were hung on either side of a large, flaming Turner. Sir Thomas was disturbed because the spectacular Turner detracted from his work. Returning the next day, he was astonished to find that Turner's painting had become strangely dark brown. "It's lampblack," Turner explained. "It'll wash off when the show is over." He had deliberately blacked out his own painting to help bring out the pictures of his friend.

Even in money matters Turner could be generous. He once lent 90,000 dollars to an old friend who had been financially ruined in a bank crash. And he bequeathed his entire fortune to aged and impoverished artists. They failed to get it only because the will was so badly drawn that Turner's relatives, all of whom he despised, succeeded in breaking it. Nevertheless, "his palm is as itchy as his fingers are ingenious," wrote Sir Walter Scott. "He will do nothing without cash and anything for it." On one occasion the Marquess of Stafford paid the painter 1200 dollars for his *Fishing Boats.* Unsatisfied, Turner wrote him half a dozen letters dunning him for the price of the frame. For all his love of money, he hated to sell his paintings. "They are my children," he would say. Whenever one of them came up for auction Turner was sure to be there to buy his "child" back. He paid 2300 dollars for the *Sun Rising Through the Vapor,* which he had originally sold for 1700 dollars, and 700 dollars for *The Blacksmith's Shop*—200 dollars above his original price.

The great flowering of this strange artist took place at a time when most men are ready to retire or have already done so—between the ages of fifty and sixty-five. These were also his melancholy years. Far less important painters were honored with knighthoods. The critics laughed and made jokes before his masterpieces. Old friends more or less abandoned him.

Today more than ever Turner has come into his own. The paintings most derided by the critics of his day are now considered his best: these fluid and beautifully chaotic landscapes have much in common with modern art. Where fifty years ago you might buy a Turner oil painting for 9000 dollars, today for the same one you would pay more than 100,000 dollars.

Toward the end of his life the round little man could not take a step without a cane. His teeth fell out; he suffered from gout and indigestion. His chief sustenance was a mixture of rum and milk. Finally, reluctantly, he sent for a doctor. When the physician told him he had only a few hours to live, Turner smiled. "Go downstairs and pour yourself a glass of sherry," he said. "Maybe you'll change your mind." Not long afterward, looking out at his beloved river Thames, the light of the sun on his face, he died.

Of all the strange men who have put brush to canvas, none is more inexplicable than William Turner. Looking at his pictures, you wonder how these golden visions of fire and sea and passion could have emerged from this unkempt beerkeg of a man. But then, who would expect volcanic fireworks to issue from the dull mass of rock we call Mount Etna? —GEORGE KENT

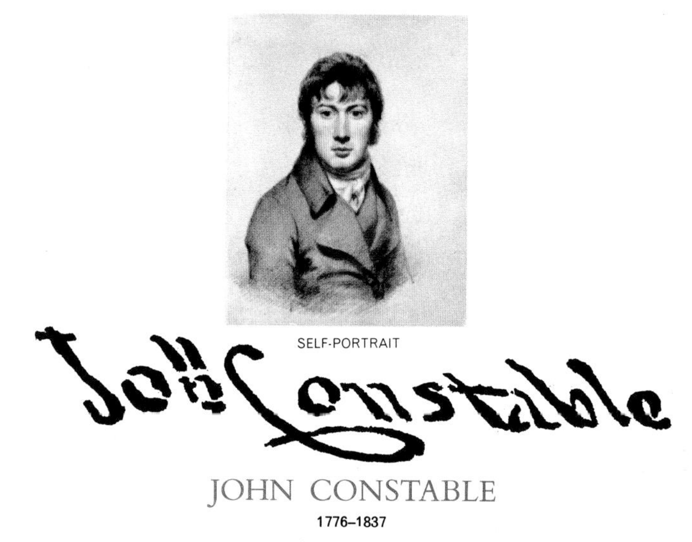

SELF-PORTRAIT

JOHN CONSTABLE

1776–1837

Worshiper of Nature

TRIUMPH WAS ON ITS WAY but no sign of it had yet reached him. His wife was suffering from tuberculosis; his eldest boy was at death's door; he himself was ill from worry over expenses. He was now forty-eight; for twenty-five years he had been struggling to gain recognition.

Gazing around his studio at stacks of pictures he had painted, he decided to sacrifice his great six-foot masterpiece to the French dealer who had offered 350 dollars for it. That was early in 1824. Later that year, when the dealer exhibited the picture at the Paris Salon along with several

WIVENHOE PARK, ESSEX

WEYMOUTH BAY

Constable never wanted to leave his native country and never did. "He brought English people face to face with England," the writer E. V. Lucas said, "the delicious, fresh, rainy, blowy England that they could identify." Above are two of his greatest landscapes, one of the countryside northeast of London, the other of the southern coast in Dorsetshire.

others by the same artist, it became famous overnight. In fact, the pictures made art history; for the artist was John Constable, pioneer English painter of nature, and his six-foot masterpiece was an Arcadian mirror of summertime England. It bore the same title as Jerome Bosch's first great painting—*The Hay Wain* (see page 76).

John Constable was born in 1776 and brought up in a Suffolk country village. Tall, strong, with fresh complexion and fine dark eyes, he was working in his father's gristmill business when he made up his mind to study art. Spurning the elegant art fashions of his times, he painted what attracted him most—the everyday fields and woods that lay around the village. But they were something more to him than just attractive. He felt that nature revealed God. Out for a walk one balmy spring day, he said: "At every step I take, that sublime expression of the Scriptures, 'I am the resurrection, and the life,' seems as if uttered near me." Artified scenery, giving only an impersonal representation of nature, had been a principal aim of landscape artists until then. Constable brought out the actual, factual realities of what he saw. In his pictures you can recognize what crops are growing, identify even the different grasses. But for a long while it was thought that since his painting looked like nature it must be a low form of art!

He tried to make others see that nature could be artistic—to no avail. Arguing the issue with one of the connoisseur lords of the day who insisted that the prevailing tone of outdoor paintings should be the dark brown of an antique violin, Constable carried an old fiddle from the house and laid it on the green lawn. His lordship turned up his nose and walked away. Again, when a fellow artist tut-tutted Constable for painting trees leaf by leaf, with single dabs of paint, Constable walked the man up to a tree and showed him that leaves *do* grow one by one. The fellow artist preferred convention to his own eyesight.

Constable painted for fourteen years before he sold a picture professionally. He would have starved to death but for the five hundred dollars a year his father gave him. To marry the woman he loved he had to wait five years because her grandfather threatened to disown her if she married a man who couldn't support her. In 1816 he won the girl, after his inheritance from his father had given him the necessary money; the painter's bride also had money, and he was from then on financially independent.

Constable's pictures were ignored year after year at the Royal Academy of Arts. For years he made application for Academy membership before he was admitted, junior grade. It took him ten years to win full membership. By that time he was fifty-three; his mother, father, wife and her scornful grandfather all were dead, and there was almost no one left with whom he could celebrate this honor that justified his life.

Englishman Constable might have gone to his grave unknown had not the French art dealer exhibited those bargain-price pictures at the Paris Salon of 1824. Constable became the shining star of the show. The French at once recognized his clear, sparkling pictures as unique; critics predicted his naturalism would sweep tradition aside. French artists stood before the pictures goggle-eyed. A visiting Londoner saw one astonished Frenchman pull another by the arm and say: "Look at these landscapes by an Englishman. The ground appears covered with dew!"

The king of France was so impressed that he decreed Constable a gold medal. The government then proposed to buy *The Hay Wain* for the national art museum of France. The dealer demurred, and sold it instead to a private collector for two thousand dollars.

You might think so much foreign acclaim would have raised his countrymen's opinion of Constable's art. But, on the contrary, the English continued to hold him in slight esteem. They still wanted their leaves indistinct, their grass a soupy brown. In fact, years later, after Constable had become a member of the Academy Council, one of his paintings accidentally got mixed in with a multitude of canvases being submitted to the jury. He sat silent as he heard the jurors reject his picture, jeering it as a "nasty green thing." Only once is he known to have cried out against his adverse fate, lamenting, to a friend, "my singularly wasted life."

Constable lived out his days in modesty and quiet, devoted to observations of nature. These were so accurate that his pictures never show even a speck of light at variance with the rest of the light, nor is even the tiniest cloud at odds with the rest of the weather in the picture. Absorbed in observation, he remained so still that once at day's end he put his hand in his pocket and found a field mouse there, sound asleep.

John Constable couldn't have imagined the triumph that has since immortalized his name. He couldn't possibly foresee that he was a harbinger of the glorious Barbizon school of nature painters who, under the inspiration of Corot (see page 133) and Millet (see page 177), among others, led artists to leave their studios and paint out-of-doors. The noted art authority, Sir Kenneth Clark, says Constable achieved "perhaps the greatest pictures ever painted in England."

—MALCOLM VAUGHAN

THE TRIUMPH OF VISION

Paris became the world's center of art by 1850, as Florence and Rome had been in the Renaissance. But now artists were exploring their craft in ways that no one had ever imagined. Photography came on the scene to wipe out portrait-painting as a means of livelihood. Artists, already alienated by the new industrial age, turned to bohemian living, in revolt against a "respectable" society that did not use their talents. They set out to shock the public with challenges in every direction. Delacroix in the early 1830's revolted against "careful" painting and resorted to dramatic action. Courbet flouted convention, exhibited in a shed and invited his fellow artists out of their studios to seek the true look of nature. The distinguished Manet delivered new shocks—using a medley of color, a blur of action and distortion of light. Following him, Renoir and Monet rained swift blows on the convention of what a picture should be. They outraged the public and the critics with their daubing style (reminiscent of Frans Hals and Rubens!) and they even chose to paint railway stations and cafés. The new movement was insultingly called "Impressionism," but the name became one of the most respected in the history of art. From many lands, painters such as the American Whistler traveled to join the revolution. They made the world see itself in a new light

SELF-PORTRAIT

Eug. Delacroix

EUGENE DELACROIX

1798–1863

He Opened the Door to Modern Art

A PARTY WAS IN progress one day in 1833 at the Paris home of novelist Alexandre Dumas. All his painter friends were there to decorate the walls with murals. Eugène Delacroix was the last to arrive. Without taking off his cloak or putting on a smock, he picked up a piece of charcoal. With three strokes, there was a horse. Another five or six, and the horse had a rider. Ten more, and there was a landscape with minor figures. The other painters stopped working to watch in awe.

Now Delacroix took brushes and palette and, with amazing swiftness, gave full color to the tottering horse and bleeding rider, feet out of the stirrups, bowed over his lance. In two hours the painting—a scene from a Spanish novel—was finished. The onlookers burst into a thunder of handclapping. Delacroix looked up in surprise. So intense was his concentration that he had not been aware of the crowd around him.

This great French painter not only could work with remarkable speed, but he could also paint in bewildering variety: portraits, animals, flowers, vast battle scenes, quiet interiors—some canvases bathed in light, others whose darkness recalled Rembrandt. All glowed with color.

Delacroix opened the door for the modern school of painting. Van Gogh came to Paris to see the master's *Pietà,* which he copied and recopied. In Cézanne's studio the only important picture conceived by another artist was a copy Cézanne had made of a Delacroix. Manet, Renoir, Matisse, Degas, Rouault were all indebted to him. Picasso's famous *Guernica* is a direct descendant of the picture Delacroix painted as a protest against the massacre of twenty thousand Greeks on the island of Chios.

Ferdinand Victor Eugène Delacroix was born in a Paris

GEORGE SAND
AND FREDERIC CHOPIN

The two portraits below were, for some unknown reason, cut out of a single painting in which George Sand, the famous woman novelist, was shown listening to the composer Chopin, then the rage of Paris, at the piano. Lovers at the time, they were portrayed together by their friend Delacroix in 1838.

WOMAN WITH A PARROT

Portraying an odalisque *(harem woman) gave Delacroix his greatest opportunity to delve into rich Oriental coloring. It fascinated him, for he had been immersed in studies of Persian miniatures and Asian art.*

DANTE AND VIRGIL IN HADES

The critics denounced the young artist's first and perhaps best painting. But the jury favored it and the government bought it—possibly because some sought favor with the great Talleyrand, Delacroix's natural father.

suburb in 1798, nine years after the French Revolution. According to most of his biographers, his real father was Prince Talleyrand, the master diplomat. (His nominal father was Minister to Holland.) There was considerable artistic talent on his mother's side of the family. It was the gift of a box of paints from an uncle which started him on his career. By the time Eugène was sixteen, both his parents had died and the family wealth had been frittered away. When he was older, he wrote: "There is no situation worse than not knowing where one will eat next week."

A highly excitable young man, he once saw a painting he admired and ran halfway across Paris to his attic room to get to his easel before its influence vanished. His first appearance before the public came when he was twenty-four, at the Paris Salon. He was too poor to buy a frame for the 8-foot-wide painting he wanted to exhibit, and it might never have been hung if a benefactor had not been so impressed with it that he provided a fine frame. The canvas, *Dante and Virgil in Hades,* showed the two poets in hell surrounded by the writhing bodies of the damned; it is now in the Louvre.

Delacroix rushed to the opening of the Salon to hear what people would say about his first picture. But instead of the praise he expected, he heard sneers and laughter. "A formless dauber," said one critic. "A charlatan!" cried another. Next day he bought the newspapers. Only one had a favorable word for him. Adolphe Thiers, later Minister of Commerce, said it was a beautiful painting, with here and there "a burst of talent." That saved the day for the young man. The adverse criticism was forgotten.

It was the beginning of an extraordinarily productive career. "Work is my only passion, but what a passion," he wrote. Awake at dawn, he breakfasted on a bit of bread, painted without pause until late afternoon. Then, drained of emotion, he read poetry to refresh himself.

In those days before the invention of the camera, painters were much in demand for re-creating current historical scenes. Delacroix lavished acres of canvas on these, with a passion for light and color that was to make him immortal. "A painting should first and foremost be a feast for the eye," he said. And he was a master chef. This specialty made him wealthy. The government was always in the market for the decoration of public buildings. Delacroix became one of the first painters in modern times to make a handsome living with his brush.

He worked for months on his *Massacre of Chios,* then lugged all 158 square feet of it across Paris to the Salon three days before the official opening. The story goes that on his way home he looked in at an exhibition of the work of John Constable, the English landscape painter. Constable's handling of clouds and the changing blues of the heavens came as a revelation to Delacroix. Realizing that the sky of his own picture was, in comparison, flat and uninteresting, he returned to the Salon and carried his unwieldy canvas back to his studio to paint an entirely new sky. Only when he was completely satisfied, two days later, did he make the return journey.

From the age of twenty-two he suffered ill health. Chronic malaria and a throat ailment frequently nailed him to his bed. Yet, though frail and sickly, softhearted and tender, he painted scenes of the greatest violence. His historical pictures were often of frightful carnage and slaughter. The *Massacre* horrified the public because of one detail: a baby suckling at the breast of a dead woman. But even in his goriest paintings his sensitive nature comes through. The dying workman in *Liberty Leading the People* has been called one of the most moving figures in the history of art.

Delacroix was among the first to paint North African scenes. He spent six months there, went everywhere, sketchbook open, drawing people and places, gathering ideas and inspiration that were to last him all his days. In Algiers he gained admission to a harem—for artistic purposes. Out of that visit came his famous *Women of Algiers.*

He has another claim to immortality besides his paintings: he kept a diary, a detailed, sensitive, three-volume record of his life. It has been ranked with the journal of Samuel Pepys. The great men and women of the period parade through his pages: Chopin, George Sand, Victor Hugo, Dumas and Mary Wollstonecraft Shelley, author of *Frankenstein* and wife of the poet.

He was also an eloquent writer of letters and a man who thought zealously about art. To an editor who asked his opinion of the influence of the official Salon, which was becoming more and more the basis for artistic recognition, he wrote in 1831: "I have just had an absurd idea. I imagined the great Rubens stretched on the iron bed of a competition . . . shrinking into a program that stifles him [and] his . . . luxuriant manner."

Olive-skinned, with somewhat Oriental eyes, his hair long and black almost to the day of his death, and with his small mustache, the painter was extremely attractive to women. They pursued him ardently, and he often allowed himself to be caught. His enduring love was the Baroness Joséphine de Forget; but for his ill health he would certainly have married her.

As Delacroix grew older, his throat ailment became

worse. There were days when he could not utter a syllable. His housekeeper, Jenny, who had been with him twenty-eight years, would stand guard at the door, barring all who might weaken his health or distract him from his painting.

Delacroix became weaker, and Jenny shut the door to everyone but the doctor. A member of the Académie des Beaux-Arts came to call. Delacroix, who had been rejected seven times before finally being elected to this august society, turned the man away. "They have insulted me enough," he told Jenny.

The honors he had longed for came to him late in life—too late. He had never been admitted into the inner circles of high society. Now he was showered with invitations. And though he had had recognition in abundance from the young, the old-line critics, almost to the end, would not accept him.

On August 13, 1863, at the age of sixty-five, he died. One of his last remarks was, "Oh, if I get well, I will do wonderful things. My mind is bubbling with ideas." The final word was written in the catalogue of the centennial exhibition of his paintings in Paris in 1963: "Eugène Delacroix is one of France's national glories." —GEORGE KENT

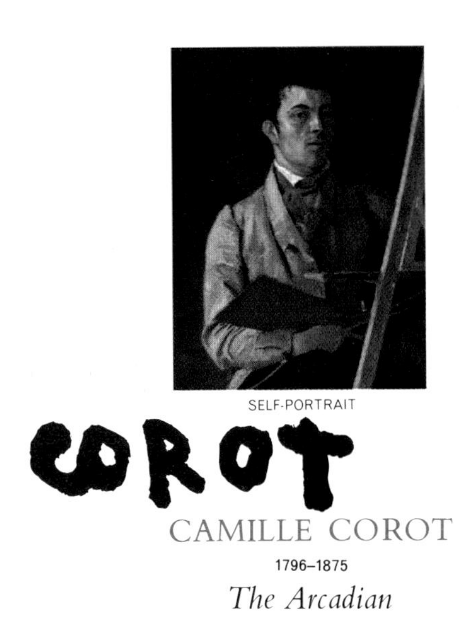

SELF-PORTRAIT

CAMILLE COROT

1796–1875

The Arcadian

THE OLD MAN'S RENT was months overdue; he could no longer earn a living because he was growing blind. The landlord threatened to evict him. But the landscape painter Corot, hearing about the poor man's plight, provided him with a cottage.

Jean-Baptiste Camille Corot could do this because he had become one of the most successful artists in France. His pictures of sylvan countrysides at daybreak or after sundown were selling at higher and higher prices to art collectors who came from all over the world. Furthermore, Corot had learned during his frugal youth how to live and be happy on a dollar a day. He saw no reason to increase his expenses just because he could afford to; he used the money to help others. His house was furnished almost humbly. Indeed he luxuriated only in modesty.

All he desired for himself was long hours of work. He would get up in the morning when it was still dark, make coffee, shoulder his pack and pick his way through the fields and woods till he came to the spot he had decided upon. There he would set up his easel, stretch a canvas, get out his paints and brushes and eagerly await the miracle of dawn. Then he'd work for hours. If all went well he could finish a picture at one sitting.

These pictures were Arcadian portraits of woods and meadows—serene landscapes with silvery-soft undertones of dawn or dusk and a charm that won praise from connoisseurs and public alike. Sometimes Corot added figures to a scene: a woman, or farm children in the dew, an oxcart or a boatman. Sometimes he turned the scene into a classical idyll by bringing in dancing nymphs and fauns. But the figures were only details; what made his pictures world-renowned was their capture of the poetry of nature.

The man himself was as serene as the pictures he painted. Of middle height, stocky build and ruddy complexion, with a storm of blond hair, he dressed in rough corduroy trousers and a cotton smock. His keen dark-blue eyes were his most striking feature.

Corot had been painting for more than twenty years when he made his first sale. He feigned grief at the event, sighing: "Up to this time I have had a complete collection of Corots, and now, alas, it has been broken."

Though gentle as a lamb, Corot possessed the strength of Hercules. Once, when attacked by ruffians, he felled the biggest of them with a single blow; the others fled. Kneeling down to revive the man he murmured: "It's astonishing—I didn't know I was so strong."

Like so many other great French artists, Corot was born of working people. His mother was a Paris milliner, and his father, a civil servant, helped her with the bookkeeping. Their business did so well that by the time their son was twenty-one they were able to buy a little house with several acres around it, on the edge of a pond outside Paris. This rustic atmosphere made a powerful impression on young Corot. He could never gaze long enough at the spreading trees, the fields of grass speckled with flowers, the willows hanging over the pond. Often he would sit at the window half the night, watching the mists and the sky.

His parents were training him to be a businessman. But

COROT

GIRL COMBING HER HAIR

Believing the public would not be interested in his paintings of human figures, the famed landscapist kept them in his studio. All three hundred were found there, after his death.

COROT'S PALETTE

THE BRIDGE AT MANTES

Corot often visited close friends in the peaceful town of Mantes, on the Seine north of Paris. Here he painted the ancient bridge (above, left)—one of his greatest canvases.

MEMORY OF CASTEL GANDOLFO

After visiting Italy, Corot fondly painted classical Roman buildings and settings. Gandolfo was built by Roman emperors on the site of a city older than Rome. Today it is the summer residence of the Pope.

his leaning toward art was so strong that finally, when he was twenty-six, they gave him an allowance of 300 dollars a year so he could do what he longed to do. On this amount Corot made ends meet. It never occurred to him or his parents that the sum was meager until, at fifty, he was decorated with the Legion of Honor and his father remarked: "Now that you wear the red ribbon in your buttonhole you must wear a better-looking coat."

Corot had a hobby: he liked to paint attractive women—not vain, self-conscious Venuses but demure, natural beauties. He painted about 250 pictures of them, and today some critics consider them even finer jewels of art than his landscapes.

Corot remained a bachelor. When his father urged him to give up bohemian life and marry he said: "I am not alone. A woman is often here in the room with me—my Muse." His other goddess was Charity. Not only did he provide a home for the half-blind old tenant, the famous painter Honoré Daumier, but when that other great artist, Jean Francois Millet, died without funds Corot sent the widow 2000 dollars. He said charity brought him good luck. "One day I let a poor fellow have 200 dollars," he said, "and the picture I painted that day was so good that I sold it for 1200 dollars. That's the way it always is. I paint better with a heart at ease."

On another occasion someone protested when an elegantly dressed woman asked Corot for 200 dollars and waited at his door in a cab. Corot got out a handful of bank notes. "Give her these," he said. "The worst kind of misery is misery dressed in silk."

Once his brush, and not his bank notes, enabled him to perform an act of charity. A stranger came to him with an "original" Corot for authentication. The painting, Corot detected, was false. The swindled art buyer's disappointment was matched by the painter's distress at his misfortune. Corot asked if he might have the canvas, and made it genuine by painting over the fake.

He was so highly regarded that the art world of Paris held a great banquet for him and presented him with a gold medal as a token of affection. Modest as ever, Corot responded with a one-line speech: "It's wonderful to be loved like this."

Unspoiled by wealth, indifferent to fame, Corot died in 1875 at the age of seventy-nine, at peace with himself and the world. He was a working artist to the end. One morning he arose to discover he had no appetite for his breakfast. "It is no use today," he said. "Papa Corot breakfasts above."

—MALCOLM VAUGHAN

SELF-PORTRAIT

h. Daumier

HONORE DAUMIER

1808–1879

Caricaturist of a Nation

THE BOY Honoré, busy with his drawing from his seventh year, roamed the streets of Paris and sneaked past the guards into the Louvre, to keep warm while looking at works of art. Nobody told him what to look at, nobody told him whom to admire. He turned to Rembrandt, attracted by the great Dutchman's sympathies with the underdog, and he was fascinated by the sculptures of Michelangelo. It is recorded that the novelist Balzac, on looking at Daumier's youthful caricatures, made this wise remark: "There is much of Michelangelo in this boy."

Daumier was born in Marseilles in 1808 and was brought to Paris in childhood. His father, a glazier and a mediocre poet yearning for literary honors, succeeded at nothing, and the family was desperately poor. The boy had no teachers, but he was always drawing and modeling little figures in clay or wax. For a while he was an usher in the courts of law, wearing a black gown and seating visitors who came to watch the lawyers perform. Later he commented, "There is nothing on earth more fascinating than the mouths of lawyers in operation."

The young Honoré also became delivery boy for a bookseller, but soon decided that it was better to starve as an artist than as a flunky. Before he was twenty he had mastered lithography, and at twenty-one he published some of the most original and powerful drawings ever done in France. His memory was almost superhuman. He hired no models to pose for him; the people of Paris in action, going about their daily business, were his models. Once he had observed a situation—a windbag of a lawyer defending a guilty woman, or a washerwoman with a child tugging at her skirts—he forgot nothing.

He discovered in people characteristics, movements, structures which escape the ordinary eye. What fascinated him was not only what they were doing but the shapes they got into and the faces they put on—not so much what they said as how they looked while saying it. He watched his victims in action, returned to his garret and, with his tenacious memory, modeled them in clay and then drew them for the press.

Daumier developed into the greatest draftsman of the nineteenth century. He drew like an Old Master, constructing heads as solid and massive as sculpture. There are no drawings of mouths, past or present, to compare with his: the mouths of drinkers, expanding into moving caverns; the mouths of lawyers opening and snapping shut like elastic traps, wheedling or condemning. No surgeon or anatomist could make such drawings. His knowledge of the human head was not surgical or scientific—it was knowledge built up by common observation intensified and sustained by his feelings of right and wrong. But you cannot make a work of art simply by loving or hating—by feelings alone. Daumier toiled like a slave to control his lines and shape his black-and-white masses into a murderous instrument.

By the time he reached his twenties he was ready to make trouble. He joined the staff of a radical paper called *La Caricature*, and in a short time he won unenviable notoriety. Respectable artists regarded him as a vicious gamin, the cat's paw of rabble-rousers; and the political cowards shook in their boots at the sight of his masterpieces of slaughter. He took a particularly hot shot at the king, Louis Philippe, representing him as a royal Gargantua swallowing moneybags stolen from the people. For this Daumier was sent to prison for six months, but he refused to mend his ways and on his release began all over again. His paper folded, and he found work on another as social satirist. For more than forty years he earned his bread by cartooning, but it was a poor living for all he did—two each week to make a grand total of four thousand lithographs.

With his wife, Marie, a dressmaker, Daumier lived on the top floor of an old house near the Seine, and in 1848, two years after his marriage, began to paint in oils. His first canvases were received with enthusiasm by the best artists of Paris, but the collectors thought them crude, if not incompetent. Twice he tried to win state decorations; twice he was rejected and with stoical courage went back to his lithographs. The strain of his arduous labors at his fine drawing was great and he was never freed from it. The streets of Paris, his first art school, never lost their hold on him; at the end of the day, from a seat by the

THE PRINT COLLECTOR
Fond affection for his craft is shown by the lithographer Daumier in many paintings of collectors browsing in the printshops. He never satirized these buyers, as he did most other people.

CRISPIN AND SCAPIN
Attracted by the unusual and the ridiculous, Daumier painted two stock characters of French comedy, both valets: the woman-chasing Crispin and the lying, mischief-making Scapin.

window, he observed the fishermen, the laundresses, and the habits of people as poor as himself. "We have our art to comfort us," he said to his friends, "but what have these wretched folk?"

His friends were celebrities—Delacroix, Courbet, Baudelaire, Corot—and they had incomes. They came to his quarters above the river as comrades; sat on the floor by the stove and drank beer together, knowing well who was the great man among them. The stocky fellow was always at work. He was a poor talker; the dialogue on his drawings was written by his editors. One night, as Daumier was peering through the smoke at a drawing—his head very close, for his sight was nearly gone—someone spoke. "Isn't it too bad," he asked the others, "that old Daumier has to work for a living?"

The old man heard the query, straightened up slowly and turned around. He had the right words this time. "It's not too bad that I have to work," he replied, "but too bad I have to work so hard, and have so little time for painting. But let me tell you something. You have incomes, every one of you, but I have a public, and between the two I'll take the public."

His lithographs, circulated by the papers, brought him a sizable audience if not much money. His friends had only dealers and a few collectors who hoarded paintings for years, eventually releasing them, one by one, to wealthy Americans.

In Daumier's last years the burden was too much for him, and he would have starved but for the help of his friends. He retired to a little cottage at Valmondois. Ten years later, on his sixty-fifth birthday, nearly blind and facing eviction because he could not pay his rent, he received a letter from Corot.

Old Friend:

I have a little house at Valmondois which I could not, for the life of me, think what to do with. Suddenly I thought to give it to you, and liking the idea, I have had your ownership legally confirmed. I had no idea of doing you a good turn. The whole scheme was carried out to annoy your landlord.

Ever yours,

Corot.

In reply Daumier said, "You're the only man from whom I can take such a present and not feel humiliated." He sent Corot a painting of some lawyers.

When offered the ribbon of the Legion of Honor, Daumier quietly refused the decoration. In 1878 a committee formed by Victor Hugo presented a large exhibition of his oils and watercolors, but the returns from sales were not enough to pay the expenses of the gallery. The following year, blind, paralyzed and alone, he died.

Honoré Daumier put his knowledge to a humane purpose, revealing a broad experience of life—of poverty, sorrow, rascality, politics, manners. Thus he makes a washerwoman a creature of epic proportions, as sublime as one of Michelangelo's prophets. His clowns and urchins are as noble as the saints of Raphael, and much more vigorous and living; his royal ministers of state, colossal and grotesque in their subversion of justice. With Daumier it was not a question of taking life lightly, of depicting all things with facility and charm, but of painting a few subjects with monumental power. The *Third-Class Carriage* (there are several versions) is a direct view of the occupants of a compartment, the figures plain and bulky but alive with the charity, the strength and the compassion poured into them from the soul of a great artist. It tells the story of forlorn humanity everywhere. —THOMAS CRAVEN

SELF-PORTRAIT

Gustave Courbet

GUSTAVE COURBET

1819–1877

Defiant Showman

YEAR AFTER YEAR the juries rejected—except for one early acceptance in 1844—the pictures Gustave Courbet wanted to get into the Paris Salon. But he talked and blew his own horn, bellowed and threatened, and he attracted a number of younger students to him. He was egotistical, thick-skinned, bellicose. He got around amazingly, and he was self-advertising. In those early days he painted his best pictures—unembellished transcripts from peasant life and strong, exact portraits. Courbet succeeded better than anyone before him in painting figures as nature made them, "without correction."

Born in 1819 in the village of Ornans, near the French-Swiss border, Courbet was the son of a prosperous farmer. The boy had enough education to aim at a career in law but decided upon art instead. He went up to Paris in 1840. His paintings were soon widely heard of, though not through official channels.

The Revolution of 1848, resulting in a change of government as well as a new roster of jurors for the Salon, gave Courbet his opportunity. The next year he received a medal of the second class for a naturalistic picture of Ornans life, an important gain because medalists had the permanent privilege of entering Salon pictures free from jury action. At the Salon of 1850 his monumental work, *Funeral at Ornans,* created violent and bitter controversy. Until then heroic-sized canvases had been reserved for "noble" subjects. That a painter should show contemporary figures—especially "common" figures—in life size was outrageous, an affront to the archaeological and historical painters, and, one would have thought, hardly less than a blow against the foundations of the Republic. During the following five years Courbet repeatedly shocked not only the conservatives but nearly everybody else with his "vulgar" pictures, his socialism, his subversive ideas about art and his boorish manners.

Generations of respectable artists in France had quoted to students a saying of Nicolas Poussin: "A noble subject matter should be chosen, one free of workaday grime." Daumier at this time was not recognized as a painter, and Millet (see page 177) still toiled in darkness. Their "lower-class" pictures remained unknown. But Courbet was too shocking and too insistent to be overlooked. His wholeheartedness, his unreserved vanity, his repeated assertion that he was the only serious artist of the century carried weight with the younger generation.

Although the well-bred painters were no longer able to exclude Courbet from the Salons, their opportunity came to snub the upstart when a great art exhibit was planned for the World's Exposition of 1855. Nothing daunted, Courbet opened a show of his own in a shed opposite the Exposition gates. Over the door he inscribed "G. Courbet: Realism." Nearly forty canvases illustrated his theory and his progress as a painter. A special scandal was caused by the immense picture entitled *A Real Allegory: My Studio After Seven Years of Art Life* (also called *The Artist's Studio).* It showed realistically, in life size, a nude model in mixed company, including the painter at work. It was as near an arranged composition, as near fantasy, as Courbet ever came. But it had little formal design and was heavy-handed as "a real allegory." The painting infuriated both the tender-minded artists and the moralists.

From then on Courbet was the idol of the rebellious students—among whom were Manet, Monet, Renoir and Pissarro—and a front-rank fighter for young authors, like Emile Zola, who were initiating the realistic movement in literature.

Courbet went on to other triumphs in the late eighteen fifties, and in the sixties received great sums for his paintings, especially for his naturalistic nudes. At the opening of the Salon of 1866 the Empress Eugénie was so scandalized at one of his displays that she threatened to close the halls if it was not removed. Such censoring only played profitably into Courbet's game of propagandizing. He had a public success again with his individual exhibit at the World's Exposition of 1867, showing 130 pictures as well as sculptures.

In 1870 the emperor offered to Courbet the decoration of the Legion of Honor. Whether sincerely or because acceptance would have less publicity value than the gesture of refusal, Courbet declined. He wrote his letter of rejection at a café gathering and went out to boast publicly that he had given the emperor "a biff in the eye." It happened that Daumier, also a staunch republican but a silent one, was awarded the Legion of Honor in the same year; he too refused, but without public announcement, explaining merely that he was too old for this recognition to mean anything.

Eighteen seventy was a fateful year for Courbet. As a socialist he was thrilled by the defeat of the Emperor Napoleon III and his surrender to the Germans at Sedan, and more so by the establishment of a republican government. Under the interim regime—before the Germans bombarded and invaded Paris—Courbet was appointed Director of Fine Arts. He busied himself with saving as many of the national art treasures as he could. In 1871 he became a member of the new revolutionary government, the Commune, and he resisted as far as he dared the popular cry for destruction of all monuments reminiscent of life under the monarchy; but he did not save, perhaps did not want to save, the Place Vendôme column built by Napoleon I. After the *communards* were ousted in "the week of blood," he was held responsible by the royalist-minded government for the razing of the Napoleonic column. He was fined and put away in prison for six months.

The following year the conservative painters took advantage of Courbet's disgrace to have his pictures excluded again from the Salon—branding his works as those of an immoral person and a convicted *communard.* Then an immense fine was assessed against him for the rebuilding of the column; when he could not pay it, his belongings, including his unsold paintings, were seized and auctioned.

Courbet fled to Switzerland and died in exile there, stripped of property, broken in spirit, embittered against his own country. For a time, he could not even paint. This was the artist who had written in the flush of his early success: "I stupefy the entire world. I have triumphed over not only the ancients but the moderns. . . . I have thrown consternation into the world of art."

It is said that no painter in France was greatly concerned about his passing. To the conservatives the episode of his triumph had been an aberration, the man himself a figure in a nightmare. It and he had passed, and now French art would settle back, doubtless, into traditional calm. On the other side, the radicals and the young progressives could do without Courbet.

Perhaps he was just as well off exiled in Switzerland during those last years. A young painter named Manet had usurped his place as chief of the rebels and purveyor of scandals, and was developing a type of realism that would become more palatable to the public than Courbet's. At a critical moment Gustave Courbet had come forward. Brutally strong, he blasted open the road for a new type of art; but since 1863, when Manet's associates exhibited the varieties of ways in which a new generation might develop an art beyond realism, the master who had taken painting back to a new beginning in nature, a new transcribing from peasant life, had not been needed.

At his death in 1877, Courbet's works were rising to a new height of international popularity that lasted to the end of the century. But once it became apparent that twentieth-century art was to pivot on painters who had abandoned his natural approach, he lost stature.

Courbet opened the way again for independent men to express themselves in paint; he set an example of virility, masculinity, power; but he was blind to one half of the artist's world—the half variously known as vision, imagination or inspiration.

Part of Courbet's service to the moderns was in his written protests and proclamations. "The museums should be closed for twenty years, so that today's painters may begin to see the world with their own eyes." "Beauty lies in nature. . . . The painter has no right to add to this expression of nature, to change the form of it and thereby weaken it." "Our century is not likely to recover from the disease of imitation by which it has been laid low."

Later artists have answered that it is no better to imitate nature slavishly than to imitate a favorite painter; but Courbet's warning was timely in 1855.—SHELDON CHENEY

THE ARTIST'S STUDIO
Courbet placed the poor on one side, his friends on the other; Truth (the nude) and Innocence (the boy) stand beside him in the middle.

THE ALARM
An eager hunter, Courbet loved to portray animals. And the snow scenes of his home in Ornans (left) rank high among all ever painted.

THE BEAUTIFUL IRISHWOMAN
Whistler graciously permitted Courbet to paint his striking companion and model Jo Heffernan (far left). She was Whistler's famous White Girl.

THE BAR AT THE FOLIES-BERGERE
A spectacular tourist attraction since the 1920's, this was just another music hall when Manet painted the barmaid Suzon in 1881. The panorama in the mirror behind her shows a gathering of Manet's friends.

OLYMPIA
Shockingly casual in her nudity, this subject caused a scandal that destroyed Manet's reputation. The public had seen nudes represented only as storied figures. Yet here was Victorine as herself, a widely known model.

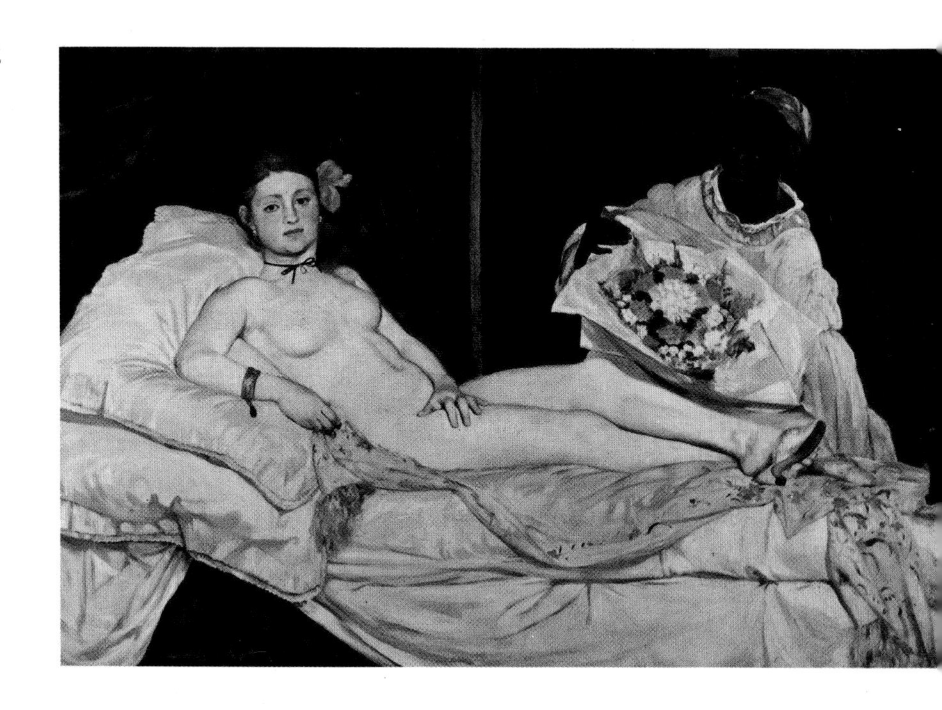

BREAKFAST ON THE GRASS
The bold portrayal of contemporaries stunned Parisians in 1863. The central figure was Victorine, the same model who two years later appeared as Olympia *(opposite page). The men were Manet's brother and his future brother-in-law.*

SELF-PORTRAIT

EDOUARD MANET

1832–1883

Reluctant Revolutionary

EDOUARD MANET MUST HAVE BEEN about thirty-two when his friend Edgar Degas, a couple of years younger, made a drawing of him. If Manet looks older, the thinning hair and the beard are part of the explanation. And the costume, from our distance of a hundred years, looks staid. Actually Manet was something of a dandy, as the spats and the bowler indicate. He might have strutted a bit, for he had a quick eye for women and they for him. But if he strutted it could also have been with some protective defiance, since during the past months the chances were better for his being recognized as a notorious figure than as an artist of consequence.

The story of Manet's life is really that of his battle as a painter, but a few other facts may enlarge the picture of him. Both of his parents came from well-to-do families. His father expected his son to follow him in a legal career. But Manet resisted, begging to paint. They compromised on the navy, and the boy went to sea as an apprentice cadet. In 1849 (he was seventeen) the ship stopped briefly at Rio de Janeiro, a city picturesque enough at that date. There are the usual stories of boyish escapades ashore. When Manet failed his examinations for the navy, his father allowed him to enter the studio of Thomas Couture, a standard academic success of much talent and little imagination. About this time Manet also entered into a liaison with Suzanne Leenhoff, his slightly older piano teacher, and in 1852 she gave birth to a son. Ten years later Manet's father died; in 1863 Manet received his legacy and married Suzanne, although he kept up a fiction that the son was her younger brother. The boy called Manet "godfather," and not until he was nearly grown did he learn his true relationship to his mother and to Manet.

During this complicated business Manet's mother supported the little family. His father never discovered the affair nor, astoundingly, did Manet's friends. His marriage (when the son was nearly twelve years old) came as a great surprise to them. During all these years Manet seems to have been deeply devoted to Suzanne, and he remained so the rest of his life. She was a plump, comfortable Dutchwoman, an expert pianist who took pleasure in joining forces with the elder Madame Manet in musicales at home. She never visited Manet's studio, and one may take the word of whichever biographer one chooses from among those who knew Manet, as to whether he was true to Suzanne, or a great womanizer, or a man of moderate indulgences. The most hackneyed of phrases most accurately states the importance of love affairs in Manet's life: his true mistress and grand passion was painting.

During the spring of 1863 Manet set the pattern for scandalous success in the art world—for attention through outrage—that has been deliberately cultivated for profit by opportunistic artists ever since. He did not need to paint for money; but even if the food on his table had depended on his changing his way of painting to a popularly and officially accepted one, he could not have done so. Although he was a lively leader of the discussions at the Café Guerbois, where a group of young artists met, he was not much of a formal intellectual.

With Manet victimized at its center, the scandal of 1863 marks the beginning of the modern artist as a man whose creative independence is subject to no check beyond his own conscience. Conservative by temperament, Manet could have seemed radical only to the reactionaries who were the entrenched jury of the Paris Salon. Until the end of his life, the reserved and somewhat puzzled man who is revealed in Degas's drawing wanted only one kind of success—the conventional success of popular acclaim and official honors, the success of the ribbon in the lapel.

Paris was the center of the art world and proud of it. The great national exposition, the Salon, was the annual climax when the arts of painting and sculpture, so assiduously cultivated, bloomed to the glory of France. The absolute power of a Salon jury in Manet's time is difficult to imagine today; in its heyday it stood alone and impregnable. Painters with new ideas worked their way into acceptance only painfully and over many years. Even before it met, Manet didn't have a chance with the 1863 jury. He had always been a little troublesome. As a student he had been unwilling to follow without question the teaching of his master. He could be standoffish to the point of snobbishness and was temperamentally incapable of currying favor. For whatever combination of reasons, the Salon jury was ready to cut Manet down to what they thought his size, and his three submissions were thrown out.

The objections of all the rejected painters in 1863 were clamorous and, in a country where the arts were so closely bound to government, the uproar amounted to more than a bit of picturesque unpleasantness in the studios. Napoleon III announced that an auxiliary Salon was to be held in conjunction with the regular one; the rejected pictures were to be hung in a *Salon des Refusés,* and the public was to judge for itself whether the jury was right or wrong. As proof of the jury's fallibility the special Salon seemed, at the time, to have backfired. Whistler had a painting in it; Pissarro (see page 178) had three. But the handful of other names that have become famous were represented by early or minor works that only an oracle could have singled out —with the exception of the three canvases by Manet. The real shocker among these was a painting called in the catalogue simply *Le Bain* ("The Bath"), which soon took on the title it still carries—*Le Déjeuner sur l'herbe* ("Breakfast on the Grass").

Basically, *Le Déjeuner* was a type of painting familiar in the Salon: combining a nude, a section of still life, and some landscape, it permitted an artist to display his skill in a set piece. The only conclusion of public and critics alike was that this fellow Manet was indifferent to moral values and that his picture was indecent. As was pointed out at the time, *Le Déjeuner* could be looked at as a modern counterpart of a Renaissance painting, *Concert champêtre,* by Giorgione (see page 69), where clothed male youths sit in a countryside with two nude females.

The main reason *Le Déjeuner* offended so deeply was that it puzzled, and by puzzling it threatened. A picture so openly matter-of-fact could not be licentious, but lacking any other way to explain it, critics and public fell back upon the stratagem of regarding it as, at worst, an offense against public morals, or, at best, as a laughable failure. We know today what *Le Déjeuner* is: a superb piece of pure painting, of art for art's sake—a translation of visual fact into forms and colors.

There is also no question today about the greatness of another painting that, in 1865, created an even more painful scandal for Manet. When Degas sketched him, the *Salon des Refusés* of 1863 had probably closed, leaving Manet bloody, a little bowed and more widely (if less favorably) known than his academic antagonists. He had either completed or was completing *Olympia,* a modern version of the old theme of the reclining nude, with special reference in this case to a portrait of a courtesan by Titian, the *Venus of Urbino* (see page 72). Manet's Parisian courtesan is a rather chunky girl of the people, arrogant not in her display of nudity but in her indifference to it. There was something brash about this girl's glance, which was infuriating; but there was something aloof, too—which was unforgivable. *Olympia,* this picture of a common girl, happens to be one of the most elegant paintings of its century; and if Manet's critics sensed this, it must have been the final and intolerable violation of their security—a reasonable explanation of their hostility toward it.

Olympia was accepted for the Salon of 1865, perhaps as a safety measure after the emperor's rebuke of 1863 and no doubt in the way an unwelcome guest may be invited to a party by a hostess who plans to give her a bad time. The attacks on *Olympia* were abominable. It was compared to "high" game, and the visitors crowding around it to sightseers at the morgue—which may have been a legitimate comment on the visitors, but not on the painting.

During the decade following Manet's *Salon des Refusés* debut as the Academy's whipping boy, the group of generally somewhat younger acquaintances who were to become known as the Impressionists were having at least equally rough going. If they were less violently attacked than Manet, it was only because they had less conspicuous reputations (a minor comfort) and most of them were going through desperate times financially. By 1874 they had despaired of the Salon as a field of fair battle, and formed a coöperative exhibiting group that held seven shows between 1874 and 1882. Manet, still with his sights set on success in the Academy's own pattern, refused to exhibit with them in spite of the urgings of Degas, whom he most nearly accepted as a close friend.

With his essentially aristocratic reserve—a self-containment that forbade all casual intimacy—Manet, as safely as any man who ever painted, may be identified with his art. His painting was his only manifesto. He seems from the first, and until the end, to have painted the way he did because it was so entirely his own way that modification was impossible. In his withdrawal from storytelling, from idealized statement, from psychological observation and from the pictorial clues that tempt the observer to *read* a painting rather than *see* it as a work of art, Manet was prophetic of the modern painters.

But his greatness is not in his prophecy; it is in the completeness with which he fused the delight of painting with a vivid record of his world. —JOHN CANADAY

MODEL FOR "THE BAR AT THE FOLIES-BERGERE"
Suzon appears here as a brunette—far more dignified than when she was painted as a blonde barmaid (page 142) in the same year. She became the companion of Manet's biographer Edmond Bazire.

SELF-PORTRAIT

Degas

EDGAR DEGAS

1834–1917

Bitter Heart, Dancing Brush

DEGAS DISLIKED MANY THINGS that belong in the normal man's life and many others that the average man finds it easiest to tolerate. He hated his own name Edgar. He came to mistrust and look down upon women. He hated flatterers among art lovers, and medal seekers among artists, and increasingly his wit turned sarcastic and cruel toward them. He disdained the sort of fame that comes with popular success. He sincerely did not want official honors, and they were consistently withheld from him. He disliked dogs, forward children and flowers on dining tables. He was disinclined to let his paintings leave his studio, always hoping to make them better at some future sitting, or, as he put it, "less mediocre." He disliked unconventionality and he loathed bohemianism, yet he lived most of his life in Montmartre and found subjects in the cafés and even in the brothels there.

Degas was born in Paris in 1834 and christened Hilaire-Germain-Edgar de Gas. His father was a successful banker who had married an aristocratic French Creole from New Orleans and maintained establishments in both Paris and Naples. As student and in his early years as painter, Degas was given whatever he needed for a comfortable living and for his work. He studied in Paris—briefly at the Ecole des Beaux-Arts—and became firmly set in the classical tradition. During a stay of several years in Italy he copied the old masters and made sketches for large historical paintings in the orthodox manner. He returned to Paris to spend years on historical works, putting in long hours also as a copyist in the Louvre. It was there that Manet first met him one day in 1862.

Although he became one of the radical group that accepted Courbet as old master of the new art and Manet

REHEARSAL OF THE BALLET ON STAGE

Degas caught the action of the split second: the master coaching the dancers, a girl yawning, a man leaning back in his chair. All the random gestures of the ballet hard at work, he made more dramatic by showing the occasional awkwardness of typically graceful figures. Slicing the edges of the picture through subjects was a device he adapted from Japanese art.

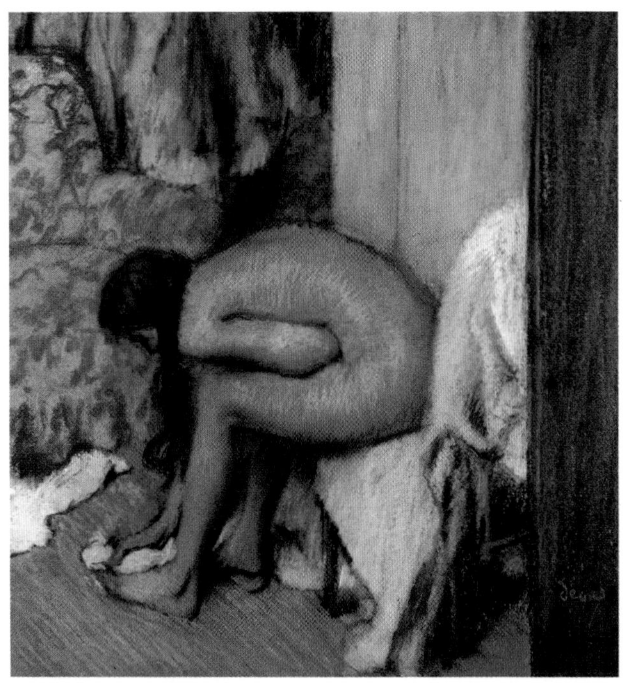

L'ABSINTHE
Two friends of the artist "dressed up" as alcoholics: the engraver Marcellin Desboutin and Ellen Andrée, a beautiful actress, but less than a beauty here.

AFTER THE BATH
His eyesight failing, Degas emphasized form rather than detail in this pastel—one of many works in which he triumphed over his disability.

as immediate leader, Degas was a laggard among the revolutionaries, and his best-known works from the sixties are realistic portraits of members of his family and friends, admirably drawn and proficiently painted, if in general a little hard. As a member of a fellowship of young rebels which met at the Café Guerbois (see page 158), he was shy, not in the uneasy way of Cézanne but with the reserve of the sensitive aristocrat. He was sympathetic to the group's aims, though doubtful of his place in it. He could be both cordial and witty; but he and Cézanne became known as the silent members of the "school," and Degas was to be less guided by it than any of the others. His reserve and unbending attitude in these years were symptomatic of the melancholy and touchiness that were to fasten upon him in later life.

Already, in his midthirties, he found himself dissatisfied with, and ready to abandon, the type of painting which he had as a student mastered with academic brilliance. A certain irresolution was setting in. He vacillated between witty gaiety and sadness, and in his art between the alluring heresies of the café radicals and the sober fundamentalism of those who had trained him.

In 1863 he had been among those rejected at the official Salon, and so was represented in the *Salon des Refusés* (see page 144). But unlike the others of the Café Guerbois group he was admitted to the Salon later in the sixties—sign enough that he was still a conformist and considered sound. Aside from his specialty of portraiture, he began to seek themes where Manet was finding his, in Parisian pleasure grounds. After 1870 Degas would seldom venture away from his chosen group of familiar subjects—racetrack scenes, theater and ballet fragments, laundresses, and women at their toilet.

Degas served as a soldier in the War of 1870, and he felt the defeat more than most artists. Not only had the Germans humiliated and dismembered France; the Republic had taken the place of the Empire, and he was temperamentally antirepublican. Perhaps this led him to embark suddenly for New Orleans, his mother's onetime home, where two of his brothers were prosperous bankers and cotton brokers. He had something of a vacation, painted at will and, not too willingly, did portraits of his relatives. Taken ill, he found himself longing for Paris. He fled for home early in 1873. It is likely that some incident of this time, if not of this visit, led to permanent bachelorhood and the critical attitude toward women that lasted the rest of his life.

Increasingly Degas moved toward the state of a recluse.

A few close friends asked him to dinner in town. In summer he went to visit them in the country, or took rare trips with artist companions. But gradually his life became artificial and thin, and the man neurotic. To his rule of avoiding intimate or frequent contact with women he made one exception: he took the American painter Mary Cassatt (see page 178) as pupil. He became a collector of paintings and of prints and amassed a great number, which he piled unsorted and unseeable against the walls of a storeroom. He joined with the Impressionists (see page 160) in their scorn of the official Salon and never again exhibited there. And his exhibits at the Impressionist shows, unlike those of Monet and Cézanne, brought acclaim and a demand for his pictures.

The theater and ballet scenes began to be a specialty soon after his return from New Orleans in 1873, and they still were after the turn of the century. The sketches of dancers in particular served to create for him a worldwide reputation. At first he made drawings from his seat in the stalls, then took to sketching in rehearsal rooms and on the stage. But the finished paintings and pastels invariably were done in his studio. Degas became celebrated for the spontaneity and verve of his work; it seemed as if he must have caught each attitude and gesture, each nuance of movement instantaneously from the stage performance or the dress rehearsal. The pictures are, however, all studio productions resulting from hard work. Usually, painstaking drawings of the chief figures exist. For the apparently spontaneous outdoor racing pictures Degas had taken only "notes" at the tracks. He had a wooden model of a horse in his studio that "stood still in the proper light." There he also kept ballet dresses and properties, used by the dancers who came to pose.

About 1890, when he had turned to the series of glimpses of women bathing, he had a bathtub specially installed in his studio to afford a semblance of that intimate milieu to which he, as a strict bachelor, had not even the slightest chance of access. They are all models carefully posed with a "prop" tub, those women seemingly caught unawares at the instant of stepping into or out of their bathwater, or toweling themselves, or binding up their hair. There is not the slightest erotic note in his gallery of intimate boudoir and bath scenes. Not one of the girls or women shown can be termed beautiful; they are seldom even pretty. Some critics assert that he was "getting even" with women, as he saw it in his warped mind, by showing them up as common creatures. It is more likely that he was interested solely in pictorial effects. His eye had been caught by certain possibilities at the theater, in the dance studios, at the milliners' and in the laundry shops; and it was easy to have the models in while he worked up the subjects at his Montmartre studio. He had become unemotional: He saw heads and torsoes, arms and legs, bouquets and ballet skirts, as so many lines, masses, accents.

For thirty years after 1873, Degas carried on experiments in what the academicians of his day termed "unconventional" picture-making. Through these experiments he made a contribution toward the manner of modern painting. Japanese art was a persistent and distinctive influence upon him. "Unnatural" angles of sight, figures or furniture or fans placed to afford the eye a starting point for its travel into pictorial space—these and other devices he took from Japanese prints. Toulouse-Lautrec's art definitely stemmed from Degas's. His example was also helpful to Gauguin and van Gogh, among others.

Degas had increasing trouble with his eyes from about 1890 on. It may be that bright color became for him a refuge when blindness seemed actually to threaten. He had long before dabbled in sculpture, and when he could no longer see well enough to paint even sketchily he took up modeling seriously. The little statuettes of horses and dancers, cast in bronze from his wax and clay originals, are divertingly natural. As for his paintings, Degas had, before the end, the doubtful pleasure of seeing his early pictures auctioned at a hundred times the price he had originally put upon them. He did not seriously care. It seemed merely one more sign of the stupidity of man in an age when the good old values of living had been lost.

Degas became a legend among the artists of Paris. Tales of his ill humor, of his inaccessibility and of his cluttered and disordered studio went the rounds. But when near-blindness ended his work, Degas tramped the streets of Paris for hours, restless and lonely, unrecognized by those he met. He had been an elegant in his earlier days, but now he came so near shabbiness that once a shopkeeper handed him a pack of cigarettes out of intended charity. He had to call a gendarme or some passerby to help him at street intersections. For twenty-five years he had lived and worked in a building on the Rue Victor-Massé in Montmartre, but this was torn down and he brokenheartedly moved to other quarters. A last picture of him is given by his friends: an old, despairing man, aimlessly walking, going finally each day to the place where his home had been—to gaze sightlessly into a hole in the ground through cracks in a fence erected by the wreckers. He died at the age of eighty-three, in 1917. —SHELDON CHENEY

SELF-PORTRAIT

JAMES McNEILL WHISTLER

1834–1903

The Embattled American

INCREDIBLE AS IT MAY SEEM, the now-famous portrait of Whistler's mother was rejected by the Royal Academy when it was first offered for exhibition in London in 1872. The jury called it rude bungling. One member of the Academy Council happily thought the picture good enough and threatened to resign unless it was accepted. So it was included in the exhibition. Yet almost all who saw the portrait found it so unconventional as to be inartistic, even funny. People stood before it laughing.

But the misfortune was nothing compared with the ordeal this American artist in London, James McNeill Whistler, suffered a few years later. His pictures were so newfangled they wouldn't sell, and he was desperately in need of money. His mother was gravely ill; he was losing his house because he couldn't meet the payments; his furniture was about to be seized for debt. He had lost his one good customer and this broke off his marriage engagement. To raise money he bartered one of his masterpieces for 50 dollars and a heavy overcoat. He pawned his marvelous painting of Thomas Carlyle for 750 dollars and tried in vain to sell, for 500 dollars, the picture that was to become the most popular of the early twentieth century—the portrait of his beloved mother. And then he got embroiled in a ruinous lawsuit.

The topmost British art critic, John Ruskin, in a vicious review of Whistler's latest exhibition, ridiculed the price of 200 guineas (1000 dollars) that Whistler wanted for one of his pictures of fireworks. It was a *Nocturne,* with flashes of color as rich as crushed jewels. "I have heard of cockney impudence before now," wrote the acid-penned Ruskin, "but never expected to hear a coxcomb ask 200 guineas for flinging a pot of paint in the public's face." This could not be called legitimate criticism. This was libel, and Whistler sued.

The trial, one of the most notorious in the annals of art, was conducted as if in jest. Whistler was treated as a mountebank, and the courtroom rang with laughter. But the embattled artist handled his case skillfully, often turning the tables on his detractors. When Ruskin's attorney demanded how long it took to paint the *Nocturne,* Whistler described it as an inspiration, which he had finished in less than two days.

"You ask 200 guineas for the labor of two days?" the attorney sneered.

"No," said Whistler. "I ask it for the knowledge of a lifetime."

At the end, the trial did render justice. Ruskin was convicted of libel. However, so little was thought of Whistler as an artist that he was awarded damages of one farthing—less than a penny! Now his creditors, learning that his art was so lightly regarded, decided he would never succeed and pressed for immediate payment. Whistler was pushed into bankruptcy; even some of his paintings were seized. He had to borrow the money to travel to visit his mother in her sickbed and pretend to her that all was going well.

A lesser man would have bowed his head in despair. Not Whistler. Slowly from this dark pit of troubles he climbed to brighter fortune. He worked at smaller pictures—etchings, pastels, drawings—and gradually began to make a living. He gave an impressive public lecture, arguing that his pictures of night revealed a beauty seldom discerned by dwellers along the Thames. He summed it up in a few glowing words: "The evening mist clothes the riverside with poetry, as with a veil; the poor buildings lose themselves in the dim sky, the warehouses are palaces in the night, and the whole city hangs in the heavens, and fairyland is before us. . . ."

Whistler's life was filled with uncommon incidents and events. Born in Lowell, Massachusetts, he spent his boyhood in Russia, where his father, an ex-army officer turned engineer, built the first Russian railroad. In his teens James entered the U.S. Military Academy at West Point, but was "bounced" three years later because he was too busy "dawdling" at art to work at his lessons. His mother, a strict Presbyterian, finally consented to his studying painting. After a period as a denizen of the art-student bohemia in Paris, he settled down in London. Here, despite financial difficulties, he was surrounded by beautiful women and a circle of celebrities such as Swinburne and Rossetti. People maneuvered for invitations to his Sunday-noon breakfasts.

PORTRAIT OF THE ARTIST'S MOTHER
Whistler insisted that the identity of a person in a portrait was of no importance, and that the public should not care about it. He titled this painting Arrangement in Gray and Black, *never dreaming that it would become celebrated throughout the world as a symbol of motherhood.*

OLD BATTERSEA BRIDGE
Directly adapted from a Japanese print, this painting was derided for its blurred quality. At the notorious Ruskin trial the defense attorney sarcastically asked if its beauty could be shown to him. Whistler replied that it would be like pouring musical notes "into the ear of a deaf man."

The whole town talked about Whistler's conspicuous dress and quick wit.

It was Clemenceau, then only a young political genius, who gave him his first big boost. Perceiving that Whistler was an extraordinary artist, Clemenceau advised the French Director of Fine Arts to buy the *Portrait of the Artist's Mother* for France's national museum, the Luxembourg. The director wrote, delicately inquiring if Whistler would part with the portrait for 4000 francs (at the time 770 dollars). This was the largest sum Whistler had ever been offered; he gratefully accepted the money and the prestige. France shortly added a further award by promoting Whistler to the rank of Officer of the Legion of Honor.

In Whistler's most controversial days, Oscar Wilde had jested that "popularity" was the "only insult" that had not been offered to the American. Yet he won fame and financial ease in the last decade of his life, and today his recognition is worldwide. —MALCOLM VAUGHAN

THE ARTIST IN HIS STUDIO

Homer

WINSLOW HOMER

1836–1910

Man and the Sea

THE GREAT WAVE CRASHED around him with an explosive roar. Spray flew in every direction. But the man who was studying this wave was snug and dry. He was working in a small waterproof cabin with a large plate-glass window, mounted on runners and anchored to the shore.

The time: early twentieth century. The hour: just after daybreak. The gale the night before had been one of the roughest the rocky Maine coast had experienced in years. The man warmed his hands at a little stove, then hurried back to the canvas on which he was recording the storm-swept ocean. The picture was destined to be one of his masterpieces, *Early Morning After a Storm at Sea.*

Winslow Homer, then one of America's foremost artists, enjoyed the roar and riot of wild waters. The

BREEZING UP
Although Homer was later famous for portraying the unruly ocean, the serene seascape above won him his first recognition in 1876.

THE LIFE LINE
As he prepared to paint this picture (far left), Homer had a lifesaving crew show him the use of a breeches buoy in rescues from ship to shore.

THE GULF STREAM
For women horrified by his castaway's fate (left), Homer wrote: "Tell these ladies that the unfortunate Negro . . . will be rescued and returned home."

rougher it got, the more violently the surf crashed, the more he reveled in it. Although he occasionally painted the ocean when it was calm, he is best known for his pictures of raging waves, the perils of the sea and the men who strive against its power. Some people thought Homer eccentric because he had become a hermit. Legend in his family says there was a woman involved, a woman he didn't marry because he couldn't afford her. We know that he kept, where he could always see it, a painting of a pretty brown-haired girl with large dark eyes. She held a hand of cards and looked straight at you. The title of the picture was *Shall I Tell Your Fortune?*

Whatever the reason, Homer, in 1883 at age forty-seven, built himself a little house on a wild, craggy promontory jutting into the Atlantic. He did his own cooking, gardening, wood-chopping. To a friend who suggested visiting him, he wrote: "I have never yet had a bed in my house. No other man or woman within a mile, and four miles from railroad and post office." Once an art collector who had come up from New York to pay homage to the great artist stopped a poorly dressed fisherman roaming the cliffs and said, "I say, my man, if you can tell me where to find Winslow Homer I have a quarter for you." "Where's your quarter?" the fisherman flashed back; then, pocketing the money, said, "I am Winslow Homer."

The ocean was not originally Homer's specialty. He began as a magazine illustrator, painting old-time American rural life—harvest dances, cornhusking, Thanksgiving and Christmas on the farm, the one-room schoolhouse.

When the Civil War broke out, a magazine sent him to the front as an "art correspondent." Scenes of war soon made him famous. His first major work, *Prisoners from the Front,* became the best-known American picture of the time. The artist was a celebrity overnight. Yet, at the peak of his success as an illustrator, Homer turned his back on it and thenceforth devoted his days to nontopical painting. He cut himself off from family and friends, sailed for England and settled in a tiny Northumberland fishing village.

It was then that the sea became his dominant theme. Two years later—his art changed as if he were another person—he returned to the United States and moved to the Maine coast. There he painted during the remaining twenty-seven years of his life the most tremendous series of sea pictures ever produced by an American, varying his Maine-coast scenes with paintings made during winter trips to Florida, Bermuda, Nassau. From such a trip came his famous *Gulf Stream.*

In Homer's paintings, as he grew older, human beings gradually played a smaller and smaller role, probably because he himself was so solitary. Now he seldom painted the ordeals of men who go down to the sea in ships, or disaster wreaked by the sea, but rather the grandeur of the ocean and its never-ending battle against the shore. "There was something in that solitary soul which responded with passionate joy to the call of the tempest," wrote a biographer, William Howe Downes.

Unlike many artists, Homer, for all his rugged life, never suffered hunger. He had no trouble selling his pictures. In time they brought large sums—up to 6000 dollars each. In recent years three have brought 50,000, 60,000 and 75,000 dollars respectively. Even one of his watercolors has now sold for 25,000 dollars.

Decade after decade Homer climbed to new heights of achievement. In his last years he was painting better than ever. Once he was asked where he got his talent. "There's no such thing," he came back. "What they call talent is nothing but the capacity for doing continuous hard work —in the right way."

—MALCOLM VAUGHAN

SELF-PORTRAIT

Renoir.

PIERRE AUGUSTE RENOIR

1841–1919

In Love with Life

IN A LARGE square room on the second floor of New York's Metropolitan Museum, visitors come to a stop and stand with a smile on their lips. They have caught sight of Pierre Auguste Renoir's portrait, *Mme. Charpentier and Her Children.* The great French artist lavished all the skill and inspiration he could muster on this 5-by-6-foot canvas. The two hundred dollars he got for it was an exceptional price for a picture in France at the time. Adding this to the even smaller amounts he had been paid for three other portraits in the Charpentier family, Renoir decided to improve his living conditions. He rented a little house in Montmartre, the artists' quarter of Paris, bought some

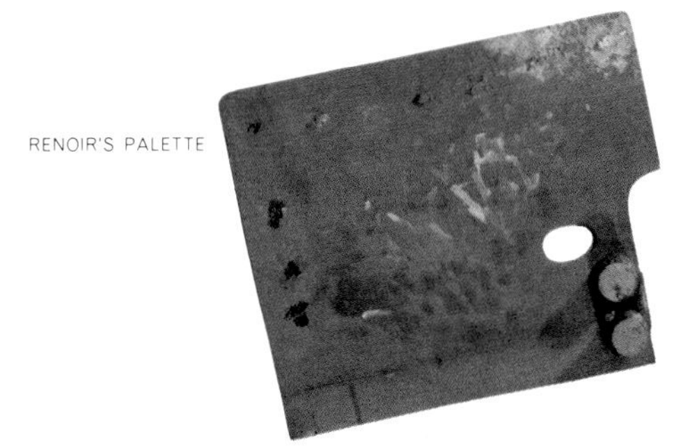

RENOIR'S PALETTE

LE MOULIN DE LA GALETTE

The young, unknown Renoir often visited the art colony of Montmartre before moving his studio there. Scenes of this lively café—named for its "galette," or pancake—were also done by Toulouse-Lautrec, Picasso and others.

BATHERS

Renoir's favorite model was Gabrielle (nicknamed "Ga"), the maid of the house. She posed for both of the bathers in the foreground, and for many other canvases. "Do you need Gabrielle in the kitchen today?" he would ask his wife. Madame Renoir did not like Ga to pose, and set up flower arrangements for him to paint.

MME. CHARPENTIER AND HER CHILDREN
The success of this picture launched Renoir's career. Perhaps no one has ever matched the enchantment of his family portraits—which he resumed painting later, when he had children of his own.

LADY AT THE PIANO
Society lady or commoner turned model? It is not certain, but she may be chestnut-haired Margot—a girl who might have posed for Renoir more often if she hadn't been "noisy." He liked quiet models.

badly needed paints, furniture and a new suit of clothes. And he gleefully said, "If I keep this up, I can afford a wife!" He already had a girl: a plump, blue-eyed, peaches-and-cream little dressmaker who was so much in love with him that she was eager to share his hand-to-mouth existence. Now he felt he could afford to marry her.

Renoir had been born to poverty. So when by the age of thirteen he showed artistic talent—he covered the margins of his textbooks with creditable drawings—his parents took him out of school and apprenticed him to a china manufacturer. There he decorated dishes with everything from floral sprigs to medallion portraits of the reigning Empress Eugénie.

When the factory failed four years later, Renoir made a living at other hackwork—painting fans, window blinds and pictures of saints at a dollar a saint. By the time he had saved up money enough to take art lessons, he was twenty-one, comparatively unlettered.

In art school Renoir was so happy that one of his teachers cracked down on him, snorting, "Painting seems only an amusement to you!" Another teacher insisted that before he could paint he must learn to draw from plaster-cast copies of marble Greek gods. Renoir obediently turned out five lifelike drawings of them. The teacher informed him that gods could *not* be lifelike. "A god must have a more majestic big toe than the toe of the local coal man!" This academic twaddle fell on Renoir like water on a duck's back. He learned the basic principles of art and he used them to paint in his own original way.

Together with Monet, Renoir pioneered the flick-fleck, dot-dash technique of painting that came to be called Impressionism. The two young artists—both within a few months of the same age—were nearly destitute in the late sixties. Renoir, thankful whenever he got a meal at his father's house, often took food to Monet.

Like his fellow pioneer, Renoir spurned the "brown mud," "green soot" and "silver haze" tones which were fashionable in his day. He turned, instead, to the colors of sunlight: bright, prismatic reds, blues, yellows and greens, with shadows running from lavender to purple or deep blue. Whatever he painted—a landscape, flowers or human beings—he preferred to work outdoors where colors were richest. They more fully expressed his intense love of life.

How far Renoir might have gone had he not painted Madame Charpentier and her children no one can say. Almost from the day the portrait was finished a marvelous tide of events began to turn in his favor. Madame Charpentier, wife of one of the richest publishers in Paris, was a celebrated hostess. She hung the portrait in her parlor, where it was seen by men and women of wealth and renown—Emile Zola, Gustave Flaubert, Guy de Maupassant, Stéphane Mallarmé, Edmond de Goncourt. She pulled the strings which landed the portrait in the great annual national art exhibition, the Paris Salon, and she used her influence to have his work shown by art dealers.

Suddenly other portrait commissions began coming to Renoir. These financed him while he painted pictures which were to make him even more famous than his portraits—sun-drenched flowers, landscapes, beautiful nudes and grouped or single figures in glowing scenes. Three years later he married his little dressmaker and swept her away on a honeymoon to Italy.

Perhaps it was her young plumpness that inspired his ideal of what a woman should look like. In any event, across the years, he developed in his pictures a type of woman not unlike her: thickset, robust, able-bodied; a woman with sun-kissed skin, large breasts, great hips—Renoir's symbol of health and fertility.

Meanwhile, the happy hubbub of a home with growing children (the Renoirs had three sons) launched him on a series of family pictures. We see the youngsters learning to eat, learning to play, learning to read, to write and to work with their hands.

In his book *Renoir, My Father,* Jean Renoir relates an incident which shows his father's complete absorption with painting. When Paris fell under the Commune in the 1870's, Renoir was out with his easel set up beside the Seine even while the bombardment went on. A guardsman, accusing him of making a map of the area bordering the river, hauled him away to the firing squad at the town hall. There, a friend who was an officer of the Commune caught sight of Renoir, embraced him and marched him to a balcony. To the crowd below, the officer shouted: "Let us sing 'The Marseillaise' for Citizen Renoir!"

"After this incident," Jean Renoir writes, "my father went right back to work again. . . . 'The devil of it,' he said, 'is that the light changes so quickly.' "

The world is always smiling in Renoir's pictures. We see it in his portraits as well as in his rainbow-tinted, almost luminous landscapes. We find no trace of the days when he was hungry or the years of struggle through which he passed on his climb to fame. During the latter part of his life he became crippled by arthritis, but his deformed hands never lay idle. Down to his last canvas in 1919 he let no unhappiness dim the buoyant, vibrant vitality of his art.

—MALCOLM VAUGHAN

SELF-PORTRAIT

CLAUDE MONET

1840–1926

Follower of the Sun

WHEN THE TWENTY-SEVEN-YEAR-OLD painter returned from the country to Paris to see the son that his mistress Camille had just presented him, he was completely without funds. His pictures, which had never found buyers, were seized and sold for a pittance to pay his debts. Not long after this he attempted suicide. The present price of only one of Claude Monet's canvases would have permitted him to live out his long life in luxury. His painting of Camille and their baby was sold in 1965 for $504,000.

He married Camille and she gave birth to a second son before she died of malnutrition in 1879. Monet noted: "Alone in the world with two children, without a penny ahead of me."

The young artist undergoing this period of poverty and anguish had received early encouragement. He was born in Paris, but his father, a grocer, had moved the family and the business to Le Havre, where Claude revealed an unsuspected aptitude: he made caricatures of customers, schoolmates and teachers, or people he noticed on the streets. After the models proved willing to buy these sketches for modest sums, Monet's drawings were shown in the window of a local framer, where the painter Eugène Louis Boudin saw them and suggested that he should go on to serious work.

So, at the age of nineteen, Monet journeyed to Paris. Here, like so many of the young artists of his time, he made copies of paintings at the Louvre. He attended the Swiss Academy where he met Pissarro (see page 178), whose ideas were to have great influence on Monet's art. At night he went to the cafés. They were the real trying ground for the newer, more revolutionary concepts in both literature and art. At the Guerbois, Nouvelle Athènes and other such

WATER LILIES

Monet loved flowers, and became devoted to wat lilies, creating about sixty paintings of them. Many other canvases he destroyed, when he felt his brush had failed to capture their beauty. "I no longer sleep because of them," he once said.

TULIP FIELDS

While on a trip to Holland to paint scenes of windmills and canals, Monet chanced upon this brilliant scene (right). For him, to see was to paint. "That man is nothing but an eye," Cézanne said of him. "But what an eye!"

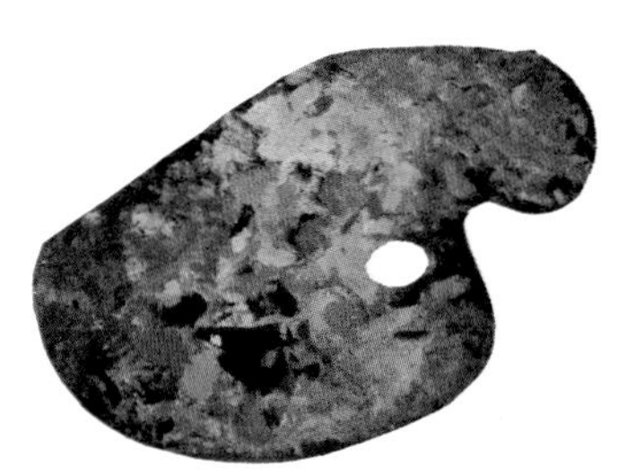

MONET'S PALETTE

meeting places, artists, poets and musicians gathered, argued and fought until the early hours of the morning, began or ended friendships, formed schools, launched movements, drew up credos. With the young Monet in the turbulent Café Guerbois group were the painters Degas, Pissarro, Renoir and Cézanne.

In the Salon of 1865, when Monet was but twenty-five, he had a measure of success: two of his seascapes were praised by the critics. About this same time he met Manet and Courbet and was influenced by both these more mature and experienced men. Monet's love of nature lured him to the country. At Bougival he painted alongside Renoir. Often both artists would render the same scene in friendly rivalry. In 1871, on a trip to London, he was introduced to the picture dealer Paul Durand-Ruel, who sold so many of his pictures in later years.

Most of Monet's finest work was done after 1873, when he was established at Argenteuil. Here he constructed a studio on a small boat, and, sailing slowly up and down the river, he painted those scenes and lively events which attracted him. By now he was the recognized leader of the new school and, along with Pissarro, was one of its ablest spokesmen.

Then, in 1874, Monet and his group staged an exhibition of their own—the first of seven they would hold in the next decade. So absurd did the critics find Monet's title for a picture, *Impression—Sunrise,* that one of them labeled all the canvases in derision as "Impressionistic." The men who exhibited their works for the first time, some thirty of them, were automatically dubbed the "Impressionists." As Courbet and Delacroix had fought their own battles against academic standards and shibboleths, so now did the Impressionists create a new movement. For Monet and the others had a firm belief in a new attitude toward the visible universe, and had developed a revolutionary manner of depicting it in color. In part, theirs was a greater concern with the out-of-door world as it appeared under varying conditions of light. They observed that a brilliant sun would so bathe a subject that outlines became vague and undulating, and colors were not neatly defined at their edges. So they tried to represent on canvas what the eye saw, and not the aspect of the objects as the *mind* knew them to be.

At one time or another, Manet, Degas, Cézanne, Toulouse-Lautrec, Gauguin and van Gogh tried their hand at producing works according to this formula. Later Signac and Seurat carried the color theory even further. But most of the painters mentioned broadened the early concepts and went off independently. By 1880 the original members were painting in diverse manners and the movement—called Impressionism—was practically at an end. Its influence on future painters was destined, however, to last for a long time.

The period of struggle for Monet was about over in 1880: he had a one-man showing of his paintings and his work was finding reception everywhere, by critics and collectors. Most of his time was now spent at the seashore or in the country; he painted the landscape at Fécamp, Poissy and Giverny, where he was to live until the end of his life. Now he was honored, and prosperous, and could afford luxurious flower gardens, lily ponds and even a private boathouse. He began to make new experiments with color, introducing pure and strong pigments into his palette. Critics and poets wrote articles analyzing and praising his works.

In 1890 he began his "systematic" studies of the effect of sunlight on the same subject from dawn to twilight. He painted, time and again, a group of haystacks in a field, as well as the facade of the cathedral at Rouen. Each day, when conditions of light were similar, he came back to the site of his painting to work on a canvas for just so long as the effect of the sunlight remained fairly constant. Then he would discard a canvas and continue with another, carrying on from where he had left it the previous session. Thus he captured, as no other man in the long history of art, the ephemeral and transient aspect of objects under changing conditions of light.

He embarked in 1902 on the masterwork that would occupy him for the last quarter-century of his life: the *Water Lilies,* an extraordinary ensemble of paintings which were installed permanently in a small building dedicated to Monet in the gardens of the Tuileries in Paris. In the Musée de l'Orangerie there are two oval rooms decorated with a continuous mural depicting the lily ponds just outside his home at Giverny. The same scene is shown as it appeared to his sensitive and poetic eye, from that time when the morning sun first lighted up the sky until at dusk it disappeared below the horizon. Here is the finest efflorescence of Impressionism in art, and the most fitting monument to Claude Monet. Not only did he give the movement its name; he was its most serious and tireless practitioner. Through a long lifetime of painting he produced hundreds of pictures which are today treasured as the purest examples of what this rebellion against the conventional represented. His name has almost become a synonym for Impressionism. —HERMAN J. WECHSLER

A READER'S DIGEST GUIDE TO PAINTERS AND PAINTINGS

Here, in the biographies of great painters, appears the story of how great paintings came into being—and of how the treasury of Western art was created by an extraordinary chain of personal events. Not only the genius of these men, but their loves, their peaceful or turbulent surroundings, their rivals and enemies—all had a role in the making of the world's finest pictures. Biblical scenes, battles, the beauty of the human form, landscapes and portraits: the array of masterpieces was shaped by the times in which their creators lived.

In order that this continuous human drama of art may be seen, these biographies have been arranged chronologically through seven centuries, from the life of the first important Western artist—Giotto—to Andrew Wyeth, an American now in the prime of his career. To locate a particular artist's biography, refer to his name in the index, where the appropriate page number is indicated in bold type.

References to a particular painting are also given in the index, by title; if the work is illustrated in the book, the page number is italicized.

To find the name of the museum, church or art collection where each painting in this book is located, consult the list of Picture Credits on page 191.

Finally, there are a number of terms that appear from time to time in the story of art—such as *frescoes, perspective* and *Impressionism.* The references to these are included in the index, indicating for each a definitive description on the page whose number is shown in bold type. For example, the reader will find an explanation of perspective on page 47, in the article about Uccello, the foremost fifteenth-century creator of visual depth.

GIOVANNI CIMABUE *Italian, 1240?–1302?* Almost nothing is known of the life of this legendary medieval artist. He worked together with other artists on mosaics, decorating churches in Florence, Rome and Pisa. But it was in painting the frescoes of the upper and lower churches of St. Francis at Assisi that his

CHRIST ON THE CROSS

major role in the drama of art occurred. Here he began a work that was completed by young Giotto, his pupil, who was to become the first great painter of the Western world. The poet Dante wrote:

Cimabue believed that in painting
He held the field, but acclaim for
Giotto is heard
And the fame of the former is
obscured.

GIOTTO *Italian, 1276?–1337.*
See article on page 41.

DUCCIO DI BUONINSEGNA *Italian, 1255?–1319*
A number of documents have come down to us about Duccio, the father of

THE CALLING OF THE APOSTLES

Sienese painting, and they are by no means all flattering. He was extravagant and did not pay his debts; more than that, he was an unruly man who again and again was forced to pay fines for various offenses to the government of Siena.

Yet he was a painter of the greatest talent and taste, a man whose pictures were the most gracious that the world had then laid eyes on. He was the artist who, above all others, had to be considered when a great work of art was wanted. And in Siena, in the year 1308, a great work was wanted: an altarpiece for the cathedral. The contract which the trustees made with Duccio provides amusing reading. They admired him, but they prudently laid out all the conditions. They guaranteed to supply him with everything needed, and he was charged with completing the picture by his own hand in three years.

For once everything worked out. Listen to a contemporary account of the celebration which occurred when the painting was finally finished: "On the day that it was carried to the Duomo [Cathedral] the shops were shut; and the Bishop bade that a goodly and devout company of priests and friars should go in solemn procession, accompanied by the Nine Magistrates and all the officers of the Commune and all the people; all the most worthy followed close upon the picture, according to their degree, with lights burning in their hands; and behind them came the women and children . . . the bells sounding joyously for devotion of so noble a picture as is this."

Those who came after Duccio had their own genius, but none surpassed him in the decorative style of Siena.

Outstanding works: *The Calling of the Apostles Peter and Andrew; Maesta; Virgin and Child Enthroned; The Marys at the Tomb.*

SIMONE MARTINI *Italian, 1284?–1344*
The great Italian poet Petrarch once wrote, "Surely my friend Simone was once in Paradise . . ." It would seem so. The paintings of Simone Martini are among the most lovely, the most paradisical that have come down to us. He was of the second generation of Sienese painters and a follower of the master, Duccio. Little else is known about him.

He was much sought after. He worked for the king of Naples, he painted in Pisa and Orvieto and decorated a chapel in Assisi. But his best works were done at home in Siena.

The exiled Pope summoned him to Avignon, France, about 1339. It was his final honor; he died there. The influence of his fastidious draftsmanship was a force for generations in Siena.

Outstanding works: *St. Francis; St. Martin Being Made a Knight; Annunciation; Guidoriccio da Fogliano; Coronation of the Virgin.*

ST. MARTIN BEING MADE A KNIGHT

STEFANO DI SASSETTA *Italian, 1392?–1450*
What we think of as the Renaissance—that is, the first great wave of invention and experiment in painting—surged forward in Florence. It rarely touched Siena, which remained a medieval town, and is so to this day. Sassetta was her last great painter. Born Stefano di Giovanni, he lived and worked almost all his life in Siena. (For some reason, he was named "Sassetta" by a writer in 1752, and he was known that way afterward.)

He took as his exemplars Duccio and Simone Martini—but he was also one of the first Sienese painters to use the innovations of the painters of Florence.

What we know of Sassetta as a man we can learn only from his paintings. But that is considerable: first of all he was a man of extraordinary taste. His

JOURNEY OF THE MAGI

drawing is delicate and inventive, his color pure and brilliant. He was an affectionate man: there is a feeling of tenderness and warmth in almost everything he did—sometimes there is even wit. And he was a religious man: his pictures have a spiritual quality equaled by very few artists.

We are fortunate in having several of his masterpieces in collections in the United States, including some in Washington, D.C., and New York.

Outstanding works: *Journey of the Magi; Madonna of the Snow; Polyptych of St. Francis; Birth of the Virgin.*

MASACCIO *Italian, 1401–1428*
His real name was Tommaso di Giovanni and he was one of the few giants of painting who died young. Probably because he was awkward, untidy and extremely absentminded, he was nicknamed Masaccio—"Big Lug Tom." But if he was absentminded, it was because he had time only for his art. Born near Florence, he spent most of his short life there. Masaccio had scarcely more than ten years to learn his trade, develop his theories and paint his masterpieces.

THE TRIBUTE MONEY

Whatever they called him, his contemporaries treated him with a respect that bordered on awe. Masaccio's discoveries influenced artists throughout the Renaissance; during the next hundred years men such as Botticelli, da Vinci, Michelangelo and Raphael went to the Brancacci Chapel in Florence to study and copy his works. He led the way in perspective and foreshortening which affected painting for more than four hundred years. No other artist achieved so much in so short a time.

Then suddenly, just after his twenty-seventh birthday, Masaccio disappeared in Rome. There were stories that he was poisoned or killed in a street brawl, but nothing is certain.

He was deeply in debt, according to the tax rolls of Florence. Perhaps absentmindedly, Masaccio neglected to obtain the money owed him by his patrons, or squandered all he had.

Outstanding works: *The Tribute Money; Crucifixion; Expulsion of Adam and Eve; Trinity of the Virgin.*

HUBERT and JAN VAN EYCK *Flemish, 1366?–1426; 1370?–1440.*
See article on page 44.

ROGER VAN DER WEYDEN *Flemish, 1399?–1464*
In about his thirty-sixth year, Roger van der Weyden was appointed City Painter of Brussels. And so great was the esteem in which he was held that no one was ever appointed to succeed him. The city fathers did not believe they could find his equal.

Van der Weyden was born in Tournai, now a city of Belgium, but he married a Brussels woman, and settled there sometime after his apprenticeship was over. In Brussels he achieved fame and a comfortable fortune.

In 1450 van der Weyden went to Italy. It would be easy to suppose that he was the first of the long line of northern painters who went south for inspiration, but such was not the case. The year 1450 was a great jubilee year of the Church, and Roger went to Rome seeking an indulgence from the Pope.

He did stop in Florence, apparently, where he painted at least two pictures for the Medicis. But he was fifty, already famous, and his style was formed. He had little to learn from anyone.

He was a painter of great elegance, a colorist the equal of the van Eycks, and a master of dramatic composition. Above all, he was deeply religious. His portrait of Peter Bladelin praying has been praised as "the purest effigy of adoration known to painting."

THE DEPOSITION

Many works by van der Weyden are in the United States, notably in Philadelphia, Washington, D.C., New York, Boston and Chicago.

Outstanding works: *The Deposition; Portrait of a Lady; Pietà; Antoine de Bourgogne; Portrait of Peter Bladelin.*

JEAN FOUQUET *French, 1420?–1480?*
No one knows what mission took Jean Fouquet—the first major painter to appear in France—from his native country to Rome in his midtwenties. Had he not gone, he would have remained a great book illuminator; easel pictures had not yet appeared in France. In his *Chevalier Hours,* a prayer book, he revealed the exquisite detail of the superb miniaturist he was.

THE STONING OF ST. STEPHEN

His exposure to the early masters of Italy made his paintings popular with members of the French court. But, though the light and shadow of his modeled figures bring to mind the works of the Italians, his ornate treatment of surfaces shows the influence of book illumination.

Legend holds that Fouquet's life at court was not without at least one spectacular artistic misadventure. He caused a scandal by painting a picture of the *Virgin and Child*! The event is not so improbable as it sounds, for his model as Mary was Agnès Sorel, mistress of King Charles VII, and in the conventional manner of courtesans of the time, the lady's bosom is exposed. To the French public this was blasphemy—but not to the king. Fouquet not only kept his job but became painter to the court under Charles' successor, Louis XI.

Outstanding works: *Etienne Chevalier and His Patron St. Stephen; Virgin and Child of Melun; The Stoning of St. Stephen,* miniature from *The Book of Hours of Etienne Chevalier.*

PAOLO UCCELLO *Italian, 1397–1475.*
See article on page 46.

FRA FILIPPO LIPPI *Italian, 1406?–1469.*
See article on page 48.

FRA ANGELICO *Italian, 1387?–1455*
It is safe to say that Fra Angelico is the most beloved painter of the Renaissance. His colors are so pure, his people so beautiful, his backgrounds so glittering with gold—he is so uncomplicated, so happy—that everyone can understand and delight in his pictures.

At about the age of twenty Guido di Pietro—his real name—entered the Dominican order at Fiesole, near Florence. From then until he reached almost forty

FLIGHT INTO EGYPT

we do not know exactly how he occupied himself, but it is reasonable to suppose he had some kind of art training.

His great opportunity came in 1437, when the ruler of Florence, Cosimo de' Medici, gave the Dominicans the Convent of San Marco in his city. Angelico was appointed to oversee all the interior decoration. He made more than fifty frescoes—many of them in the cells of the brothers—which in their simplicity and beauty have seldom been surpassed. With the inauguration of the convent, which the Pope himself attended, Angelico became famous.

It was a fame he did not want. For he was said to be a devout man who prayed each time before he began to paint and whose cheeks were wet with tears when he worked on a *Crucifixion*. He wished to remain obscure, a servant of God.

But twice papal summonses brought him to Rome, and from these visits we have inherited the Niccolina Chapel in the Vatican, which is still radiant with his colors. According to Vasari, the sixteenth-century biographer, Pope Nicholas V admired him so much that he offered to make him Archbishop of Florence. Angelico declined, but he did serve for three years as Prior of the Convent of San Domenico at Fiesole.

It is hard to find the human being behind this saintly man. Perhaps only once does his human side show through, and that is in his great *Last Judgment*, where this staunch Dominican painted a number of Franciscan Friars—and placed them in hell.

Outstanding works: *Flight into Egypt; Coronation of the Virgin; Annunciation; Angel Musicians; Last Judgment.*

PIERO DELLA FRANCESCA *Italian, 1418?–1492*
In many ways there was no painter in the second half of the fifteenth century to compare with Piero. But he did all his work away from the large cities of Rome and Florence—in Arezzo and Urbino, in Borgo San Sepolcro and Ferrara, in northern Italy. All, that is, with one exception—his frescoes in the Vatican, and these are gone. Just after Piero came those giants Michelangelo, da Vinci, Raphael. It is said that Pope Julius II ordered the Vatican frescoes of Piero, Perugino and others whitewashed, and engaged Raphael to paint new works over them (see page 68).

Piero's reputation declined, partly of course because his pictures were so hard to visit. Hundreds of years later—toward the end of the nineteenth century

THE NATIVITY

—he was rediscovered and restored to his rightful position. His portrait of the Duke of Urbino is now recognized as one of the great portraits of the world, and his masterpiece, the series of frescoes in the Church of San Francisco in Arezzo, ranks among the half-dozen most magnificent achievements in that form.

We know little about Piero. We know he was born in Borgo San Sepolcro; we can date his progress from town to town; but about the man we can only surmise.

We also know he was interested in mathematics, in fact wrote a treatise on perspective, and his pictures give a feeling of mathematical precision. His colors are cool. His figures are heroic, almost Greek in feeling and sternly honest.

Outstanding works: *The Nativity; Federigo, Duke of Urbino; Queen of Sheba; Resurrection.*

ANDREA DEL CASTAGNO *Italian, 1423?–1457*
Unfortunate charges darken the reputation of Andrea del Castagno—the worst of them, at least, false. He was famous throughout Florence for a temper that even by Renaissance standards was furious; his first documented painting, now

YOUTHFUL DAVID

lost, was the curiously morbid depiction of two hanged criminals; and he was charged by the gossipy biographer Vasari with the murder of his teacher and rival, Domenico Veneziano. There is proof, though, that Castagno died four years earlier than Veneziano—which disposes of at least one charge.

However hot his temper, Castagno was extremely influential among the artists of Florence, a master of perspective and the adapter of the sculptural style of Donatello into painting. He is renowned for his group portraits, *Famous Men and Women,* which included *Boccaccio, Petrarch* and *Dante.*

Outstanding works: *Youthful David; The Last Supper; Dante* (from *Famous Men and Women*).

ANTONIO POLLAIUOLO *Italian, 1432?–1498*
Pollaiuolo was an early example of the Renaissance man of universal talents. He was not only a painter, but a goldsmith, a sculptor, a ceramist, an engraver—even a maker of embroidery patterns—as well. He was born in Florence, the son of a poultryman presumably, and early apprenticed to a goldsmith. But he must have done everything at once, for sometime in his late twenties (we know this from a letter he wrote) he was a good

enough painter to be commissioned by Lorenzo de' Medici, of the ruling family of Florence, to execute three large canvases on the labors of Hercules.

The large pictures are lost, but Antonio himself made small copies, and in them we are able to glimpse for the first time his ferocious interest in anatomy. It is for his experiments and inventions in the drawing of the nude male body that Antonio is most famous. His celebrated engraving, *The Battle of the Nudes,* inspired not only Signorelli but so gentle a painter as Botticelli, who may have adapted its composition for his *Primavera.* Pollaiuolo was also an influence on da Vinci and Michelangelo.

There is an interesting incident in connection with two of his small *Hercules* panels. For years they hung in the Uffizi Gallery in Florence, but sometime during World War II they disappeared. Then — mysteriously, dramatically — nearly twenty years later they turned up hanging in the living room of a house in Pasadena, California. The owners were not aware of the treasure they possessed.

HERCULES KILLING THE HYDRA

Now, happily, the panels are back in Florence where they belong.

Outstanding works: *Hercules Killing the Hydra; The Battle of the Nudes; David; St. Sebastian.*

HUGO VAN DER GOES *Flemish, 1440?–1482*
A great painter rarely ends up in a madhouse: a clear and powerful mind is too necessary a part of his equipment. But there have been unhappy exceptions; Hugo van der Goes was one.

The first sure date we have for him is 1467, when he was admitted to the Painters' Guild in Ghent. From then on his rise to fame was spectacular. There are many mentions of him in the Guild records—he was made its dean in 1474. The following year, suffering from extreme depressions—a first breakdown—he entered the monastery of the Red Cloisters, near Brussels, of which his half

ADORATION OF THE SHEPHERDS

brother was a member. He did not stop painting; in fact it was there that his masterpiece was done. This was the *Portinari Triptych,* an altarpiece which now hangs in the Uffizi Gallery in Florence and is certainly one of the most splendid paintings by a foreigner there.

It was commissioned by Tommaso Portinari, a powerful banker who represented the Medici family in Bruges. It is an immense work, about 19 feet long and 8 feet high, on the theme of the Adoration of the Shepherds. A composition of genius, magnificently painted—it is hard to believe that an unstable mind could have conceived such a picture.

The monks did everything they could for him: the Father Superior even had music played for him to calm his frenzies. But the painter died when he was no more than forty-two, hopelessly insane.

Outstanding works: *Portinari Triptych; Portrait of a Man; Death of the Virgin.*

HANS MEMLING *Flemish, 1440?–1494*
Memling was a quiet man. After the passions and experiments of his countrymen van der Weyden and van der Goes, he was content to make pictures that were calm, tender, beautiful—and popular. He may have studied with van der Weyden in Brussels, but after the time of the master's death and the breakup of the studio, he moved to Bruges, where he lived the rest of his life.

Memling's success is shown by the fact that he became one of the creditors of the government of Bruges. And he was an honored citizen. The Hôpital St. Jean, a religious house, ordered many paintings from him. The Hôpital is now a museum, known for its many beautiful works by Memling.

He produced a great body of pictures which are now scattered over the world. His portraits are excellent; the subjects always appear serene and untroubled.

In contrast to his own sedate life, one of Memling's pictures figured in a melodramatic incident. This is his *Last Judgment,* an enormous composition commissioned by Jacopo Tani, a wealthy Italian in Bruges. When the picture was finished it was sent off to Italy. But at sea the ship was captured by pirates, who took their prize back to Danzig. There they presented the picture to the Church

SEVEN JOYS OF THE VIRGIN

of Our Lady, where it still hangs today.

Outstanding works: *Seven Joys of the Virgin; Madonna and Child; Adoration of the Magi; The Mystic Marriage of St. Catherine; The Shrine of St. Ursula.*

GENTILE AND GIOVANNI BELLINI *Italian, 1429?–1507?; 1430?–1516.*
See article on page 50.

ANDREA MANTEGNA *Italian, 1431–1506*
Before the age of ten—he may have been an orphan—Mantegna was taken into the household of a painter named Squarcione. When the boy was enrolled in the Painters' Guild of Padua he was described as Squarcione's "adoptive son," though the relationship was apparently nothing so gentle as "son," because when Andrea reached twenty-four, he went to court to win his release from his "father."

But Mantegna's stay in Squarcione's house was of vital importance to his career, for his master's studio was a meeting place for the professors of the University of Padua. From them Mantegna acquired his knowledge of the classical world of ancient Rome.

Mantegna was a corrector and an innovator, a tough and fastidious workman; a whole generation of painters were to look on him as master. When he was twenty-two he married the daughter of Jacopo Bellini, and her two brothers, Gentile and Giovanni, eagerly followed

CIRCUMCISION

his style (see page 50). By the time he was twenty-eight and had finished an altarpiece at the church of San Zeno in Verona, his fame was such that he had offers from everywhere. He chose to go to Mantua, where the rulers, the Gonzagas, were the great art patrons of that time. He stayed there, off and on, for the rest of his life. For the Gonzagas, Mantegna did his masterpiece, the decoration of the bridal chamber in their palace.

Like so many artists, he was a man hard to get along with. The Gonzagas treated him with kindness, indeed with forbearance, considering his truculent behavior. He lived in constant need of funds, for Mantegna was cursed with that most expensive of diseases: art collecting. His collection must have been a great one—Lorenzo the Magnificent came away from it envious.

Mantegna's death in 1506 was as momentous as that of a ruling Gonzaga, but the fit of apoplexy that carried him off came as no great surprise to anybody.

Outstanding works: *Circumcision; Dead Christ; St. James on His Way to Execution; Gonzaga Family.*

ANDREA DEL VERROCCHIO
Italian, 1435–1488
Verrocchio holds a peculiar position in the history of painting. Various pictures are ascribed to him by various critics, but there is only one which all experts agree is surely his—the *Baptism of Christ* in the Uffizi Gallery in Florence. And even in that painting, one of the angels and the background are attributed to the young Leonardo da Vinci.

Verrocchio lives through artists on whom he was a powerful influence: Leonardo, Perugino and Ghirlandaio, to name only the most celebrated. He was an extremely conscientious workman, insisting upon elegance and care and dignity. Think what a blessing he was in the training of the young da Vinci, who entered his workshop at the age of thirteen and stayed for more than ten years. Leonardo's genius was nothing if not mercurial; he needed a strong hand to tame and control it.

Verrocchio's real fame rests upon his sculpture. His *David* is a marvel of aristocratic poise. And his powerful Colleoni monument in Venice is one of the greatest equestrian statues ever made.

BAPTISM OF CHRIST

Outstanding works: *Baptism of Christ; Virgin and Child;* and—possibly by Verrocchio—*Tobias and the Angel.*

SANDRO BOTTICELLI *Italian, 1444?–1510.* See article on page 52.

PERUGINO *Italian, 1445?–1523*
As a rule, an artist's temperament and personality are reflected in his work. Perugino was an exception to that rule. Though he was an atheist, his pictures of religious subjects are among the most serene and beautiful that have ever been

FRANCESCO DELLE OPERE

painted. His lovely Madonnas and saints are set in soft and spacious landscapes. He was Raphael's teacher, and as such influenced the style of Italian painting for a long time after.

He was born Pietro Vannucci in Perugia, taking his name from that hill town in central Italy. Along with da Vinci he studied in Florence at the studio of Verrocchio. In his midthirties he had completed a series of frescoes in the Sistine Chapel in Rome and was one of the most celebrated artists in Italy. Commissions poured in from everywhere, and for the rest of his life he executed them with an almost uniform greatness.

Yet when Perugino died he was refused Christian burial, along with other victims of the plague that killed him. This man—whose whole life had been dedicated to the painting of Marys and saints and Christs—put his trust in money, not immortality. He had not cared who knew of his atheism. However, in due time, the members of the confraternity of the Annunciation transferred his remains to their church.

Outstanding works: *Francesco delle Opere; Crucifixion; Entombment; St. Michael; The Holy Family.*

LUCA SIGNORELLI *Italian, 1445?–1523*
Signorelli was, with Perugino, one of the most famous of the Central Italian artists before Raphael. Our knowledge of the first part of his life is sketchy: we know that he was born in Cortona, studied with Piero della Francesca, but was most influenced by the anatomical works of Pollaiuolo.

Signorelli's masterpiece—frescoes depicting the *End of the World* in the cathedral at Orvieto—is not ennobling, but it is powerful and terrifying, in its great masses of naked bodies.

There is an enlightening story told about him. One of his sons was murdered, and Signorelli, though heartbroken, sat down and sketched the body of the dead young man. Later he incor-

ANGEL

porated the sketch into his painting of the *Entombment*, which is in Cortona.

Raphael imitated Signorelli's structure, and Michelangelo himself was affected by his handling of the heroic nude.

Outstanding works: *Angel; Souls of the Damned; End of the World.*

DOMENICO GHIRLANDAIO *Italian, 1449–1494*
Ghirlandaio was a painter who was contented with the time and place in which he lived. Florence was at the height of her glory—no other city in history except Athens has ever been more concerned with art—and all Ghirlandaio wanted was to make the most of his every opportunity.

The son of a goldsmith, his aim was to please. In one of his first frescoes, a *Madonna of Mercy*, he has so crowded the composition with portraits of the family who ordered the picture that the Madonna seems almost an afterthought. This was the way to please—and to find customers; and find them he did. His output was enormous and popular right up to the end of his life.

His studio was almost a factory; it was overflowing with assistants and apprentices. No commission was ever turned down. Anything would be painted, from the handle of a basket to a *Last Supper*.

Ghirlandaio's real importance lies in his portraits—he has left scores of them. They are among the best ever painted and are said to have influenced Raphael. One of Ghirlandaio's claims to fame he never lived to know about. While he was working on his final frescoes in the Florentine Church of Santa Maria Novella, there was a brash young apprentice climbing about on the scaffolding. We have no way of knowing whether Ghirlandaio even really noticed him, but probably he did. For it is likely that sooner or later the pupil—Michelangelo

GIOVANNA TORNABUONI

Buonarroti—got in the master's way.

Outstanding works: *Giovanna Tornabuoni; Old Man and Boy; Birth of the Virgin.*

JEROME BOSCH *Flemish, 1450?–1516.*
See article on page 76.

VITTORE CARPACCIO *Italian, 1465?–1526?*
Carpaccio has left us some of the most splendid spectacles of Venice that we have. The last of the great storytelling artists, he stands aside from the mainstream of art. In his day the high Renaissance was at hand, with its monumental religious and classical works.

He is a surprising artist, for he has left us a few pictures which are quite at odds with his usual manner. One is his *Courtesans*. Here he has painted two women in full sunlight, and the truthful view he

COURTESANS

has given of their empty, tragic life is completely modern in feeling.

Lightly regarded by his contemporaries, he was already almost forgotten when he died. It was only a hundred years ago that the great critic John Ruskin helped to rediscover Carpaccio and set his reputation on the road to the esteemed place it enjoys today.

Outstanding works: *Courtesans; St. Ursula.*

LEONARDO DA VINCI *Italian, 1452–1519.*
See article on page 56.

ALBRECHT DURER *German, 1471–1528*
It could not have been easy for Albrecht Dürer to leave Italy and return to Germany. "I shall freeze at home, longing for the sunshine of Venice," he wrote. But he knew he must leave, and because he did he was able to establish a bridge between the great Italian age and his own northern tradition. Few men are able to lift the level of their own times so that all artists may walk on higher ground, but Dürer was such a man.

In Italy, Dürer had found not only a new art, but a new kind of life for artists. In Germany painters were regarded as artisans; here they associated with scholars, philosophers and other prominent people, and were greatly admired. Still, as a painter, Dürer knew he would never be able to say what he had to say in an alien land. He had grown up in a sterner climate. When he returned to Germany in 1507, he was a painter with a new outlook—and a very specific mis-

SELF-PORTRAIT IN A FUR COAT

sion. He would not only continue to develop his craft, he would develop his mind as well. In the breadth and depth of his interests he had only one equal—the great Leonardo. Dürer also felt a responsibility to share what he had learned.

Fortunately his role of missionary was made somewhat simpler by his being an engraver. He knew he could turn out hundreds of pictures which might "instruct as well as please," and since engravings were smaller than paintings, they could be transported anywhere and even produced in such quantities as to fall within the price range of almost everyone.

Born one of eighteen children, Dürer served the usual apprenticeship, then traveled for several years before settling in Nuremberg and marrying a girl his family had picked out for him. According to some accounts, she soon developed into a nagging shrew. At any rate, he promptly set out on a brief trip to Italy. Later, when he made his famous series of woodcuts, *The Apocalypse,* he went to Italy again to execute a painting for a group of German merchants in Venice. With this work—*The Feast of the Rose Garlands*—the acknowledged master of the woodcut also earned the Italians' praise for his painting. Even Bellini, the grand master of Venetian art (see page 50), requested one of Dürer's pictures and offered to pay well for it; the great Raphael sent him a work of his own.

When Dürer returned to Nuremberg, his next thirteen years were devoted to studying and writing and work on engravings and paintings which combined the monumental forms of Italy with his own human touch. He was trying—somehow always successfully—to capture the loftiness of Rome and at the same time to bring his subjects down to earth and make them meaningful to his own people. When we consider that these were years when Germany was going through the emotional strains of the Reformation and breaking away from the Roman Catholic Church, we can begin to sense his genius.

In 1520 he traveled again, this time to the Netherlands, and again he was lionized. His carefully kept journals give full details of the banquets and parades tendered in his honor. On his way home, always curious, he wandered into the swamplands of Zeeland—he had heard a rumor that a whale had been washed ashore. Here he contracted a fever that was never to leave him. His last years were spent mostly in writing, and in 1528 he died.

It has been said that Dürer was his own best subject—and surely he was his best biographer. At thirteen he did a drawing of himself, perhaps the greatest adolescent picture ever drawn: for the man is completely foretold in the boy; the eagerness, the curiosity, the determination are there.

Outstanding paintings: *Self-Portrait in a Fur Coat; Sts. John, Paul, Peter and Mark; Portrait of the Artist as a Young Man* (three); *The Feast of the Rose Garlands.*

LUCAS CRANACH THE ELDER *German, 1472–1553*

The life of Lucas Cranach has all the elements of a success story. He was living in Germany as a Catholic in the age of the Reformation—and at the same time was a close friend of Martin Luther's. He had good associations on both sides. What a fascinating character this Cranach must have been!

He learned painting from his father, an engraver, in whose shop he worked; and he traveled widely in the Danube country, painting serious, almost macabre, religious pictures. In 1505 Cranach was called to Wittenberg to become a court painter for Elector Frederick the Wise of Saxony. As a courtier his style of work, as well as of living, underwent many changes; on a diplomatic mission to the Netherlands he was exposed to the Flemish masters, who also affected his style. In time, he was made a noble. When he returned, his portraits were suddenly in great demand. Fortunately, along the way Cranach had developed a keen business sense. He now employed assistants, and his studio became a veritable assembly line. He illustrated books and sold them. He held a monopoly on the sale of medical drugs and at one point was even given a patent on the printing of the Bible. Still he found time to turn out propaganda pictures to help Luther hasten his Reformation.

This extraordinary productivity never let up. Cranach continued to paint his handsome scenes—usually with a most lifelike animal worked into the composition. It was said that his stags "were so natural dogs barked when they saw them." Even more remarkable were his nudes. These beautifully painted, slender young women are unlike any other nudes in Western art—for they have great humor. No other painter had succeeded in putting humor into a portrait of a nude without seeming coarse or lewd; but even though these merry women wear necklaces, bracelets and, sometimes, ridiculous hats, they never appear self-conscious. They are Cranach's masterpieces, and he painted them with a charm all his own.

VENUS AND CUPID

Some critics have held that he tried too much, that he might have been a greater painter if he had not been such a successful one. Even Dürer commented once that Cranach could "depict the features, but not the soul," and indeed in Cranach's self-portrait we see more of the successful dignitary than we do of the artist. His tombstone states simply "pictor celerrimus" (fastest painter), but that may not be the whole story. Cranach was a man who shared the actions and passions of his time, and he left paintings that delight, amuse and impress us.

Outstanding works: *Venus and Cupid; Nymph of the Spring; Duke Henry of Saxony; Venus.*

MICHELANGELO BUONARROTI *Italian, 1475–1564.*
See article on page 60.

RAPHAEL SANZIO *Italian, 1483–1520.*
See article on page 65.

GIORGIONE *Italian, 1477–1510.*
See article on page 68.

TITIAN *Italian, 1477–1576.*
See article on page 71.

ANDREA DEL SARTO *Italian, 1486–1530*
While an apprentice in the studio of Piero di Cosimo in Florence, del Sarto went often to draw from the famous Leonardo and Michelangelo sketches hanging in the Council Hall of the

PORTRAIT OF A YOUNG MAN

Republic. It was from these models that the young and soon-to-become-famous Andrea learned his trade. He was enormously admired in his own lifetime. At the age of twenty-three he began a series of frescoes which, on their completion eleven years later, brought him acclaim as the equal of Raphael.

Apparently he was an easygoing young man who enjoyed life with his fellow artists in Florence. He belonged to a couple of dining clubs, he recited comic poetry—and he fell in love with a married woman. As rarely happens in the resolution of such triangles, the husband suddenly died, and in 1517 Andrea was able to marry his Lucrezia. In 1518 he accepted from the king of France an invitation to come to Paris. But he was moved by the appeals of the lonely Lucrezia; so in less than a year, promising faithfully to return, he went home to Florence. When he left, the king gave him a sum of money for work that he agreed to do in the future; with the money Andrea built a house for Lucrezia and never returned to Paris. He painted for the rest of his life, and all his women, all his Virgins and Madonnas somehow resembled Lucrezia.

His reputation is no longer what it was when he was alive. He is recognized as a supreme technician, but he lacked the genius of a very great painter.

Andrea del Sarto died of the plague about 1530. Lucrezia lived on for nearly forty years. For all his adoration of her, it is said that she led him a tragic life: according to the people who knew her, she was faithless, jealous and overbearing.

Outstanding works: *Portrait of a Young Man; Madonna of the Harpies; Madonna del Sacco; The Last Supper; St. John the Baptist.*

ANTONIO ALLEGRI DA CORREGGIO
Italian, 1498?–1534
One thing can be said for the Italian people of the Renaissance: they had good taste. When a great painter came along—and it happened with dizzying frequency—he was immediately recognized, he was appreciated, he was rewarded. Raphael lived like a prince, as did Titian and others. All this makes it difficult for us to understand the scant recognition Correggio received from his contemporaries. Without doubt he was one of the supreme painters of Italy.

He was born in Correggio, near Parma in northern Italy, and never ventured far away. As a youth he was in Mantua, where he saw the marvelous pictures of Mantegna. From these, it seems certain, he developed his mastery of perspective and foreshortening.

His masterpieces are in Parma, where he frescoed the domes of the Church of San Giovanni Evangelista and of the cathedral. These domes he has transformed into cloudy glimpses of heaven, peopled by hordes of angels, of Evangelists, of church doctors. The profusion, the vitality, the joy of life are unforgettable. You have to go to Michelangelo's Sistine Chapel to find a ceiling more awe-inspiring.

The cautious citizens of Parma were resentful. Looking at the tangle of legs of the ascending angels in the dome of the cathedral, they called it a "frog pond."

ANTIOPE ASLEEP

In fact, there is a legend that they were so displeased that they called upon Titian to look at it: the price, they said, was far too high—did he not agree? Titian told them that if they turned the dome upside down and filled it with gold ducats, the sum would not be too much to pay.

Correggio died at forty, at the height of his powers, but unmourned. It was a hundred years before a stone was put on his grave.

Outstanding works: *Antiope Asleep; Mystic Marriage of St. Catherine; Jupiter and Antiope; Nativity*

MATHIAS GRUNEWALD *German, 1480–1528*
For years, less was known about Grünewald than about any other great artist. His first biographer tells us only that "he lived a solitary and miserable life and was wretchedly unhappy in his marriage." Later art historians, digging through ancient documents, unearthed

mentions of his name showing that he was an unsuccessful engineer.

Such data may be of interest to historians, but they give us no picture of the artist. He remains a mystery and a wonder. His fame rests now upon his

CRUCIFIXION

incredible *Crucifixion,* part of a large four-winged altarpiece he painted for the monastery at Isenheim. When open, this reveals, in luminous colors, scenes of great joy and exultation: the glad tidings of the Annunciation told by the angel to Mary, a heavenly orchestra playing for the amusement of a happy Madonna and Child, and a triumphant Christ rising in a burst of glory. When the two outer panels are closed, one picture appears, the gruesome, overpowering Crucifixion—by far the most emotional rendition of death ever attempted in art. Christ—larger and more Godlike than the mortals who surround Him—is all too human in His agony. He has been beaten and is now covered with bruises, sweat and dried blood.

Painting in a Germany that was feeling the influence of the Italian Renaissance and concerned primarily with disciplined, "reasonable" art, Grünewald dared to portray a tragedy—one not of Italy, or Germany or even of ancient Palestine, but rather one that cries out from deep within the artist himself.

Historians may continue to search for information about Grünewald; doctors may even argue about his anatomical drawing; but most men who stand before his *Crucifixion* are silenced by the thought of the suffering the artist must have known. We are awed by the miracle of anyone transcending such anguish and placing it on canvas.

Outstanding works: *Isenheim Altarpiece; The Mocking of Christ; St. Dorothy; Portrait of a Man.*

HANS HOLBEIN *German, 1497?–1543.*
See article on page 78.

FRANCOIS CLOUET *French, 1510?–1572?*
His father's name was Jean Clouet, and out of respect for this great man who had taught him so much, young François often signed his paintings "Janet," the name his father used. The elder Clouet had come to France from the Netherlands, married a Frenchwoman and been appointed an official court painter. When the father died, his estate reverted to the crown, since he was legally a foreigner. But just after his death a court order declared that the estate should be returned to his family and that his son should continue in the father's role as court painter. According to the document, François had "followed his father very closely in the science of his art." Therefore his salary was to begin where his father's had left off.

François did more than follow. In his careful, lifelike portraits he surpassed his famous father and most of his contemporaries. In a period when the artistic activities of the French court were primarily decorating ballrooms or copying Roman pastoral scenes, when kings traveled from castle to castle constantly surrounded by bevies of courtier-painters, Clouet lived simply in a small house near that of an apothecary. Here under four successive monarchs he met and painted most of the eminent men and women of Europe, yet he continued to live and to work very much as would any other

DIANE DE POITIERS

industrious craftsman of his generation.

His scrupulously detailed portraits speak to us of his time and of the nobles who posed for him. In their eyes we see reflected their personal feelings, their fears and hopes. But perhaps they also tell us something of the artist Clouet. Except for his paintings of Diane de Poitiers—lifelong mistress of Henry II—his most important portrait is of a private citizen, his neighbor Pierre Quthe, the sensitive, highly intelligent apothecary.

Outstanding works: *Diane de Poitiers* (two); *Elizabeth of Austria; Henry II; Pierre Quthe.*

PIETER BRUEGHEL *Flemish, 1520?–1569.*
See article on page 81.

TINTORETTO *Italian, 1518–1594*
Tintoretto is supposed to have nailed a sign on his studio wall: "The drawing of Michelangelo, the color of Titian." Whether this is so or not, it tells us a

ORIGIN OF THE MILKY WAY

great deal about his ambition, and indeed his achievement.

This last of the giants among native Venetian painters was born Jacopo Robusti, and was nicknamed after his father's profession—a dyer, or tinter.

Tintoretto was a man of enormous ambition, with a desire for fame so overwhelming that he had little time for the amenities. For the most part he was self-taught—Titian threw him out of his studio after only a few weeks. He achieved success at twenty-seven with his *Miracle of St. Mark.*

A famous story illustrates his temperament. The Confraternity of San Rocco announced a competition for a painting of their patron saint. Many famous painters were invited to compete. When the day came for the judging, the contestants arrived with their sketches—except Tintoretto, who brought a huge finished painting. That was the way he worked, he said; he hoped they would understand. Needless to say, he got the job, and in fact soon after signed a contract as official painter for the Confraternity. He worked intermittently on its two great halls and their anterooms for nearly thirty years.

In his way he was able to marry the style of Michelangelo and the color of

Titian, but the result was wholly Tintoretto. He wrought his own miracle by a new and dramatic use of light, with which he gave form to lithe, monumental bodies and picked up lush color as well. His pictures often give the feeling they were painted just as a storm was passing.

His output was enormous. He had orders from Philip II of Spain and the Gonzaga family of Mantua, but he cared really only for fame in Venice. It is there you must go to see most of the marvels Tintoretto accomplished.

Outstanding works: *Origin of the Milky Way; Flight into Egypt; Miracle of St. Mark; Venetian Senator; St. George Killing the Dragon; The Crucifixion.*

PAOLO VERONESE *Italian, 1528–1588*
The circumstances of Paolo Caliari's youth probably do much to explain his artistic behavior as a man. It was perhaps in reaction to the dreary poverty of his early years that this son of a stonecutter of Verona—the town for which he was named—painted the kind of picture he did: the most stylish, the most sumptuous, the most opulent of Venetian art.

He was twenty-five when he arrived in Venice, already an accomplished master. The life of the rich city seemed just what his brush was waiting for. He loved the brilliant society, its ease, its pomp, its frank enjoyment of all the good things in that day of flourishing materialism.

His picture *Marriage Feast at Cana* illustrates his method. Cana was the scene

FINDING OF MOSES

of Christ's first miracle, the turning of water into wine, and the feast at which it took place was most likely a simple one. But it was a jovial miracle and Veronese set out to elaborate on it: Beginning with a marble pavement, he constructs a series of levels with columns, archways and balconies, and peoples the scenes with more than 100 guests. And what guests! Francis I of France is there, the Sultan Suleiman the Magnificent, Vittoria Colonna, a noblewoman and friend of Michelangelo. In the foreground he has painted himself with Titian and Tintoretto, playing viola, bass and cello. The picture has about as much religious significance as a photograph of a fancy-dress ball, but it does have unparalleled splendor.

This lack of religious feeling once got him into trouble with the Court of the Inquisition. He had painted a *Last Supper.* In his usual manner he laid it in an enormous palace, crowded it with hordes of people—even "modern" German soldiers and a dog. The Court did not approve. Veronese defended himself on the grounds of artistic license—after all Michelangelo had introduced nudes into the Sistine Chapel—but he failed to move the Inquisitors. They ordered him to correct the picture at his own expense. What he did was change its title: it hangs now in the Venice art school, the Academy, and is called *The Feast in the House of Levi.*

Outstanding works: *Finding of Moses; The Feast in the House of Levi; Marriage Feast at Cana; Mars and Venus.*

EL GRECO *Spanish, 1541–1614.*
See article on page 84.

CARAVAGGIO *Italian, 1573–1610*
Caravaggio shocked his contemporaries. He painted what he really saw, and they did not approve.

Michelangelo Merisi, called Caravaggio after the small town in northern Italy where he was born, arrived in Rome while still in his teens. For a few years he painted lighthearted pictures of Bacchus and gay youth; then suddenly he turned to extremely dramatic religious subjects. He continued these almost exclusively for the rest of his life.

An early commission from a church, *The Calling of St. Matthew,* caused such a scandal that the church rejected it. The Romans of the time could not accept a picture of the saint portrayed as a common peasant with dirty feet. It was not Caravaggio's only picture to be rejected. The Church of Santa Maria del Popolo would not accept his *Conversion of St. Paul,* and the Church of Santa Maria della Scala called his *Death of the Virgin* blasphemous. Always before, people had been used to seeing the Virgin touched with glory; Caravaggio painted a peasant woman, obviously dead.

Fortunately Caravaggio had a few influential admirers. These were the rich connoisseurs of the day—both in and out of the Church. They bought his paintings and protected him. But the people, including his fellow artists, hoped to

THE CALLING OF ST. MATTHEW

discredit his pictures and slandered him.

He gave them some cause for their charges. He was arrogant; he was reckless, a lover of low life; and he killed a man in a duel. In fact he had to flee Rome. He spent the next three years wandering, and died on a beach near Naples shortly after being released from a brief imprisonment for some misadventure.

But the influence of his strange new dramatic lighting outside Italy was enormous, especially on the Spaniards Ribera and Velázquez. It was Peter Paul Rubens who advised the Duke of Mantua to buy the rejected *Death of the Virgin.*

Outstanding works: *The Calling of St. Matthew; Death of the Virgin; Bacchus; Supper at Emmaus.*

PETER PAUL RUBENS *Flemish, 1577–1640.*
See article on page 87.

FRANS HALS *Dutch, 1581?–1666.*
See article on page 96.

ANTHONY VAN DYCK *Flemish, 1599–1641.*
See article on page 90.

GEORGES DE LA TOUR *French, 1593–1652*
A seventeenth-century historian has told us that Louis XIII so admired La Tour's *St. Sebastian* and considered it "in such perfect taste that the king had all other paintings removed from his chamber,

leaving only this one." Later scholars, however, have doubted Louis's motives. According to them Louis was visiting in Lorraine near the home of La Tour during the plague of 1633 and, knowing that the best way to ward off a plague was to place oneself at the mercy of this

ST. SEBASTIAN

kindly saint, he chose St. Sebastian. La Tour at this time had painted many saints; always happy to make a copy, he presented Louis with a *St. Sebastian.* The king, fearing that the other pictures on his wall might distract him at his prayers, or even be distasteful to the saint himself, had all but La Tour's carted away.

Whichever interpretation is true, we know that later French kings—and especially Louis XIII's successor—had a disastrous effect on the reputation of Georges de La Tour. He was a powerful and a very simple painter who told Biblical stories in terms of humble everyday life. His are "night pictures" in which the beam of a single candle often blocks out all distracting details while illuminating the faces and thoughts—even the souls—of his characters.

It was this very simplicity that became disagreeable to Louis XIV. La Tour's humanity seemed anti-aristocratic and utterly opposed to the classical art which the king at his grandiose Palace of Versailles was trying to impose upon France. But that any man—even one as forceful as Louis XIV—could so completely destroy the reputation of a great artist that his name would remain unknown for almost three hundred years is one of the most incredible stories of art. In histories of his own province you will find no mention of Georges de La Tour. Not until our times have scholars, searching through ancient churches and museums, rediscovered his masterpieces and restored La Tour to his rightful place among the great painters of France.

Outstanding works: *St. Sebastian; Fortune Teller; Education of the Virgin; Joseph the Carpenter.*

NICOLAS POUSSIN *French, 1594–1665*

Nicolas Poussin was born and spent his early years on a farm in Normandy; his mother was illiterate, a sheriff's daughter, and his father a soldier in the army of King Henry IV. It was a strange beginning for one who was to become the great intellectual artist of France.

His fascination with art began when he saw a painter decorating a church and he begged for lessons. Then, when the church assignment was completed and the painter had moved on, young Nicolas ran away to Paris to continue his studies. Soon after his arrival at the capital he discovered a set of reproductions of the works of Raphael—an event which was to alter his entire life. He knew then that somehow he must get to Rome—to study there "in the birthplace of all true art." For nine years he worked at all manner of jobs, saving every franc. Twice he even set out for Italy, but twice was forced to return. Finally, one of his jobs was to illustrate a book of poems, and the results were so pleasing that the author not only arranged other commissions but gave Poussin letters of introduction to a few prominent Romans.

At last in Rome, he waited four years

ARCADIAN SHEPHERDS

before being presented to Cardinal Barberini, who ordered him to create a painting based on the death of the Roman, Germanicus. Poussin produced a masterpiece, and from that day on he was offered more work than he possibly could accept. He settled down and began, slowly, methodically, developing his theories of art. He read constantly—especially the technical writings of Dürer—and he examined old masters, looking always for the reason that lay behind various kinds of beauty. He was seeking, not an emotional inspiration, but some concept to guide him in his work. In fact, Poussin was never a man to trust emotions; he regarded them as a sin, a weakness he must learn to control.

In 1640 Cardinal Richelieu ordered him to return to Paris to work on the great hall at the Louvre. He was reluctant to go, and found the petty jealousies of the French court so depressing he left as soon as he could. Back in Italy, he turned more and more to the Bible and mythology for his subjects, but the actual story his pictures were telling was of small interest to him—his concentration was riveted on form. One unusual theme keeps recurring: In the foreground we see his characters, in the background a group of magnificent ancient buildings; and between the two lies a vast body of water. Is Poussin saying that the past (the background) is always there, but that we are always separated from it?

Because of his absorption with such ideas, Poussin often neglected color, and today most of us miss this element in his paintings. His disciplined, precise compositions have continued, however, to exalt other artists. In 1944, almost three hundred years after the death of Poussin, Picasso created a *Bacchanalia* based, he proudly admitted, on a painting by Nicolas Poussin.

Outstanding works: *Arcadian Shepherds* (two); *The Funeral of Phocion; Venus Asleep; Orpheus and Eurydice; The Holy Family on the Steps.*

CLAUDE LORRAIN *French, 1600–1682*

At a time when France was importing art—and artists—wholesale from Rome, when Paris itself was called "an Italian island," a few Frenchmen reversed the trend and spent their lives in Italy. Among these few was Claude Lorrain, a simple, uneducated, contented painter.

Born in the province of Lorraine, he was trained as a pastry cook. Orphaned at twelve, he somehow made his way to Rome, where he was employed by a landscape artist. He cooked, helped in the studio and, most important of all, he learned the first rudiments of art.

In his early works Lorrain's style was somewhat marred by the fashions of his time, which demanded that some symbol of antiquity—a broken column or an ancient statue—be present in every canvas. He undoubtedly also was influenced by his neighbor and friend, the intellectual Poussin, but he gradually broke free and gave himself completely to the one overwhelming passion of his life: realistic pictures of nature.

He loved the Italian fields, he loved the sun moving, changing the colors of distant hills. He would arise before dawn to watch the first beginnings of light—and stay out of doors all day, sketching, mixing colors, trying to catch the subtle differences. Then he would hurry back to his studio to capture the glories he had beheld. If he continued to add occasional characters to his canvases, it was perhaps done merely to satisfy customers who could not respond as he could to the miracles of light.

This former pastry cook was called an "inspired idiot," but by working directly with nature he captured a kind of sunshine never seen in painting before. With no formal training and no intellectual approaches to distract him, he added his own special light to the world of art, a light that was to influence the whole Impressionist school of painting two hundred years later.

MARRIAGE OF ISAAC AND REBECCA

Outstanding works: *Marriage of Isaac and Rebecca; Flight into Egypt; Cleopatra at Tarsus; The Embarkation of the Queen of Sheba.*

DIEGO VELAZQUEZ *Spanish, 1599–1660.*
See article on page 93.

FRANCISCO DE ZURBARAN
Spanish, 1598–1664
For an artist to live at the same time as a genius can be both a blessing and a curse. We do not know how much inspiration Zurbarán derived from Velázquez, but surely the shadow that has fallen across his art is due in part to the overwhelming brilliance of his friend.

Zurbarán went to Seville when he was about sixteen, and several years later his reputation was established. He did not remain in Seville, but retired to a small town where he met and married the first of his three wives. The important commissions at this time came primarily from religious institutions; monks and priests wanted pictures to honor their saints and founders. The talent of this simple, pious man seemed ideally suited to such a task, and it was not only Spain that appreciated him. Zurbarán was one of the first masters whose pictures were exported to the colonies in South America and Mexico.

LEMONS, ORANGES AND ROSE

Strangely, most of his best work was done during his younger years, as if he had been driven by a youthful religious fervor. Later, he seemed to have worked himself out. Many reasons have been given for this. His export pictures may have been painted too hastily—or with less refinement, in an effort to appeal to the more rugged taste of the New World. Also, by the time Zurbarán was middle-aged the young painter Murillo had become quite popular, and there are signs of his trying to capture something of Murillo's sugary touch. Such sweetness somehow appears incongruous and a little sentimental on Zurbarán's somber canvases.

In 1658 he traveled to Madrid, perhaps to seek help from his old friend, but Velázquez was to live only two more years. Zurbarán stayed on at the capital and in 1664 he died, and few marked his passing. It was not until Napoleon's armies invaded Spain almost 150 years later that his pictures were rediscovered. Many of them were requisitioned and carted off to the Louvre and other northern galleries, where they still hang, giving us a strong, colorful view of Spain in the seventeenth century.

Outstanding works: *Lemons, Oranges and Rose; Death of St. Bonaventure; St. Casilda; Fray Jerónimo Pérez.*

REMBRANDT VAN RIJN *Dutch, 1606–1669.*
See article on page 98.

JAN VERMEER *Dutch, 1632–1675.*
See article on page 104.

GIOVANNI BATTISTA TIEPOLO
Italian, 1696–1770
Many artists open doors or windows to let sunshine flow into a room, but Tiepolo blasted off the very roofs of churches and palaces to give us a view of the sky and the heavens soaring above. Because most eighteenth-century painting had dealt with religious subjects in a solemn, highly serious manner, Tiepolo's exuberance must have been quite a shock. Indeed, in his student days he too had worked with a somber, dark palette, but in the year 1719 he married the painter Guardi's sister and immediately—as if his life and his imagination suddenly had been freed—began to form his own light, loose, wondrous style. One of his earliest important commissions was to do decorations for the palace of the Patriarch in Udine, northern Italy, and here we have a glimpse of the heady arrangements, partly architectural and partly painting, which rambled beyond the actual picture. From Udine he traveled in the grand manner with his own retinue, working constantly on murals and altarpieces. Two of his sons were always at their father's side, assisting him in his enormous works.

TRIUMPH OF ZEPHYR AND FLORA

In 1750 Tiepolo was invited to Germany to do the prince-bishop's residence in Wurzburg, considered by many to be his masterpiece. He returned to Venice and in 1756 was elected president of the Venetian Academy, but was soon traveling again. He reached Madrid at the invitation of Charles III. The Royal Palace had only recently been completed, and Tiepolo was obviously the choicest painter to glorify its ceiling.

He never left Spain. He and his assistants spent four years working in the palace, then Charles had other commissions for him. But many feel that his last years were bitter years, for the younger generation considered his work trivial, missing completely the power and glory of his gigantic imagination.

Outstanding works: *Triumph of Zephyr and Flora; The Banquet of Cleopatra* (two); *The Triumph of Faith; Sacrifice of Iphigenia.*

CANALETTO *Italian, 1697–1768*
One sometimes hears it said of actors that they were born in a trunk and that the only nursery they knew was the backstage of a theater, but this was also the story of a great painter. Antonio Canal, called Canaletto, was the son of a scene designer, and it was in the Venetian

VIEW OF THE GRAND CANAL NEAR SAN MARCO

theaters of the early eighteenth century that he was trained to reproduce on canvas lifelike scenery. Here, too, he learned to use a sort of magic lantern. Outdoor scenes reflected through the lens of a "camera obscura" could be thrown onto his canvas and painted over.

Fortunately for Canaletto—and for us—just beyond his stage door lay Venice, with its miraculous lagoons, its warm light and luminous colors. His Venetian scenes have rarely been equaled.

Outstanding works: *View of the Grand Canal near San Marco; Feast of the Ascension; View of London; Ducal Palace.*

FRANCESCO GUARDI *Italian, 1712–1793*
From earliest times, long before postcards and cameras, the footloose wanderers of this world have wanted to carry home pictures to remind them of the strange and wondrous sights they have seen. It is not surprising therefore that in Venice, the goal of all romantic sightseers, there has always been a demand for views-of-the-city, and that in the eighteenth century there were so many painters willing and happy to supply such a demand.

Among the happiest of these was one Francesco Guardi. During his lifetime

VENETIAN GALA CONCERT

his gay, colorful pictures were somewhat overshadowed by those of his contemporaries, indeed even by works done in his own family. His father was a well-known artist; his brother Giovanni, with whom he often painted, was much more highly regarded; and his brother-in-law was the world-famous Tiepolo. People thought of Francesco as a pleasant enough painter, but no one took him too seriously (he was not elected to the Academy until shortly before his death).

From all accounts, Guardi had enough leisure, enough money and time to work exactly as he chose. On an old gondola he built a sort of floating studio in which he would drift along from canal to canal sketching the city he loved, and he loved all sections of Venice—the grand piazza with its bright pageants, and the less fashionable areas with their ancient, crumbling villas and deserted courtyards.

Shortly after his death Napoleon's forces moved in, the Doge abdicated, the Venetian Republic was abolished and the legendary "city of pleasure" was forever changed, but Guardi's joyful impressions—their dots of light glittering from the water and bouncing back from the shiny gondolas—live on as skillful, affectionate mementos.

Outstanding works: *Venetian Gala Concert; Vaulted Arcade, Doge's Palace; Departure of the Bucentauri; Ascent in a Balloon; The Little Piazza, Venice.*

JEAN ANTOINE WATTEAU
French, 1684–1721
Groups of strolling players were the rage of Paris when Watteau first arrived in the city, and from their lighthearted comedies he took his inspiration and many of the subjects he wanted to paint. He did not depict their theatrical settings; instead he borrowed their style, their gaiety, their coy ways of making love. Then, dressing his characters in shiny silks and satins, he placed them in idyllic parks and leafy groves, an arrangement which became the height of eighteenth-century fashion.

In many ways Watteau was a product of his society, and it was his privilege to have lived in an age of elegance and pretense. The nobility wanted art to reflect only their ideals, their dreams. Anything coarse or plebeian was out of place, and fortunately young Watteau had exactly the feathery touch to capture these dreams. He was never disturbed by patriotic messages.

His private life, however, was often the reverse of the high-comedy world he painted. As a youth he had been forced to work in a factory that turned out routine devotional pictures. He was poor and at an early age developed tubercu-

THE MEZZETIN

losis. When he finally achieved some recognition, the first money he earned was lost in unwise investments. His work was not recognized by Louis XIV at Versailles, but rather among the many secondary courts made up of state officials, pretenders and visiting nobles. It may have been his sense of being an outsider, as well as his poor health, that lent a note of sadness to many of his gayest pictures. The *Embarkation for Cythera* depicts groups of young lovers about to set sail for their island of dreams; yet the landscape behind this earthly paradise is tinged not with the colors of spring but of autumn and approaching winter. In 1719 he visited London, in search of commissions. But his health grew worse. He returned to France and died in 1721 at the age of thirty-seven.

Watteau recorded dreams on canvas. Although we know that this particular dreamer was haunted by illness, still he managed to conjure up a series of scenes which by some poetic magic of his own give us a fleeting glimpse of what life might be.

Outstanding works: *Gilles; Embarkation for Cythera; The Mezzetin; Gersaint's Shop Sign.*

JEAN BAPTISTE CHARDIN
French, 1699–1779
Chardin first commanded attention by what we would call today a shrewd piece of advertising. When a doctor commissioned him to do a sign, instead of using the conventional symbols of the medical profession Chardin painted a dramatic scene: A man lay dying of a wound as the doctor came to his aid. The doctor's offices, of course, could be seen quite clearly in the background.

Born the son of a cabinetmaker, Chardin passed through life completely untouched by the fashionable world—whose extravagances and frivolities were already paving the way for the French Revolution. While court painters busied themselves with decoration and pretense, with elegant goddesses frolicking in pastoral settings, Chardin concentrated on his neighbors, on domestic servants and still lifes, and young children at play. He left his home city of Paris only for one brief trip. It was said that he lacked imagination, that his mind never went beyond the kitchen, but Chardin had a way of giving the most ordinary subjects a special luster. Although he would spend hours arranging his models, they never seemed posed. It was as though a candid camera had caught them unaware—and always at a most significant moment: A mother waits until her child has finished saying grace; a boy hesitates as he plays at building a house of cards.

STILL LIFE WITH PIPE

Perhaps a *Self-Portrait* gives us our greatest insight. He has painted a plain man in glasses, wearing an eye shield, with a simple cap-headdress. He added no elegance and no feeling of artificial importance here.

Once, so the story goes, when a fellow artist tried to teach him a more sophisticated use of color, Chardin answered that he did not paint with color. He used color, he said, but he painted with emotion. This emotion was so deeply felt, so loving, that it lent dignity to the simplest of people and added stature to their most commonplace chores.

Outstanding works: *Still Life with Pipe; Boy with Top; Back from Market; Boy Preparing to Draw; Card Player.*

JEAN HONORE FRAGONARD
French, 1732–1806
His paintings have been called sensuous, erotic; they have been dismissed as sentimental works created only to amuse the aristocracy. There may be some truth in these accusations, but Jean Honoré Fragonard had such a contagious zest for living that his healthy, carefree works have survived, and many of them speak to us now as delightfully as they did to the Paris of Louis XV.

As a youth he tried to study with the unpretentious Chardin, but their outlooks were so diametrically opposed that their association lasted only a few months. Fragonard left to study with Boucher. By the time he was twenty he had won the coveted Prix de Rome and soon went south to complete his education. In Rome, instead of studiously copying only old masters, his youthful spirit reached out to the life around him, to its colors and sunshine. Finally, after years of travel, he returned to Paris and was an immediate success, earning a handsome income.

It has been said that as a young man Fragonard painted in many different styles. If so, we can be sure it was not from any desire to steal from others, it was merely that he found all forms of art—and of living—irresistible. Not until he was thirty-seven did he settle down—in marriage to a woman of twenty-four. Then he concentrated for a time on somewhat simpler, more domestic scenes.

Naturally such lighthearted exuberance found its greatest response among the nobility. At one point Madame du Barry commissioned him to do a series of decorations for her drawing room, then unaccountably rejected them.When the Revolution broke, commissions for paintings became increasingly rare and Fragonard went to live for a year with relatives in Grasse, his home town. The Reign of Terror virtually put an end to his career. Although he was given a position in the Government Museum Service, he died in 1806 almost totally forgotten.

THE SWING

Outstanding works: *The Swing; Storming the Citadel; Love Letters; Bathers; Mme. du Barry.*

WILLIAM HOGARTH *English, 1697–1764.*
See article on page 108.

JOSHUA REYNOLDS *English, 1723–1792.*
See article on page 111.

GAINSBOROUGH *English, 1727–1788.*
See article on page 114.

GEORGE ROMNEY *English, 1734–1802*
When he had finally got together a hundred pounds or so, George Romney presented his wife with half of the money, then with the other half in his pocket he struck out for London. They would not live together again for more than thirty years.

In London there must have been anxious times, but once the public became aware of his talent, his future was never in doubt. He was sensitive, determined and gifted, and he was an extremely rapid painter. He had to be. As an itinerant artist wandering through Lancashire, he painted country folk who could not pay much for a portrait. So, in order to support a family and save for the

London trip he trained himself to turn out an incredible number of likenesses every week.

Today Romney is perhaps best remembered for his *Lady Hamilton* pictures. This ravishing, vivacious girl (who was to become the mistress of Lord Nelson) first came into Romney's studio—and into his life—when she was about eighteen and he was almost fifty. He was immediately willing to turn away any client and break any appointment for an

A CONVERSATION

opportunity to paint her fantastic beauty.

But even without this distraction, his business affairs would have been in a peculiar state, for more and more as he grew older he lacked the perseverance necessary to complete his paintings. He would begin a canvas with tremendous enthusiasm, but after a few sittings his interest would jump to another subject and he would be off starting a new work. Often it would have required only a half hour's labor to finish—filling in a drapery, or completing a background—but these details were drudgery, and he was too proud to allow an assistant to do them for him. They say that families broke up or died, wives were divorced and favorite ladies dismissed before Romney would make the little necessary effort to complete commissioned pictures. Literally thousands of pounds were lost by the unfinished—and unsalable—portraits that cluttered his studio.

In 1799, his health broken, he returned to the north of England, where his wife nursed him until his death in 1802. Romney may not be one of the great painters—he had no interest in penetrating the character of his sitters. We learn no more from his subjects than if we were to meet them at a formal state function. Yet his beautiful women radiate a refined, ingratiating manner that makes us quite pleased to have seen them.

Outstanding works: *A Conversation; Portrait of Mrs. Davenport; Lady Hamilton* (several); *Mrs. Anne Carwardine and Her Child.*

JOHN SINGLETON COPLEY *American, 1738–1815.*
See article on page 116.

GILBERT STUART *American, 1755–1828*
Gilbert Stuart would have been a remarkable portrait painter in any age. One critic said of him that he could "nail the face to the canvas," so it was his rare good fortune to have lived at a time when so many of the founding fathers of the young United States were willing to come to his studio and have their faces "nailed."

Born the son of an unsuccessful snuff manufacturer, he began as a boy to draw rough likenesses of his fellow townsmen in Newport, Rhode Island. By the time he was nineteen he had set sail for England to study under masters there. Within a few years his fame had been established and he was busily painting the nobility of both England and Ireland. But Stuart, it seems, had inherited his father's business "sense"; he lived lavishly and was con-

MRS. RICHARD YATES

stantly pursued by bill collectors and lawyers. It was reported that he owed four hundred dollars for snuff alone.

Stuart's decision to return to America apparently rested on "pecuniary reverses" and an overwhelming desire to paint his hero, General George Washington. He was soon engaged for commissions in New York. Martha Washington probably persuaded the general to sit for Stuart, but she, poor soul, was never to get possession of the portrait. It is said that whenever she demanded it, the artist insisted it was still unfinished. Perhaps he was never satisfied with this work, but he is known to have painted some seventy-five copies of it. Indeed, whenever Gilbert Stuart needed a little extra money he would repaint his famous portrait of Washington and sell it. These copies he referred to as his "hundred-dollar bills."

Outstanding works: *George Washington* (three); *Mrs. Richard Yates; Skater.*

FRANCISCO GOYA *Spanish, 1746–1828.*
See article on page 119.

JACQUES LOUIS DAVID *French, 1748–1825*
He was called the "guillotine artist," but Jacques Louis David was far more than that. Occasionally, it is true, he did sketch his friends—as well as Marie Antoinette—on their way to be guillotined, but David saw himself as not just an artist. He dreamed of being a political force. Paris was a hotbed of revolution and counterrevolution; at one stage David was condemned to the guillotine he had often sketched.

As a young man he had painted for the court of Louis XVI, but he sensed the unrest that was sweeping France. More and more his pictures began to glorify Freedom. By the time the Revolution broke, his works were regarded as "symbols of democracy" and he was made a leader. Then, as so often happens, when the revolutionaries turned on their own, David was arrested and sentenced to die. At this point his wife, Charlotte—a beautiful young aristocrat who had left her husband when he had rebelled against the king—came to his rescue. At some risk to herself, she went from door to door pleading for his release. David was so touched by Charlotte's loyalty that he immediately set to work on *The Sabines,* an immense canvas showing a group of women throwing themselves between warriors in an attempt to end the conflict. This canvas caught the eye of Napoleon Bonaparte. Now, by depicting the little Corsican as augustly as if he were a direct descendant of the Caesars, David again became a political power.

After Waterloo, he was exiled to Belgium, and here, perhaps for the first time, we are given a glimpse of what might have been. The weight of ambition no longer on his shoulders, he did a

NAPOLEON IN HIS STUDY

series of gentle portraits. With only townspeople to pose for him, he seems to have relaxed and at last to have discovered in their faces a few simple, touching and beautiful human traits.

Outstanding works: *Napoleon in His Study; The Dead Marat in His Bath; Mme. Récamier; Death of Socrates.*

JEAN-AUGUSTE-DOMINIQUE INGRES
French, 1780–1867
There are many paradoxes in the life of Ingres. He was a gambler willing to bet everything on himself as an artist, yet he had no struggle to establish himself.

TURKISH BATH

From childhood he was encouraged by an understanding father and at seventeen was already in Paris studying with the great Jacques Louis David and happily making sketches of anyone who would sit for him. Apparently everyone would sit—he was an attractive young man and his portraits were always charming and flattering. In his early twenties the painter captured the Prix de Rome, an award which enabled him to go to Italy. His friends in Rome felt he should marry, and one suggested he write to her cousin. His "mail-order" proposal was accepted and Ingres and Madeleine, a young dressmaker, were soon married. From all accounts, they lived together quite contentedly for the next thirty-five years. If at times life seemed difficult in Italy, still he was able to get commissions and to continue his studies. Returning to Paris later, he was hailed as a master.

In his successful middle years, a strange streak of bitterness began to show. Ingres demanded respect and could not abide criticism—especially from younger men. With no children of his own, he would have liked to adopt the entire younger generation of artists. His attitude toward them was that of an indulgent father who loves and pampers his children so long as they look up to him. But the moment they showed signs of any independence, this "father" could see only ingratitude. Ingres was feared as much as he was loved.

In 1849 Madeleine died and again his friends worried. He seemed desolate and was unable to paint, but in 1852, at the age of seventy-two, he fell in love again, married and returned to his work with all the verve of a young bridegroom.

Line and form were the important elements to Ingres, and here he knew no equal. We may say of his life what we choose, but always painters have turned to Ingres to study and copy his superb draftsmanship.

Outstanding works: *Turkish Bath; Mme. Rivière; François Bertin; Mme. Moitessier.*

WILLIAM TURNER *English, 1775–1851.*
See article on page 123.

JOHN CONSTABLE *English, 1776–1837.*
See article on page 126.

EUGENE DELACROIX *French, 1798–1863.*
See article on page 130.

CAMILLE COROT *French, 1796–1875.*
See article on page 133.

JEAN FRANCOIS MILLET
French, 1814–1875
They called him a "Socialist" and insisted that only a political rebel would be interested in painting peasants working in their fields. His name was Jean François Millet, and he was a man of peasant stock himself, whose only "politics" consisted of repeatedly denying he had any political motives.

Millet had known poverty and hunger. A few years after his marriage, he had stood at the bedside and watched his young wife, unable to stand the strains of their life, die miserably. An art lover had prevailed upon the town council to give him the money to study in Paris. He was considered an outsider in the city, a crude country fellow with no finesse, and was rejected.

In an effort to earn enough to buy food for his children he tried to do portraits in imitation of the fashionable painters of the Paris Salons, but he had no talent and no real desire to cater to a public whose taste ran to sentimental allegories and canvases filled with cupids

THE ANGELUS

and nymphs. He yearned to paint simply and to capture the plain truths he had learned from men and women of his own kind, who spent their days quietly tilling the soil. Finally, in 1849, he left Paris and settled in Barbizon, near Paris (for Barbizon school, see page 128), where he went on painting—often in an unheated barn.

It was not until five years before his death that he gained any recognition, and by then it was too late; his health was shattered. The honors meant nothing. Ironically, with his death in 1875 his paintings were immediately in great demand, single canvases bringing more money than Millet earned from all the pictures he had sold.

Outstanding works: *The Angelus; The Gleaners; The Woodcutters.*

GUSTAVE COURBET *French, 1819–1877.*
See article on page 138.

HONORE DAUMIER *French, 1808–1879.*
See article on page 136.

CAMILLE PISSARRO *French, 1830–1903*
This beloved man was a leader in many of the experimental excursions in the art of his day—Impressionism (see page 160), the "open air" school of landscape painting known as *plein-air,* and the color effects of Pointillism (see page 20) championed by Seurat. He belonged to the famous Café Guerbois group (see page 158). A prolific artist, he gave the world some of its loveliest pictures.

The son of a Jewish hardware merchant and a Creole woman of St. Thomas, in the Virgin Islands, Camille Pissarro came to Paris in 1855. A warm, selfless man, he was soon the friend of many of the advanced painters at a time when they were often in conflict.

In 1871 Pissarro suffered an artistic disaster such as few other painters have ever experienced. After the Franco-Prussian War he and his family returned from London to their lodgings in Louveciennes, outside Paris, to find that the invading Germans had looted their house and destroyed hundreds of his paintings—almost the whole of his life work. Many had been used as mats to make paths in the muddy garden while the house served as a butchery.

LA COTE DES BOEUFS AT L'HERMITAGE

In his last years Pissarro's pictures started to sell and he bought a small house at Eragny. Despite failing eyesight, he continued to paint to the end—befriended and respected by all.

Outstanding works: *La Côte des Boeufs at L'Hermitage; Bather in the Woods; Entrance to Voisin; View from Louveciennes.*

EDOUARD MANET *French, 1832–1883.*
See article on page 143.

EDGAR DEGAS *French, 1834–1917.*
See article on page 146.

CLAUDE MONET *French, 1840–1926.*
See article on page 158.

PIERRE AUGUSTE RENOIR
French, 1841–1919.
See article on page 154.

MARY CASSATT *American, 1845–1926*
Many American girls have traveled to Europe, but not many have looked into a shop window and seen something that

BOATING PARTY

changed their entire lives. This is what happened to Mary Cassatt, who came from a Pittsburgh banking family. At twenty-seven she was living in Paris, studying art, when one day she saw a small pastel by Edgar Degas hanging in a window. From that moment on, Mary Cassatt knew that she would dedicate her life to painting in his style.

Later she met Degas and became his close disciple. Quite often she exhibited her works with Degas and the other great Impressionists, yet she did not enter into their manner of living but remained the proper, wealthy American spinster that she was. Except for her father and her brother Alexander (who became president of the Pennsylvania Railroad), men seem to have played a small part in her life and seldom appear in her paintings. She was content to use as her models young women and children—usually most gracefully draped in the flowing gowns of the late Victorian era. Through these she created many beautiful, if somewhat idealized, studies of motherhood.

By 1917 she became partially blind, gave up painting, and afterward spent her time encouraging her fellow Americans to invest in art. After several years of total blindness, Mary Cassatt died, leaving behind many touching portraits which tell of her tender way of life.

Outstanding works: *Mother and Child* (several); *Boating Party; The Toilet; Young Girls.*

JAMES MCNEILL WHISTLER *American, 1834–1903.* See article on page 150.

PAUL CEZANNE *French, 1839–1906.*
See article on page 8.

HENRI ROUSSEAU *French, 1844–1910.*
See article on page 20.

PAUL GAUGUIN *French, 1848–1903.*
See article on page 12.

VINCENT VAN GOGH *French, born in Netherlands, 1853–1890.*
See article on page 15.

GEORGES SEURAT *French, 1859–1891.*
See article on page 18.

HENRI DE TOULOUSE-LAUTREC
French, 1864–1901.
See article on page 23.

WINSLOW HOMER *American, 1836–1910.* See article on page 152.

ALBERT RYDER *American, 1847–1917*
Albert Pinkham Ryder, the youngest

DEATH ON A PALE HORSE

son of a seafaring family, was born in New Bedford, Massachusetts. From the time he was a small boy and began sketching old whaling ships along the New England coast, there was never any doubt about what "Pinkie" Ryder's inner voices were telling him to do. In his own words, he wanted simply "to see nature springing to life" on his canvas.

Arriving in New York in his early twenties, he lived and worked without recognition for some fifteen years during which he was forced to accept support from his family. Then, about 1880, his works began to sell and from there on his art paid his modest way.

In his middle twenties he entered the National Academy of Design, where he was set to copying replicas of ancient Greek statues. Though he exhibited there, and even sold some works, it was not until he left the Academy and gave himself completely to painting the seas and ships of his boyhood that he found himself as a mature artist.

In the next forty years Albert Ryder rarely left Manhattan. Twice he visited the great galleries of Europe at the urging of friends. His reaction to the works he saw there was typical. "Not for me," he remarked. "If I am to do anything I must paint my own experience in my own way." This he always did, sometimes spending ten or fifteen years on a single canvas. The small collection of paintings which he left may seem somber, even tragic, to us today. There are not many human figures in his works, and these are most often used to illustrate man's helplessness against the great forces of nature. Yet in all of them we can sense a stubborn Yankee spirit of perseverance and, above all, the determination of a man to speak his own mind.

Outstanding works: *Moonlight—Marine; Death on a Pale Horse; The Flying Dutchman; Night Clouds; Siegfried and the Rhine Maidens.*

JOHN SINGER SARGENT
American, 1856–1925
When John Singer Sargent was still in his twenties, Henry James wrote that his was "a talent which on the very threshold of its career has nothing more to learn." This must have been a happy phrase for a young painter to read, but Sargent knew it was far from true. Till the end of his days he would be learning about life and art. The son of a wealthy American couple who traveled in Europe (he was born in Florence, Italy), Sargent spent his early years moving

EL JALEO

from hotel suites to rented villas, yet nothing seems to have distracted him from his goal. In 1884 he finished his portrait of Madame Gautreau, the most famous beauty in France. Parisian society was buzzing with excitement awaiting the portrait, on which the artist had worked for two years. When it was unveiled, a scandal broke upon Sargent's head which he was never to forget. He was accused of having caricatured the great woman when actually he had painted her as she really was. "I chronicle," he said, "I do not judge." In this case he had chronicled a professional beauty in a most revealing, tight-fitting gown—his portrayal was true even to the violet tone of her skin. From the absurdly unreasonable reactions to this work, now known as the *Portrait of Madame X,* Sargent became notorious.

From Paris he moved to England and then on to America, where the fashionable world flocked to his studio offering vast sums to be immortalized by his brush. He recorded the high life of two continents. Princes and princesses, actors, musicians, statesmen and American millionaires lionized him. King Edward VII wanted to knight him as the most distinguished portrait painter in England and was stopped only when Sargent's American citizenship was revealed.

A true internationalist, he was a constant, indefatigable observer of cultures, none of which was really native to him. It has been said that he was an American who was born in Italy and educated in France, and who looked like a German, spoke like an Englishman and painted like a Spaniard. He left behind more than five hundred portraits, handsome tributes to a society that was once powerful, wealthy and charming, but is now, except for his glowing reminders, all but forgotten.

Outstanding works: *El Jaleo; Portrait of Madame X; Asher Wertheimer; The Daughters of Edward D. Boits.*

THOMAS EAKINS *American, 1844–1916*
In Thomas Eakins we find no eccentric bohemian, but a man who looked upon art as a problem to be solved, who studied each canvas as an engineer might study a building. After graduating from a Philadelphia high school he studied at a fine-arts school and a medical college, and then spent some three years in Europe absorbing the works of old masters and new, but he never looked to any of them for inspiration or imitation. He was searching only for techniques which might serve him when he had mastered his craft. He returned to Philadelphia, to the same house his family had lived in since he was a child, and set to work painting realistic studies of his neighbors and relatives, a world that was completely familiar to him.

His inquisitive mind never relaxed, and in time he went back to medical school for classes in anatomy and dissection. His attitude was close to the great spirit of science abroad in the nineteenth century, but it was little understood in polite art circles. Eakins' masterpiece, *The Clinic of Dr. Gross,* caused an uproar—he had dared show blood on the surgeon's hand—and he was labeled a "butcher." An art jury in Philadelphia in 1876 refused to hang the picture and he sold it for only two hundred dollars to a medical school.

MAX SCHMITT IN A SINGLE SCULL

Though he returned to more conventional subjects, he continued to search for what went on beneath the surface; the results were not always pleasing to those he painted. Finally his neighbors refused to take his portraits even as gifts. There was, however, one rare exception: Walt Whitman kept Eakins' portrait hanging on his wall. "The more I get to realize it, the profounder seems its insight," Whitman said. "Eakins is not a painter, he is a force."

Outstanding works: *The Clinic of Dr. Gross; Max Schmitt in a Single Scull; Concert Singer; Walt Whitman.*

HENRI MATISSE *French, 1869–1954.*
See article on page 26.

MAURICE VLAMINCK *French, 1876–1958*
Vlaminck bragged that he had never set foot in the Louvre. He was a man of the people, an earthy soul, who was a writer, a violinist, a lover of folk arts, a farmer, a championship bicycle racer—and an artist on the side. Nevertheless, he found time to paint canvases that today are in nearly every major museum with a collection of modern art.

Maurice Vlaminck was born in Paris; his father's people were Flemish, his mother was from Lorraine. His parents tended toward the bohemian life and he managed to receive little formal education. If he was as likely to be carrying a violin (he supported himself by playing in a café orchestra) as a paint box, art was nevertheless a passion.

He became the most violent of the Fauves (see page 29), who were devoted

HOUSES AT CHATOU

to the use of bright, and sometimes riotous, splashes of color. Vlaminck turned to Fauvism after a short-lived enthusiasm for the manner of van Gogh ("he means more to me than my own father") and, in the span of fifteen years, also embraced and discarded the influences of African sculpture, Cézanne and Cubism.

In 1915 he settled down to more than forty years of painting in a mature style of his own. What was that style? Curiously enough, one that moved ever closer to the old masters he said he had not studied—one that became increasingly realistic, and whose colors and subjects were more and more subdued.

Outstanding works: *Winter Landscape; Portrait of Derain; Laundry Barges; Houses at Chatou.*

RAOUL DUFY *French, 1877–1953*

When a young doctor arranged to have Raoul Dufy brought to a Boston hospital for a series of treatments to relieve his arthritis, the aged painter made a most typical gesture—he gave the attendants, interns, nurses and doctors lessons in sketching, because, as he told them, "there is no medicine like painting."

For Raoul Dufy there was no joy like painting, either. One of nine children of a poor family at Le Havre, he had to leave school at an early age to find work. His few leisure hours were spent in art classes and soon he got himself to Paris. At first he was uncomfortable, "scared" by the old masters at the Louvre, but there was another Paris, one that was alive and bursting with new artists and revolutionary ideas, and here he felt completely at home.

Early in our century theories of modern art also were affecting the world of fashion. Before long young Dufy, with his love of color, had established himself as a designer of fabrics which were later made up into the most successful dresses in Paris. Often at exhibitions of his painting he would hear ladies deploring his pictures, then notice that they were wearing silks he had designed.

One day his partner took him to a racetrack at Deauville, by the English Channel, to study the current fashions. But Dufy saw only the race. In the speed of the horses and the extraordinary combinations of color on the jockeys he found a perfect subject for his zestful style. That night he painted his first *Racecourse.*

There were soon others. He did regattas and esplanades as well, and they all displayed his personal touch, his tricks of technique. There is something theat-

RACETRACK AT DEAUVILLE

rical about Dufy's paintings; they are shows, great gala scenes glimpsed for a fleeting moment.

Outstanding works: *Racetrack at Deauville; Mozart Concerto; The Studio; Black Cargo.*

MAURICE UTRILLO *French, 1883–1955*

At first glance, the story of Maurice Utrillo seems to have all the ingredients of a cheap and rather sordid novel of the streets of Montmartre.

He was born on Christmas Day in 1883 to an unmarried woman, Marie-Clementine, later known as Suzanne Valadon, one of the most famous models of France. For eight years Suzanne tried to find a man who would give her son his name, and finally in 1891 she discovered a Spanish journalist who agreed to register the boy. After the necessary legal ceremonies he was rechristened Maurice Utrillo. This arrangement,

CHARTRES

however, was so displeasing to young Maurice that he continued to call himself Valadon. Even after he had started to paint he often signed his pictures "Maurice Utrillo V."

Left to wander the streets on his own as a child, he began to drink—at first only wine, but he soon switched to absinthe—and by the time he was eighteen he was a confirmed alcoholic. At the suggestion of a doctor who felt that art might serve as a form of therapy, Suzanne taught her son to paint. For a time—and at various intervals throughout his life—painting became as great an obsession as alcohol.

He painted what he knew, the streets and buildings of Paris. And he painted well, with a simple yet quite individual balance of colors. Soon his pictures were in demand, and it was not long before dealers were outbidding one another for his canvases. One of them would invite him out for an evening, ply him with liquor and after a while lock him into a room with some paints, brushes, food—and enough liquor to keep him going. Then after a few days they would turn him loose again, keeping his pictures "in payment" for his lodgings.

For Utrillo there were many long periods of being shut up in institutions and asylums, where different "cures" were attempted. At one of these he painted some views of Paris on his cell doors, and within hours the doors were removed and carted off to a gallery.

In 1935 he married a widow, Lucie Pauwels, who gave his life the stability that enabled him to survive twenty years longer.

Few careers had been more tragic, and the wonder of Utrillo is that out of his personal hells he was able to leave us so many sensitive views of the city he loved.

Outstanding works: *Chartres; Cabaret du Lapin Agile; La Rue St. Rustique; Snow in Montmartre; Church at Deuil; L'Eglise St. Pierre.*

CHAIM SOUTINE *French, born in Lithuania, 1894–1943*
Even when his pictures had begun to sell and there was enough money for his simple needs, Chaim Soutine could never bring himself to paint on new canvas. He would give his dealer a few cents to get him used or soiled canvases in the Flea Market.

Soutine had come out of the ghetto of a small Russian village, near Minsk. He was seventeen when he arrived in Paris, and he knew no French, only Hebrew and a little Russian. At first he settled at La Ruche, a beehive-like building where other "displaced artists" huddled together. But Soutine had nothing to learn from other artists. The scars of the ghetto were still raw—and they were to remain raw all his life—as if he carried with him a memory of suffering that colored every sight and every influence that tried to enter his life.

La Ruche was located near the slaughterhouses, and Soutine would often borrow huge sections of beef from the butchers, hang them in his room and use them as models. One of his first friends—and there were not to be many in this

PAGE BOY AT MAXIM'S

strange, tortured life—was Modigliani, who sensed his power and introduced him to the dealer Zborowski. Zborowski managed to sell a few of his paintings and, more important, arranged for him to live in Ceret, in the Pyrenees. Here he turned to landscapes, but even in Ceret he was not painting the quiet countryside of France; he saw only the dark shadows, the tortured land and a sky filled with nightmarish clouds.

The contours of a picture were of such small interest to him that he never bothered to draw preliminary sketches. He needed an immediate contact with paint to express his feelings, with the result that the distortions which fill his canvases never come from any new intellectual concepts, as they did with most of his contemporaries—they spring directly from his emotions.

His only guides seem to have been his intuitions and his passion for perfection. He would go over and over the same subject, and would often try to buy back his canvases to improve them. There were many stories of his sitting in his studio, surrounded by his works, studying each one, then in a rage of frustration slashing at them with a knife. His friends would collect the mutilated paintings and try to repair them. Surprisingly, it was an American who first appreciated Soutine. Dr. Albert Coombs Barnes bought over a hundred pictures in 1923. Today many of Soutine's best works hang in American galleries.

Some critics claim that he was in love with all forms of life. Behind his tortured studies of death and starving children they hear his frantic cry for help. We can only guess now about his real motivations, but we do know that he was a man who painted with passion and violence, as though driven by demons.

Outstanding works: *Page Boy at Maxim's; Woman in Red; Tree at Vence* (two); *The Choir Boy* (two); *The Flayed Ox.*

AMEDEO MODIGLIANI *French, born in Italy, 1884–1920.* See article on page 33.

GEORGES ROUAULT *French, 1871–1958*
Rouault was the exact opposite of the careless, lighthearted bohemian. He was deeply religious, exacting and formal; when he sat down to paint he wore a stiff collar, a necktie, a vest and a well-pressed suit. As a young man he was trained in the making of stained-glass windows, and never forgot his early lessons. His pictures are easily recognized by their heavy black outlines enclosing brilliant patches of color. He is most famous for his paintings of clowns and his religious subjects.

Toward the end of his life Rouault did a remarkable thing. Dissatisfied with hundreds of his pictures which were in the hands of his dealer, he sued to get them back. The court decided in his favor, ruling that only the artist knew when a picture was finished. Then

THE OLD KING

Rouault, at seventy-seven, fearing he would not live to alter the pictures to his satisfaction, burned 315 of them. It was a multimillion-dollar holocaust.

After his death his heirs presented the state with about two hundred of his works. They will hang in France's new Museum of the Twentieth Century. His pictures can be seen in almost every museum which shows modern art.

Outstanding works: *The Old King; The Judge; Holy Face; Head of Christ.*

WASSILY KANDINSKY *German, born in Russia, 1866–1944*
Believers in an international world of art had every reason to be hopeful in 1913. Works of contemporary painters were being exhibited in foreign capitals and examined by fellow artists everywhere. Articles explaining the newest trends were avidly read in many countries. And the writings of Kandinsky, setting forth his views on painting, were translated into English, making him an international leader of art.

The new "modern artists" of Munich were indeed fortunate to have Wassily Kandinsky as their spokesman. He not only had paintings to illustrate his theories—he had the clear analytic mind of a lawyer, and he had a gift for writing. Born in Moscow, he had been trained in economics, law and science. Not until he was thirty did he decide to move to Munich to become a painter.

There he sought a new way to express himself, his state of mind. In 1908 he found it—in a series of improvisations marking a complete break with the recognizable subject. Lines, forms and colors danced across his canvases for only one purpose: to establish a mood.

Though it broke with the artist's traditional belief that beauty must derive from nature, Kandinsky's novel style had its roots in the past. The Norwegian Edvard Munch's grotesque studies in neurosis—portraying hysteria, primarily—had exercised a profound influence on German painters through an exhibition in Berlin in 1892. Other forerunners were van Gogh (see page 15), with his swirling lines and garish colors, aimed at conveying intense emotion, and Toulouse-Lautrec (see page 23), with his caricature-like emphasis on prominent aspects of people and places.

Exaggerations of line, color and shape—these became the elements of the style of the Expressionists, a group of painters who sought to communicate what they felt, as opposed to the Impressionists,

IMPROVISATIONS WITH GREEN CENTER

who tried to represent what they saw. Prominent Expressionists after Kandinsky were Kokoschka (see page 183) and Soutine (see page 181).

With the outbreak of war in 1914, Kandinsky's brief, bright period ended and he returned to Russia. In 1922 he was back in Germany, painting and teaching artists eager to follow him. Hitler's advent in 1933 forced him to flee to Paris, but his noble search for the new possibilities of his art went on.

At his death in 1944 it could be said that the former lawyer had won his case: moods and emotional states had been established as legitimate subjects for paintings.

Outstanding works: *Improvisations with Green Center; Improvisation No. 30, 1913; Landscape with Red Spots No. 2.*

LYONEL FEININGER *American, 1871–1956*

He was a budding violinist who became a cartoonist, then a painter of great originality whose works expressed his love of

GELMERODA IV

music, boats and the sea, and the buildings of his native Manhattan.

By twelve, Lyonel Feininger had given violin concerts. And so his musician parents sent him several years later to their homeland of Germany to study for a career. The youngster was soon attracted to the new movements in art then sweeping through Europe, and he set out to become a painter.

Though he was slow to find his own linear style, he quickly solved the problem that proves so difficult for many artists—making a living. At twenty-three he was a cartoonist in Berlin; a weekly comic page by Feininger appeared for a time in the Chicago *Tribune*.

About 1912, following the patterns of Cubism, he began to create works that are notable for their expression of a mood, their solidity of design, their interplay of light. Surprisingly for modern painting, the viewer can readily identify the scene; yet he can also sense the abstract design and force of it.

In 1933 the Nazis included his work in an exhibit of "degenerate art," and by 1937 political pressures had grown so intense that Feininger left Germany to return to New York City. There he continued to produce his oils and watercolors, as remarkable as ever for their modern approach to romantic subjects and feelings—until his death in 1956.

Outstanding works: *Towers of Halle; Sailing Boats; Gelmeroda IV.*

PAUL KLEE *German, born in Switzerland, 1879–1940*

"A drawing," Paul Klee said, "is taking a line for a walk." All his life Klee was a drawer; it was only reluctantly that he admitted he was a painter as well. It was not until he was almost forty that he began to use oils consistently.

Born in Switzerland, he had his early training in Munich. His first works were drawings, fantastic etchings and a few watercolors. In 1914, when he went to Tunisia, the hot country impelled him toward heightened color. Then came World War I, during which he spent several years in the German army. In 1920 he was elected professor at the famous Bauhaus school for artists in Weimar, Germany.

It can never be claimed that Klee ranks with the greatest painters, but his works were charming, witty and ironic. What he did was to make brilliant footnotes to the life of his times—so brilliant, in fact, that the Nazis labeled him a degenerate artist and confiscated 102 of his works. Fleeing Germany, he died in Locarno, Switzerland, in June 1940. He has remained one of the most pleasing talents

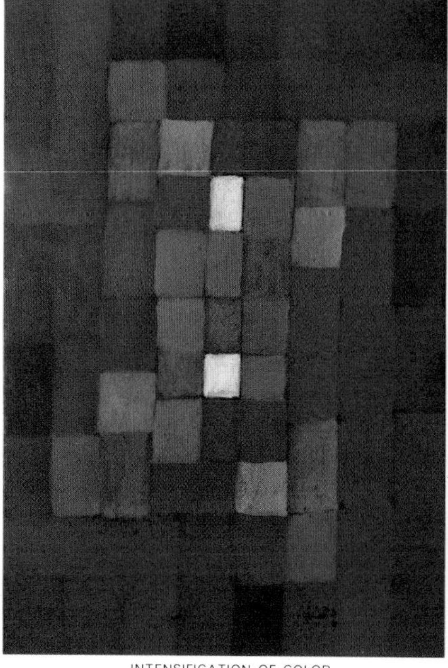

INTENSIFICATION OF COLOR FROM THE STATIC TO THE DYNAMIC

of the first half of the twentieth century.

Outstanding works: *Fish Magic; Landing Boat; Twittering Machine; Intensification of Color from the Static to the Dynamic.*

OSKAR KOKOSCHKA *German, 1886–*
When a play he had written was produced in Vienna, the young artist-playwright Oskar Kokoschka insisted upon making up the actors himself. On some he painted tiger stripes, and on all of

HARBOR OF MARSEILLES

them he drew little crooked pen strokes which gave the impression that the actors' nerves were outside of their skin. Nothing was ever more typical of the artist's passion to distort surface reality and show us the truth that lies beneath.

Brought up in a suburb of Vienna, Kokoschka found his first job painting postcards and teaching at the School of Arts and Crafts. Even there his revolutionary outlook was being shaped and he was in close daily contact with the most progressive minds in the city. His first entries in an exhibition were considered so unconventional they created a "public scandal" and in turn caused him to lose his teaching assignment. Through the exhibit, however, he had made a few staunch friends, who arranged some commissions for him, and from then until 1914 he concentrated his fierce energies on a series of psychological portraits. Trying to do on canvas what Sigmund Freud was doing in analysis, he cared nothing for the physical appearance of his subjects—he strove only to expose their inner lives.

After being wounded in World War I, he traveled for many years painting landscapes and views of cities, hoping to widen his outlook. But just as he had disdained lifelike reality in his portraits, so here colors and forms were distorted to reflect his own feelings.

In the Germany of the nineteen thirties, his drawings were burned by the Nazis, his paintings were removed from museums, and soon he was forced to flee to Prague, and then to England. For the next few years money was scarce. At one point he was offered 1000 pounds (5000 dollars) to paint Ivan Maisky, the Russian ambassador to Great Britain. He accepted the commission but donated the full amount to a wartime hospital fund in Stalingrad.

Outstanding works: *Harbor of Marseilles; Professor Forel; Self-Portrait; Father Hirsch; The Bride of the Wind.*

PABLO PICASSO *French, born in Spain, 1881–* . See article on page 35.

GEORGES BRAQUE *French, 1882–1963*
Braque met Picasso when he was twenty-five, and in the next seven years they joined their talents to create the great painting innovation of the twentieth century—Cubism. Although some say the first impulse came from Braque, it was avowedly a joint venture, which is surprising considering the different temperaments of the two men. Certain paintings of the period are so alike that it is difficult for anyone but an expert to tell who painted which. The style of Cubism—largely abandoning the use of color for a new approach to form and space—affected almost all the young painters of the time.

Separated by the First World War, Braque and Picasso did not resume their artistic partnership. After being seriously wounded in the war, Braque left Cubism behind him and took a new look at nature. It was his personal view: "I do not wish to copy nature," he said. "I am more concerned with the possibility of being on an equal level with her."

He began to use color again, with dazzling success: it has been said of him—with reason—that he had the most

STILL LIFE, LE JOUR

distinguished sense of color of any man who ever lived.

His life after the war was uneventful. He had married happily, and he devoted himself wholly to painting. He won honors and vast acclaim. Braque never allowed himself to become a public figure. Although he was one of the great French painters of his time, he saved all his energy and invention for his work.

He was first of all a craftsman. His father had owned a decorating-paint shop, and the boy had early learned to imitate a variety of surfaces, such as the paneling of doors, the graining of wood, the veining of marble; these were skills he used all his life.

At the end of his career, in a sudden burst of energy (as so often happens with great painters), he did a series of eight large interiors of his studio. These pictures rank with the masterpieces of the twentieth century.

Outstanding works: *Still Life, Le Jour; The Table; Man with Guitar; Atelier VIII; Beach at Dieppe; Washstand by a Window.*

FERNAND LEGER *French, 1881–1955*
It is strange to realize now that Léger did not visit the United States until he was a man of fifty, for there is something

THE BIRD CHARMER

about Léger's temperament, even about the world he painted, that seems strangely attuned to Americans. A close study of his art, of course, reveals certain influences—Cézanne, the Cubist movement and others—which were entirely European.

Born in Normandy, he was apprenticed to an architect at the age of sixteen. Even after going to Paris he continued to support himself as an architectural draftsman—and the knowledge acquired in his office there was never to leave him. His pictures are put together with the authority of a man organizing stones for the construction of a great cathedral.

At the time of his arrival in Paris, artists were desperately seeking new ways, "a new language" to keep painting somehow in tune with the changing world. Before many years, Léger himself became a voice to be listened to. Called into the army in 1914, he was impressed by the machinery of war; after being gassed near Verdun, he was discharged. Soon huge machines became prominent in his canvases.

In the twenties the artists were no longer alone—the buying public also became interested in understanding the "new language." Of course many things helped in this: the Russian and Swedish ballets, the new plays and even motion pictures were searching for fresh forms. Léger designed scenery and costumes, and at one time even tried his hand at experimental movies. But it was in large murals that he spoke most freely. Here, in describing the human being and his relationship to an industrial civilization, he found the fullest outlet for his energies.

Such a man would of course respond to America. "It's not a country," he wrote, "it's a world. . . . In America you are confronted with a power in movement, with force in reserve without end. . . . It is all here for the painter to organize. . . ."

Léger has been called "the most truly modern artist of our times"—and certainly no artist has painted our mechanistic world more vividly. Occasionally he seems to go beyond the present and to be giving us a glimpse of what may be in store. The arms and legs of his human figures appear to be hinged and jointed onto their bodies, and his characters look out at us as expressionless as robots.

Outstanding works: *The Bird Charmer; Viaduct, 1925; La Danseuse aux Clés; Woman Bathing; Four Cyclists; The Grand Parade.*

SALVADOR DALI *Spanish, 1904–*

All his life Dali has felt a frenzied need to call attention to himself. When he was a youth he threw himself down the stone staircase of his school several times so he would be the center of concern of his classmates. In his late fifties he sported the longest waxed mustaches ever seen. He has never let the world forget that he is alive and kicking—and working.

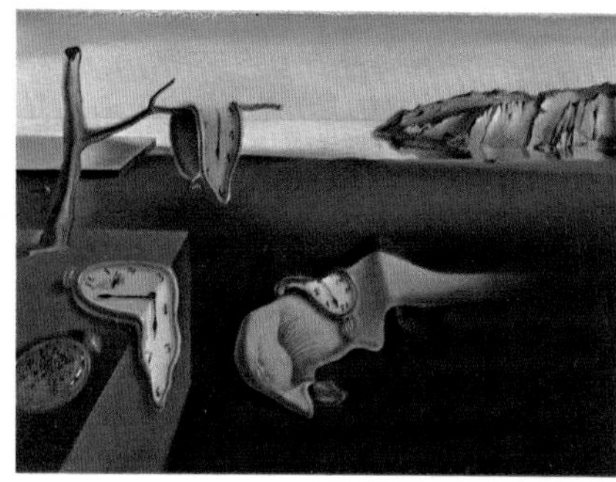

PERSISTENCE OF MEMORY

He spent his youth in Spain, where he experimented in various styles and perfected his marvelous manual dexterity. His technique easily rivals the realism of the early masters. He was twenty-four before he made his first quick trip to Paris, and the following year he moved there, officially joining the Surrealist movement—that school of "dreams and madness." For many years Dali was the most famous member of the group—in fact his painting of the limp watches, *The Persistence of Memory,* brought him world prominence. In the thirties, besides painting he also designed sets for ballets, made movies, wrote books and created an attraction at the 1939 New York World's Fair called "Dali's Dream of Venus."

Recently his painting has undergone a change. He has done a number of large canvases—some on religious subjects—which have achieved tremendous popularity. His *Crucifixion* at the Metropolitan Museum in New York is an example.

Dali lives in Spain, but travels widely. He continues to draw—and draw attention to himself—prodigiously.

Outstanding works: *Persistence of Memory; Bacchanale; Crucifixion; Sacrament of the Last Supper.*

PIET MONDRIAN *Dutch, 1872–1944*

Piet Mondrian may be the most influential artist of the twentieth century—not among other artists (his followers have been few) but in architecture, commercial design, typography and advertising. Look at any modern building, or open any magazine, and you will be aware of his influence.

In his youth in Holland, Mondrian was not an exceptional painter. His subjects were the usual ones: windmills, flowers, landscapes—all of which he did with dignity and ease. But in 1911 he went to Paris, where he saw the new Cubism, and his life changed. He embraced Cubism as no other artist did, even its inventors—Braque and Picasso. Although they eventually abandoned the movement, he carried it on to its logical conclusion: the areas of flat red, blue, yellow and white enclosed by vertical or horizontal black lines, which have become so celebrated and familiar.

Mondrian spent the First World War in Holland, painting and writing. He became the most important contributor to a famous Dutch art magazine called *De Stijl.* He continued writing all his life. After the war he took the first train from Amsterdam to Paris. There he lived and worked for the next twenty years.

Mondrian never made much money, but this did not disturb him. He was both an ascetic and an aristocrat. Possessions meant nothing to him. His various studios in Paris and London and New York were all much the same—sparse, painted pure white and decorated only by cardboard squares of color which he often rearranged to please himself.

In 1938, convinced war was coming, he left Paris and spent two years in London before journeying to New York, where, at sixty-eight, he began a new life. He fell in love with the city—to such an extent that he made arrangements to become an American citizen.

A change came over his painting as well. The black lines disappeared; the compositions became more complex. Two of his most famous pictures, *Broadway Boogie-Woogie* and *Victory Boogie-Woogie,* were done in New York. Here he died in 1944.

COMPOSITION WITH BLUE AND YELLOW, 1932

Outstanding works: *Opposition of Line, Red and Yellow; Broadway Boogie-Woogie; Composition with Blue and Yellow, 1932; Oval Composition (Tableau III).*

JOAN MIRO *Spanish, 1893–*

In Paris, in the early nineteen twenties, Ernest Hemingway bought a picture by Joan Miró. It is called *The Farm* and is one of the masterpieces of twentieth-century art. Miró was very poor when he painted *The Farm*—he says he had money for only one lunch a week—but he spent nine months at work on it.

Hemingway too was short of money, and although the picture was cheap, he had to pay Miró's dealer on the installment plan. When the final payment was due, Hemingway, completely broke,

DUTCH INTERIOR

had to roam the bars and restaurants of Montmartre borrowing money from friends. Finally, in triumph, he carried off the picture from the dealer. Hemingway himself described the moment: "At home we hung it and everyone looked at it and was very happy. I would not trade it for any picture in the world." He owned it as long as he lived.

The Farm was among the last of Miró's realistic pictures. Afterward he was attracted by Surrealism, and finally his painting became almost totally abstract. But his pictures have almost always been gay in their bright blues and yellows and reds, with their infinitely varied and witty forms.

Modest, even timid, Miró nevertheless has lived the drama of our times. He painted the agonies of the civil war in his native Spain with the "intensity of a scream in the night." An exile in France from 1936, he fled the Nazi invasion with his wife in 1940, returning to Spain, though he did not know what his reception there would be.

Miró was always admired by other artists and writers in Europe, but it was America which actually started him on worldwide popularity. The Museum of Modern Art in New York gave him an enormous exhibition in 1941, and from that moment on he was recognized as the master he is—one of the few great modern Spanish painters.

Outstanding works: *Dutch Interior; The Mauve of the Moon; Dog Barking at the Moon; Flight of the Bird over the Plain III; The Farm.*

MARC CHAGALL *French, born in Russia, 1889–* . See article on page 30.

JACKSON POLLOCK *American, 1912–1956*
Pollock's youth was spent in the Far West. He was seventeen before he went to New York and began to study under Thomas Hart Benton. Much has been made of the fact that this most abstract of Americans should have studied under such a realist as Benton. But Pollock tested many masters and manners before he evolved his own style: the Mexicans, the Surrealists, Picasso and others. When, at the age of thirty-four, he began his famous "drip" paintings, he was well grounded—he knew what he wanted.

The paintings literally were dripped. The huge canvases—monumental pictures often ten or fifteen feet long—were placed on the studio floor. Then with a stick dipped in a bucket of thinned color (house paint, sometimes) the painter guided a stream of the liquid onto the canvas. Pollock said he had a "getting-acquainted period" with each picture, and that each had a "life of its own," which made some of his detractors think his whole production was accidental. But his descriptions are painters' phrases which would have been well understood by Tintoretto or Daumier. Actually the pictures now look rich, lively and anything but accidental.

Pollock became the most famous of abstractionists both in America and Europe. During the ten years from 1945 to 1955 the center of interest in the art world shifted from Paris to New York, and Pollock to a large extent was responsible for this.

NUMBER 1, 1948

His exhibition at the Museum of Modern Art, in a series titled "Artists in Mid-Career," was suddenly turned into a memorial when he was killed in an automobile accident in 1956.

Outstanding works: *Blue Poles; Number 1, 1948; Number 12, 1952.*

ANDREW WYETH *American, 1917–*
No painter was ever more fortunate in his selection of parents than Andrew Wyeth. His father, an illustrator of such children's books as *Treasure Island* and *Robin Hood,* was a man to whom formal schooling meant little, but to whom the world of the imagination was everything. In Chadds Ford, Pennsylvania, a town with a population of 140, N. C. Wyeth and his family formed a small art colony among themselves. There his five children were free to race across the countryside, act out scenes from their father's books and, in the case of young Andrew, learn to transpose childhood dreams onto canvas.

One might think that such an uninhibited childhood would produce a free-wheeling, abstract bohemian, but Andrew Wyeth is the exact opposite. He is not only financially the most successful painter working in America now, he is the most disciplined artist in the realist technique. Obviously greatly influenced by his father—whose death was the first dark cloud across his life—he has developed his own style. Reducing the extravagant, romantic bravura of the elder Wyeth, he has found his own way of hewing drama down to one highly charged instant. Andrew shows us a crippled woman struggling to climb a hill, or a boy all alone bicycling across vast open spaces. These carefully recorded "moments" have moved Wyeth so deeply that people in all walks of life respond to them; emotion is so concentrated in these paintings that time itself seems to have stopped.

CHRISTINA'S WORLD

A Wyeth study of some frail curtains blowing into a deserted room was Robert Frost's favorite painting, and President John F. Kennedy also felt its eerie fascination. He chose Andrew Wyeth to be among the first painters to be awarded the Medal of Freedom. The citation read by President Johnson after Kennedy's death stated, "He has in the great humanist tradition illuminated and clarified the verities and delights of life."

Outstanding works: *Christina's World; Distant Thunder; Far Away; Northern Point.*

INDEX

For the locations of paintings in museums, churches and collections, see the Picture Credits on pages 191-92.

Bold type indicates main entries; *italics* denote illustrations

Bold type indicates main entries; *italics* denote illustrations

ACKNOWLEDGMENTS

BY JOHN CANADAY:
RELUCTANT REVOLUTIONARY, cond. from HORIZON (Winter 1964, Vol. VI, No. 1), © The American Heritage Publishing Co., Inc.

BY SHELDON CHENEY:
SOUL IN TORMENT, **WIZARD OF COLOR**, **DEFIANT SHOWMAN** and **BITTER HEART, DANCING BRUSH**, cond. from THE STORY OF MODERN ART, © 1941, 1958, Sheldon Cheney, pub. by The Viking Press, U.S.A.; The Macmillan Company of Canada, Ltd. Reprinted by permission from The Viking Press, Inc.

BY THOMAS CRAVEN:
OLD MASTER OF MODERN PAINTING, **THE DISCOVERERS**, **SATIRIST EXTRAORDINARY** and **THE SAVAGE EYE**, cond. from MEN OF ART, © 1958, Thomas Craven, pub. by Simon and Schuster, Inc. **THE EXPERIMENTER**, cond. from A TREASURY OF ART MASTERPIECES, © 1939, 1952, 1958, and pub. by Simon and Schuster, Inc. **A DYNASTY OF VENICE**, cond. from MEN OF ART, © 1958, Thomas Craven, pub. by Simon and Schuster, Inc., from THE RAINBOW BOOK OF ART, © 1956, Thomas Craven, pub. by The World Publishing Company, and from A TREASURY OF ART MASTERPIECES, © 1939, 1952, 1958, and pub. by Simon and Schuster, Inc. **THE DIVINE PAINTER** and **EXQUISITE CRAFTSMAN**, cond. from A TREASURY OF ART MASTERPIECES, © 1939, 1952, 1958, and pub. by Simon and Schuster, Inc., and from THE RAINBOW BOOK OF ART, © 1956, Thomas Craven, pub. by The World Publishing Company. **CARICATURIST OF A NATION**, cond. from MEN OF ART, © 1958, Thomas Craven, pub. by Simon and Schuster, Inc., and from THE RAINBOW BOOK OF ART, © 1956, Thomas Craven, pub. by The World Publishing Company.

BY WILL DURANT:
AMOROUS MONK and **BEHOLDER OF DREAMS**, cond. from THE RENAISSANCE, © 1953, Will Durant, pub. by Simon and Schuster, Inc. **SPECTATOR IN A PEASANT LAND**, cond. from THE REFORMATION, © 1957, Will Durant, pub. by Simon and Schuster, Inc.

BY WILL AND ARIEL DURANT:
THE PATRICIAN, **PERFECT COURTIER** and **THE INCOMPARABLE**, cond. from THE AGE OF REASON BEGINS, © 1961, Will and Ariel Durant, pub. by Simon and Schuster, Inc.

BY FRANK JEWETT MATHER, JR.:
EXPLORER OF THE AFTERWORLD, cond. from WESTERN EUROPEAN PAINTING OF THE RENAISSANCE, © 1939, Holt, Rinehart and Winston, Inc. Reprinted by permission.

BY BERNARD S. MYERS:
CAPTIVE OF FAME, cond. from FIFTY GREAT ARTISTS, © 1953, reprinted by permission of Bantam Books, Inc., and from LESSONS IN ART APPRECIATION, © 1937, The National Committee for Art Appreciation, Ltd.

BY DONALD CULROSS PEATTIE:
GENIUS OF ALL ARTS, cond. from THE CATHOLIC WORLD, © 1946, The Missionary Society of St. Paul the Apostle in the State of New York.

BY HENDRIK WILLEM VAN LOON:
HE PORTRAYED AN ERA, cond. from THE ARTS, © 1965, Estate of Hendrik Willem van Loon, pub. by Simon and Schuster, Inc. Reprinted by arrangement with the estate of the author through the Margot Johnson Agency.

BY HERMAN J. WECHSLER:
STRANGE GENIUS OF THE MOULIN ROUGE, **THE ULTIMATE BOHEMIAN** and **FOLLOWER OF THE SUN**, cond. from LIVES OF FAMOUS FRENCH PAINTERS, © 1952, Herman J. Wechsler, reprinted by permission of Washington Square Press, Inc.

Also to GIMBEL'S RARE COIN DEPARTMENT for providing equivalents in U.S. dollars of foreign monies through the centuries.

PICTURE CREDITS

The following references are arranged by pages in the same sequence as in the book. The museum, church or collection in which a painting is located may be found by referring to the page, below, on which the picture appears.

Front cover, (detail) **KLEE's** INTENSIFICATION OF COLOR FROM THE STATIC TO THE DYNAMIC (Collection Bienert), photo: Skira.
Back cover, (detail) **CIMABUE's** CHRIST ON THE CROSS (Church of San Domenico, Arezzo, Italy), photo: Scala.
Back of jacket, **VAN GOGH's** SUNFLOWERS (Stedelijk Museum, Amsterdam).

PART I • ART IN OUR TIME

CEZANNE: p. 8, SELF-PORTRAIT (Louvre Museum, Paris), photo: Agraci; pp. 8–9, LANDSCAPE WITH VIADUCT (The Metropolitan Museum of Art, New York); p. 10, CARD PLAYERS (Louvre Museum, Paris), photo: Giraudon; p. 10, STILL LIFE WITH APPLES (The Art Institute of Chicago). **GAUGUIN:** p. 12, SELF-PORTRAIT (The National Gallery of Art, Washington, D.C., Chester Dale Collection); p. 13, THE BURAO TREE [TE BURAO] (The Art Institute of Chicago, The Joseph Winterbotham Collection); p. 13, TWO TAHITIAN WOMEN (The Metropolitan Museum of Art, New York); p. 13, GAUGUIN'S PALETTE (Louvre Museum, Paris), photo: Agraci. **VAN GOGH:** SELF-PORTRAIT, 1887 (Stedelijk Museum, Amsterdam); p. 16, SUNFLOWERS (Stedelijk Museum, Amsterdam); p. 16, LA MOISSON EN PROVENCE, 1888 (Collection of Mr. and Mrs. Paul Mellon); p. 17, THE HARVEST (Stedelijk Museum, Amsterdam); p. 17, BEDROOM AT ARLES (The Art Institute of Chicago, Helen Birch Bartlett Memorial Collection). **SEURAT:** p. 18, SEURAT, by Ernest Laurent (National Museum of Modern Art, Paris), photo: Agraci; p. 19, LA GRANDE JATTE (The Art Institute of Chicago, Helen Birch Bartlett Memorial Collection); p. 19, THE CIRCUS (Louvre Museum, Paris), photo: Musées Nationaux. **ROUSSEAU:** p. 20, SELF-PORTRAIT (Narodni Museum, Prague), photo: Giraudon; p. 21, THE CART OF PERE JUNIET (private collection), photo: Giraudon; THE EQUATORIAL JUNGLE (The National Gallery of Art, Washington, D.C., Chester Dale Collection). **TOULOUSE-LAUTREC:** p. 23, TOULOUSE-LAUTREC, by Jean Edouard Vuillard (Toulouse-Lautrec Museum, Albi, France), photo: G. Groc; p. 23, THE LAUNDRESS (from the book LAUTREC BY LAUTREC, by Ph. Huysman and M. G. Dortu, EDITA, Lausanne, Switzerland); p. 23, THE JOCKEY (lithograph: Sterling and Francine Clark Art Institute, Williamstown, Mass.); p. 24, AT THE MOULIN ROUGE (The Art Institute of Chicago, Helen Birch Bartlett Memorial Collection); p. 24, YVETTE GUILBERT (Toulouse-Lautrec Museum, Albi, France), photo: G. Groc; p. 24, POSTER, LE MOULIN ROUGE (Bibliothèque Nationale, Cabinet des Estampes, Paris), photo: Guilbert; p. 24, MOULIN ROUGE, 1900, photo: Roger-Viollet; p. 25, JANE AVRIL DANCING (Louvre Museum, Paris), photo: Musées Nationaux. **MATISSE:** p. 26, SELF-PORTRAIT (private collection), photo: J. Lacoste; p. 27, ODALISQUE IN RED PANTS (National Museum of Modern Art, Paris), photo: Agraci; p. 27, WHITE PLUMES (Minneapolis Art Institute); p. 27, THE PLUMED HAT (drawing: The Detroit Institute of Arts); p. 27, LADY IN BLUE (Philadelphia Museum of Art, Wintersteen Collection); p. 28, THE ANEMONES AND THE MIRROR (Reader's Digest Collection, Pleasantville, N.Y.); p. 28, HEAD OF HAIR (private collection), photo: J. Lacoste; p. 28, THE DANCER (private collection); p. 28, THE DANCE (Hermitage, Leningrad), photo: Editions Cercle d'Art. **CHAGALL:** p. 30, SELF-PORTRAIT WITH SEVEN FINGERS (Stedelijk Museum, Amsterdam); p. 31, THE THREE CANDLES (Reader's Digest Collection). **MODIGLIANI:** p. 32, MME. HEBUTERNE (Reader's Digest Collection); p. 33, SELF-PORTRAIT (private collection, São Paulo, Brazil), photo: Giraudon; p. 33, THE APPRENTICE (Collection of Mme. Jean Walter), photo: J. Lacoste. **PICASSO:** p. 35, SELF-PORTRAIT, 1906 (Philadelphia Museum of Art, A. E. Gallatin Collection); p. 35, WOMAN IN BLUE (Museum of Contemporary Art, Madrid), photo: Giraudon; p. 35, LOLA, 1899 (Picasso Museum, Barcelona), photo: Ediciones Llorca; p. 36, WOMAN IN WHITE (The Metropolitan Museum of Art, New York); p. 36, THE THREE MUSICIANS (Museum of Modern Art, New York); p. 36, GERTRUDE STEIN (The Metropolitan Museum of Art, New York); p. 36, FAMILY OF SALTIMBANQUES (The National Gallery of Art, Washington, D.C.); p. 36, POOR PEOPLE ON THE SEASHORE (The National Gallery of Art, Washington, D.C.); p. 37, WOMAN AND TWO GIRLS (Philadelphia Museum of Art, Wintersteen Collection); p. 37, GIRL BEFORE MIRROR (Museum of Modern Art, New York); p. 37, GUERNICA (Museum of Modern Art, New York); pp. 36–37, THE BULLS (Kohlhammer Verlag-Abrams, New York).

PART II • THE AGE OF GREATNESS

GIOTTO: p. 40, THE MASSACRE OF THE INNOCENTS (Scrovegni Chapel, Padua, Italy), photo: Scala; p. 40, THE FLAGELLATION OF CHRIST (Scrovegni Chapel, Padua, Italy), photo: Scala; p. 41, EXTERIOR OF SCROVEGNI CHAPEL, photo: Alinari-Anderson; p. 42, ST. FRANCIS PREACHING TO THE BIRDS (Upper Church of San Francesco, Assisi, Italy), photo: Scala; p. 43, MEETING AT THE GOLDEN GATE (Scrovegni Chapel, Padua, Italy), photo: Scala; p. 43, THE BETRAYAL BY JUDAS (Scrovegni Chapel, Padua, Italy), photo: Scala. **THE VAN EYCKS:** p. 44, SELF-PORTRAIT (?) by Jan van Eyck (courtesy of the Trustees, The National Gallery, London); p. 45, MARRIAGE OF GIOVANNI ARNOLFINI AND GIOVANNA CENAMI (courtesy of the Trustees, The National Gallery, London). **UCCELLO:** p. 46, ST. GEORGE AND THE DRAGON (courtesy of the Trustees, The National Gallery, London); p. 46, Uccello's signature, from Uffizi panel, THE ROUT OF SAN ROMANO, (courtesy Uffizi Museum, Florence), photo: Alinari; p. 47, National Gallery panel, THE ROUT OF SAN ROMANO (courtesy of the Trustees, The National Gallery, London); p. 47, PERSPECTIVE STUDY OF A CHALICE (Uffizi Museum, Florence), photo: Alinari; p. 47, PERSPECTIVE STUDY OF A MAZZOCCHIO (Uffizi Museum, Florence), photo: Alinari. **FRA FILIPPO LIPPI:** p. 49, ADORATION OF THE MAGI (The National Gallery of Art, Washington, D.C., Samuel H. Kress Collection), said by some to have been painted, in part, by Fra Angelico and completed by Lippi. **GIOVANNI BELLINI:** p. 51, PIETA (Brera Museum, Milan), photo: Elettra Cliché. **GENTILE BELLINI:** p. 51, PROCESSION OF THE TRUE CROSS (Galleria dell' Accademia, Venice), photo: Scala. **BOTTICELLI:** p. 52, SELF-PORTRAIT from ADORATION OF THE KINGS (Uffizi Museum, Florence), photo: European Art Color Slide Co.; p. 53, YOUNG MAN WITH A MEDAL (Uffizi Museum, Florence), photo: Scala; pp. 54–55, SPRINGTIME [LA PRIMAVERA] (Uffizi Museum, Florence), photo: Scala; p. 55, THE BIRTH OF VENUS (Uffizi Museum, Florence), photo: Scala. **DA VINCI:** p. 56, SELF-PORTRAIT (courtesy Biblioteca Reale, Turin, Italy), photo: Rampazzi; p. 57, THE VIRGIN OF THE ROCKS (Louvre Museum, Paris), photo: Giraudon; p. 58, PORTRAIT OF CECILIA GALLERANI (National Museum, Krakow, Poland, Czartoryski Collection); p. 58, THE LAST SUPPER (Santa Maria delle Grazie, Milan), photo: European Art Color Slide Co.; p. 59, MONA LISA (Louvre Museum, Paris), photo: Giraudon. **MICHELANGELO:** p. 60, LIKENESS OF THE ARTIST FROM HIS SCULPTURE (detail from a PIETA in the Florence Cathedral—the Duomo), photo: Scala; p. 61, THE LIBYAN SIBYL (Sistine Chapel, The Vatican, Rome), photo: de Antonis; p. 61, Drawings for THE LIBYAN SIBYL (The Metropolitan Museum of Art, New York, Joseph Pulitzer Bequest, Purchase 1924); pp. 62–63, THE CREATION OF MAN (Sistine Chapel, The Vatican, Rome), photo: de Antonis; p. 62, JEREMIAH (Sistine Chapel, The Vatican, Rome), photo: de Antonis; p. 62, JONAH (Sistine Chapel, The Vatican, Rome), photo: de Antonis; p. 63, THE SISTINE CEILING (The Vatican, Rome); photo: Scala. **RAPHAEL:** p. 65, SELF-PORTRAIT (Uffizi Museum, Florence), photo: European Art Color Slide Co.; p. 65, PLATO AND ARISTOTLE, detail from SCHOOL OF ATHENS (The Vatican, Rome), photo: Scala; p. 65, HOME OF RAPHAEL, photo: Arborio Mella; p. 66, MARRIAGE OF THE VIRGIN (Brera Museum, Milan), photo: Scala; p. 67, PORTRAIT OF A CARDINAL (Prado Museum, Madrid), photo: European Art Color Slide Co. **GIORGIONE:** p. 69, CONCERT CHAMPETRE (Louvre Museum, Paris), photo: Agraci; p. 69, ADORATION OF THE SHEPHERDS (The National Gallery of Art, Washington, D.C.). **TITIAN:** p. 71, SELF-PORTRAIT (Prado Museum, Madrid), photo: Dominguez Garcia; p. 71, NYMPH AND SHEPHERD (Kunsthistorisches Museum, Vienna), photo: Meyer; p. 71, MALTESE DOG (Nationalmuseum, Stockholm); p. 72, PORTRAIT OF A YOUNG MAN (Pitti Palace, Florence), photo: Scala; p. 72, VENUS OF URBINO (Uffizi Museum, Florence), photo: Scala; p. 73, LA BELLA (Pitti Palace, Florence), photo: Scala.

PART III • MASTERS OF OLD EUROPE

BOSCH: p. 76, BOSCH, by Jacques LeBoucq (Bibliothèque Municipale, Arras, France), photo: J. Lacoste; p. 76, THE HAY WAIN [or HAY WAGON] (Prado Museum, Madrid), photo: European Art Color Slide Co.; p. 77, CHRIST BEARING THE CROSS (Musée des Beaux-Arts, Ghent, Belgium), photo: European Art Color Slide Co.; p. 77, THE CONJUROR (Saint-Germain-en-Laye Museum, France), photo: Giraudon. **HOLBEIN:** p. 78, SELF-PORTRAIT (Uffizi Museum, Florence), photo: Scala; p. 79, HENRY VIII (National Gallery, Rome), photo: Giraudon; p. 79, ANNE OF CLEVES (Louvre Museum, Paris), photo: Giraudon; p. 79, SIR THOMAS MORE (The Frick Collection, New York); ERASMUS OF ROTTERDAM (Louvre Museum, Paris), photo: Giraudon; p. 79, PORTRAIT OF A MAN (The Metropolitan Museum of Art, New York, The Jules S. Bache Collection, 1949); p. 79, JANE SEYMOUR (Kunsthistorisches Museum, Vienna), photo: Meyer; p. 79, EDWARD VI (The Metropolitan Museum of Art, New York, The Jules S. Bache Collection, 1949). **BRUEGHEL:** p. 81, SELF-PORTRAIT (Albertina Museum, Vienna), photo: Ritter; p. 82, CHILDREN AT PLAY (Kunsthistorisches Museum, Vienna), photo: Meyer; p. 83, HUNTERS IN THE SNOW (Kunsthistorisches Museum, Vienna), photo: Meyer. **EL GRECO:** p. 84, SELF-PORTRAIT (?) (Prado Museum, Madrid), photo: Oronoz; p. 84, THE ANNUNCIATION (Iglesia del Hospital de la Caridad, Illescas, Spain), photo: Oronoz; p. 84, THE BURIAL OF COUNT ORGAZ (Iglesia de Santo Tomé, Toledo, Spain), photo: Oronoz; p. 85, VIEW OF TOLEDO (The Metropolitan Museum of Art, New York). **RUBENS:** p. 87, SELF-PORTRAIT (Kunsthistorisches Museum, Vienna), photo: Meyer; p. 88, RAPE OF THE DAUGHTERS OF LEUCIPPUS (Bayerische Staatsgemäldesammlungen, Munich), photo: Blauel; p. 89, THE STRAW HAT (courtesy of the Trustees, The National Gallery, London); p. 89, DESCENT FROM THE CROSS (Notre Dame Cathedral, Antwerp, Belgium), photo: ACL Brussels. **VAN DYCK:** p. 90, SELF-PORTRAIT (Bayerische Staatsgemäldesammlungen, Munich), photo: Blauel; p. 90, CHILDREN OF CHARLES I (The Metropolitan Museum of Art, New York, Bequest of Collis P. Huntington, 1925); p. 91, CHARLES I OF ENGLAND (Louvre Museum, Paris), photo: Agraci. **VELAZQUEZ:** p. 93, SELF-PORTRAIT (Museo Provincial de Bellas Artes de Valencia, Spain), photo: Fragar; p. 94, PHILIP IV (The Metropolitan Museum of Art, New York, Bequest of Benjamin Altman, 1913); p. 95, VENUS AND CUPID [THE ROKEBY VENUS] (courtesy of the Trustees, The National Gallery, London); p. 95, PRINCE BALTASAR CARLOS (Prado Museum, Madrid), photo: Oronoz; p. 95, INFANTA DONA MARGARITA (Prado Museum, Madrid), photo: Oronoz. **HALS:** p. 96, SELF-PORTRAIT from OFFICERS AND SUBALTERNS OF THE CIVIC GUARD OF ST. GEORGE, HAARLEM (courtesy Frans Hals Museum, Haarlem, Netherlands), photo: Nico Zomer; p. 97, THE JESTER (private collection, France), photo: J. Lacoste; p. 97, THE BOHEMIAN GIRL (Louvre Museum, Paris), photo: European Art Color Slide Co.; p. 97, THE LAUGHING CAVALIER (by permission of the Trustees of the Wallace Collection, London). **REMBRANDT:** p. 99, SELF-PORTRAIT (Uffizi Museum, Florence), photo: European Art Color Slide Co.; p. 99, SELF-PORTRAIT, 1630 (Mauritshuis, The Hague, Netherlands), photo: European Art Color Slide Co.; p. 99, SELF-PORTRAIT (São Paulo, Brazil), photo: European Art Color Slide Co.; p. 99, SELF-PORTRAIT, GOLD CHAIN, 1633 (Louvre Museum, Paris), photo: Giraudon; p. 99, SELF-PORTRAIT, 1652 (Kunsthistorisches Museum, Vienna), photo: European Art Color Slide Co.; p. 99, SELF-PORTRAIT, 1655 (Kunsthistorisches Museum, Vienna), photo: European Art Color Slide Co.; p. 99, SELF-PORTRAIT, 1656–1658 (Kunsthistorisches Museum, Vienna), photo: European Art Color Slide Co.; p. 99, SELF-PORTRAIT, HIS LAST ONE (Mauritshuis, The Hague, Netherlands), photo: European Art Color Slide Co.; pp. 100–01, JUDAS RETURNING THE THIRTY PIECES OF SILVER (private collection, England), photo: by kind permission of Gilchrist Photo Service; p. 102, THE ARTIST'S SON TITUS (The Metropolitan Museum of Art, New York, Bequest of

Benjamin Altman, 1913); p. 102, YOUNG GIRL AT AN OPEN HALF-DOOR (The Art Institute of Chicago, Mr. and Mrs. Martin A. Ryerson Collection); p. 102, THE NIGHT WATCH (Rijksmuseum, Amsterdam). **VERMEER:** p. 104, THE LACE-MAKER (Louvre Museum, Paris), photo: Giraudon; p. 104, THE LITTLE STREET (Rijksmuseum, Amsterdam); p. 104, THE ARTIST IN HIS STUDIO (Kunsthistorisches Museum, Vienna), photo: Meyer; p. 105, THE MUSIC LESSON (The Queen's Collection, England: Copyright reserved).

PART IV • THE NEW TRADITION

HOGARTH: p. 108, SELF-PORTRAIT (courtesy of the National Portrait Gallery, London); p. 108, HOGARTH'S HOUSE, photo: by permission of Middlesex County Council, England; p. 108, HOGARTH'S PALETTE (Royal Academy of Arts, London); p. 108, THE SHRIMP GIRL (courtesy of the Trustees, The National Gallery, London); p. 109, MARRIAGE A LA MODE (courtesy of the Trustees, The National Gallery, London). **REYNOLDS:** p. 111, SELF-PORTRAIT (courtesy of the National Portrait Gallery, London); p. 112, COLONEL TARLETON (courtesy of the Trustees, The National Gallery, London); p. 113, MRS. SIDDONS AS THE TRAGIC MUSE (courtesy Henry E. Huntington Library and Art Gallery, San Marino, Calif.). **GAINSBOROUGH:** p. 114, SELF-PORTRAIT (Collection of the late Captain E. G. Spencer-Churchill, by kind permission of Christie's, London); p. 114, MASTER NICHOLLS (courtesy of The National Trust, Waddesdon Manor, England); p. 115, THE HON. MRS. THOMAS GRAHAM (courtesy of The National Gallery, Edinburgh, Scotland), photo: Tom Scott; p. 115, ROBERT ANDREWS AND HIS WIFE (courtesy of the Trustees, The National Gallery, London). **COPLEY:** p. 116, SELF-PORTRAIT, PASTEL (courtesy Henry Francis du Pont Winterthur Museum, Wilmington, Del.); p. 117, BROOK WATSON AND THE SHARK (courtesy Museum of Fine Arts, Boston), photo: Barney Burstein; p. 117, BOY WITH A SQUIRREL (private collection), photo: Barney Burstein. **GOYA:** p. 119, SELF-PORTRAIT (Prado Museum, Madrid), photo: Fred Fehl; p. 119, DONA ISABEL COBOS DE PORCEL (courtesy of the Trustees, The National Gallery, London); pp. 120–21, THE NUDE MAJA (Prado Museum, Madrid), photo: Oronoz; p. 121, THE CLOTHED MAJA (Prado Museum, Madrid), photo: European Art Color Slide Co. **TURNER:** p. 123, SELF-PORTRAIT (courtesy of the National Portrait Gallery, London); pp. 124–25, THE SHIPWRECK (courtesy of the Trustees of the Tate Gallery, London). **CONSTABLE:** p. 126, SELF-PORTRAIT (courtesy of the National Portrait Gallery, London); p. 127, WIVENHOE PARK, ESSEX (The National Gallery of Art, Washington, D.C., Widener Collection); p. 127, WEYMOUTH BAY (courtesy Museum of Fine Arts, Boston), photo: Barney Burstein.

PART V • THE TRIUMPH OF VISION

DELACROIX: p. 130, SELF-PORTRAIT (Louvre Museum, Paris), photo: Agraci; p. 130, GEORGE SAND (Ordrupgaard Museum, Copenhagen), photo: Agraci; p. 130, FREDERIC CHOPIN (Louvre Museum, Paris), photo: Agraci; pp. 130–31, WOMAN WITH A PARROT (Musée des Beaux-Arts, Lyon, France), photo: Giraudon; p. 131, DANTE AND VIRGIL IN HADES (Louvre Museum, Paris), photo: Agraci. **COROT:** p. 133, SELF-PORTRAIT (Louvre Museum, Paris), photo: Giraudon; p. 134, THE BRIDGE AT MANTES (Louvre Museum, Paris), photo: Agraci; p. 134, MEMORY OF CASTEL GANDOLFO (Louvre Museum, Paris), photo: Giraudon; p. 135, GIRL COMBING HER HAIR (Louvre Museum, Paris), photo: Giraudon; p. 135, COROT'S PALETTE (Louvre Museum, Paris), photo: Agraci. **DAUMIER:** p. 136, SELF-PORTRAIT (Museum Calvet, Avignon, France), photo: La Photothèque Giraudon; p. 137, THE PRINT COLLECTOR (Petit Palais, Paris), photo: Agraci; p. 137, CRISPIN AND SCAPIN (Louvre Museum, Paris), photo: Agraci. **COURBET:** p. 138, SELF-PORTRAIT, L'HOMME A LA PIPE (Musée Fabre, Montpellier, France), photo: Claude O'Sughrue; p. 140, THE BEAUTIFUL IRISHWOMAN (Nationalmuseum, Stockholm); pp. 140–41, THE ARTIST'S STUDIO (Louvre Museum, Paris), photo: André Held; p. 141, THE ALARM (Ordrupgaard Museum, Copenhagen. **MANET:** p. 142, THE BAR AT THE FOLIES-BERGERE (Courtauld Institute Galleries, London); p. 142, OLYMPIA (Louvre Museum, Paris), photo: Musées Nationaux; p. 143, SELF-PORTRAIT (Mr. and Mrs. John L. Loeb), photo: Skira; p. 143, BREAKFAST ON THE GRASS (Louvre Museum, Paris), photo: Agraci; p. 145, MODEL FOR "THE BAR AT THE FOLIES-BERGERE" (Musée des Beaux-Arts, Dijon, France), photo: Giraudon. **DEGAS:** p. 146, SELF-PORTRAIT (Louvre Museum, Paris), photo: Giraudon; pp. 146–47, REHEARSAL OF THE BALLET ON STAGE (The Metropolitan Museum of Art, New York, Gift of Horace Havemeyer, 1929, the H. O. Havemeyer Collection), photo: J. D. Barnell; p. 148, AFTER THE BATH (Louvre Museum, Paris), photo: La Photothèque Giraudon; p. 148, L'ABSINTHE (Louvre Museum, Paris), photo: La Photothèque Giraudon. **WHISTLER:** p. 150, SELF-PORTRAIT (courtesy of The Detroit Institute of Arts); p. 151, PORTRAIT OF THE ARTIST'S MOTHER (Louvre Museum, Paris), photo: Giraudon; p. 151, OLD BATTERSEA BRIDGE (courtesy of the Trustees of the Tate Gallery, London). **HOMER:** p. 152, THE ARTIST IN HIS STUDIO, photo: Brown Brothers; pp. 152–53, BREEZING UP (The National Gallery of Art, Washington, D.C., Gift of the W. L. and May T. Mellon Foundation); p. 152, THE LIFE LINE (Philadelphia Museum of Art, George W. Elkins Collection), photo: A. J. Wyatt; p. 153, THE GULF STREAM (The Metropolitan Museum of Art, New York, Wolfe Fund, 1906). **RENOIR:** p. 154, SELF-PORTRAIT (courtesy of the Fogg Art Museum, Harvard University, Cambridge, Mass., Maurice Wertheim Collection [Class of 1906]); p. 155, LE MOULIN DE LA GALETTE (Louvre Museum, Paris), photo: Giraudon; p. 155, RENOIR'S PALETTE (Louvre Museum, Paris), photo: Agraci; p. 155, BATHERS (Louvre Museum, Paris), photo: Giraudon; p. 156, MME. CHARPENTIER AND HER CHILDREN (The Metropolitan Museum of Art, New York, Wolfe Fund, 1907); p. 156, LADY AT THE PIANO (The Art Institute of Chicago, Mr. and Mrs. Martin A. Ryerson Collection). **MONET:** p. 158, SELF-PORTRAIT (private collection), photo: J. Lacoste; pp. 158–59, WATER LILIES (Reader's Digest Collection); p. 159, TULIP FIELDS (Sterling and Francine Clark Art Institute, Williamstown, Mass.); p. 159, MONET'S PALETTE (private collection), photo: J. Lacoste.

A READER'S DIGEST GUIDE TO PAINTERS AND PAINTINGS

CIMABUE: p. 162, CHRIST ON THE CROSS (Church of San Domenico, Arezzo, Italy), photo: European Art Color Slide Co. **DUCCIO:** p. 162, THE CALLING OF THE APOSTLES PETER AND ANDREW (The National Gallery of Art, Washington, D.C., Samuel H. Kress Collection). **MARTINI:** p. 162, ST. MARTIN BEING MADE A KNIGHT (Lower Church, San Francesco, Assisi), photo: Scala. **SASSETTA:** p. 162, JOURNEY OF THE MAGI (courtesy of The Metropolitan Museum of Art, New York, Bequest of Maitland F. Griggs, 1943). **MASACCIO:** p. 163, THE TRIBUTE MONEY (Brancacci Chapel, Santa Maria del Carmine, Florence), photo: European Art Color Slide Co. **VAN DER WEYDEN:** p. 163, THE DEPOSITION (Prado Museum, Madrid), photo: European Art Color Slide Co. **FOUQUET:** p. 163, THE STONING OF ST. STEPHEN from THE BOOK OF HOURS OF ETIENNE CHEVALIER (Musée Condé, Chantilly, France), photo: Giraudon. **FRA ANGELICO:** p. 164, FLIGHT INTO EGYPT (Museo di San Marco, Florence), photo: Elettra Cliché. **DELLA FRANCESCA:** p. 164, THE NATIVITY (courtesy of the Trustees, The National Gallery, London). **CASTAGNO:** p. 164, YOUTHFUL DAVID (The National Gallery of Art, Washington, D.C., Widener Collection). **POLLAIUOLO:** p. 165, HERCULES KILLING THE HYDRA (Uffizi Museum, Florence), photo: Scala. **VAN DER GOES:** p. 165, ADORATION OF THE SHEPHERDS, detail from PORTINARI TRIPTYCH (Uffizi Museum, Florence), photo: European Art Color Slide Co. **MEMLING:** p. 165, SEVEN JOYS OF THE VIRGIN (Bayerische Staatsgemäldesammlungen, Munich), photo: Blauel. **MANTEGNA:** p. 166, CIRCUMCISION (Pitti Palace, Florence), photo: European Art Color Slide Co. **VERROCCHIO:** p. 166, BAPTISM OF CHRIST (Uffizi Museum, Florence), photo: European Art Color Slide Co. **PERUGINO:** p. 166, FRANCESCO DELLE OPERE (Uffizi Museum, Florence), photo: Scala. **SIGNORELLI:** p. 167, ANGEL (Santuario, Loreto, Italy), photo: A. Villani. **GHIRLANDAIO:** p. 167, GIOVANNA TORNABUONI (Collection Baron Thyssen, Lugano, Switzerland), photo: Brunel. **CARPACCIO:** p. 167, COURTESANS (Correr Museum, Venice), photo: European Art Color Slide Co. **DURER:** p. 168, SELF-PORTRAIT IN A FUR COAT (Bayerische Staatsgemäldesammlungen, Munich), photo: Blauel. **CRANACH:** p. 168, VENUS AND CUPID (Bayerische Staatsgemäldesammlungen, Munich), photo: Blauel. **DEL SARTO:** p. 169, PORTRAIT OF A YOUNG MAN (courtesy of the Trustees, The National Gallery, London). **CORREGGIO:** p. 169, ANTIOPE ASLEEP (Louvre Museum, Paris), photo: Giraudon. **GRUNEWALD:** p. 170, CRUCIFIXION, detail from ISENHEIM ALTARPIECE (Unterlinden Museum, Colmar, France), photo: Braun. **CLOUET:** p. 170, DIANE DE POITIERS (The National Gallery of Art, Washington, D.C.). **TINTORETTO:** p. 170, ORIGIN OF THE MILKY WAY (courtesy of the Trustees, The National Gallery, London). **VERONESE:** p. 171, FINDING OF MOSES (The National Gallery of Art, Washington, D.C., Mellon Collection). **CARAVAGGIO:** p. 171, THE CALLING OF ST. MATTHEW (Church of San Luigi dei Francesi, Rome), photo: Scala. **LA TOUR:** p. 172, ST. SEBASTIAN (Stiftung Preussischer Kulturbesitz, Gemäldegalerie der Staatlichen Museen, Berlin-Dahlem). **POUSSIN:** p. 172, ARCADIAN SHEPHERDS (Louvre Museum, Paris), photo: Agraci. **LORRAIN:** p. 173, MARRIAGE OF ISAAC AND REBECCA (courtesy of the Trustees, The National Gallery, London). **ZURBARAN:** p. 173, LEMONS, ORANGES AND ROSE (Collection Contini-Bonacossi, Florence), photo: Scala. **TIEPOLO:** p. 173, TRIUMPH OF ZEPHYR AND FLORA (Ca' Rezzonico, Venice), photo: Ferruzzi. **CANALETTO:** p. 174, VIEW OF THE GRAND CANAL NEAR SAN MARCO (Brera Museum, Milan), photo: Scala. **GUARDI:** p. 174, VENETIAN GALA CONCERT (Bayerische Staatsgemäldesammlungen, Munich), photo: Blauel. **WATTEAU:** p. 174, THE MEZZETIN (The Metropolitan Museum of Art, New York, Munsey Fund, 1934). **CHARDIN:** p. 175, STILL LIFE WITH PIPE (Louvre Museum, Paris), photo: Giraudon. **FRAGONARD:** p. 175, THE SWING (by permission of the Trustees of the Wallace Collection, London). **ROMNEY:** p. 176, A CONVERSATION (Collection of Mr. & Mrs. Paul Mellon), photo: Barney Burstein. **STUART:** p. 176, MRS. RICHARD YATES (The National Gallery of Art, Washington, D.C., Mellon Collection). **J. L. DAVID:** p. 177, NAPOLEON IN HIS STUDY (The National Gallery of Art, Washington, D.C.). **INGRES:** p. 177, TURKISH BATH (Louvre Museum, Paris), photo: Agraci. **MILLET:** p. 177, THE ANGELUS (Louvre Museum, Paris), photo: Giraudon. **PISSARRO:** p. 178, LA COTE DES BOEUFS AT L'HERMITAGE, NEAR PONTOISE (courtesy of the Trustees, The National Gallery, London). **CASSATT:** p. 178, BOATING PARTY (The National Gallery of Art, Washington, D.C., Chester Dale Collection). **RYDER:** p. 178, DEATH ON A PALE HORSE (The Cleveland Museum of Art, Purchase from the J. H. Wade Fund). **SARGENT:** p. 179, EL JALEO (Isabella Stewart Gardner Museum, Boston), photo: Barney Burstein. **EAKINS:** p. 179, MAX SCHMITT IN A SINGLE SCULL (The Metropolitan Museum of Art, New York, Alfred N. Prunnett Fund and Gift of George D. Pratt, 1934). **VLAMINCK:** p. 180, HOUSES AT CHATOU (The Art Institute of Chicago, Gift of Mr. and Mrs. Morris E. Culberg). **DUFY:** p. 180, RACETRACK AT DEAUVILLE (Fogg Art Museum, Cambridge, Mass., Maurice Wertheim Collection), photo: Barney Burstein. **UTRILLO:** p. 180, CHARTRES (Reader's Digest Collection, Pleasantville, N.Y.). **SOUTINE:** p. 181, PAGE BOY AT MAXIM'S (Albright-Knox Art Gallery, Buffalo, N.Y.). **ROUAULT:** p. 181, THE OLD KING (Carnegie Institute, Pittsburgh), photo: Barney Burstein. **KANDINSKY:** p. 182, IMPROVISATION WITH GREEN CENTER (The Art Institute of Chicago), photo: Barney Burstein. **FEININGER:** p. 182, GELMERODA IV (Guggenheim Museum, New York), photo: Barney Burstein. **KLEE:** p. 182, INTENSIFICATION OF COLOR FROM THE STATIC TO THE DYNAMIC (Collection Bienert), photo: Skira. **KOKOSCHKA:** p. 183, HARBOR OF MARSEILLES (City Art Museum of St. Louis, Mo.). **BRAQUE:** p. 183, STILL LIFE, LE JOUR (The National Gallery of Art, Washington, D.C., Chester Dale Collection). **LEGER:** p. 183, THE BIRD CHARMER (Collection A. H. Maremont, Chicago, Brandeis Exhibition), photo: Barney Burstein. **DALI:** p. 184, PERSISTENCE OF MEMORY (Museum of Modern Art, New York). **MONDRIAN:** p. 184, COMPOSITION WITH BLUE AND YELLOW, 1932 (Philadelphia Museum of Art, A. E. Gallatin Collection), photo: A. J. Wyatt. **MIRO:** p. 185, DUTCH INTERIOR (Museum of Modern Art, New York, Mrs. Simon Guggenheim Fund). **POLLOCK:** p. 185, NUMBER 1, 1948 (Museum of Modern Art, New York). **WYETH:** p. 185, CHRISTINA'S WORLD (Museum of Modern Art, New York).